Dividing Paradise

Dividing Paradise

RURAL INEQUALITY AND THE DIMINISHING AMERICAN DREAM

Jennifer Sherman

UNIVERSITY OF CALIFORNIA PRESS

University of California Press
Oakland, California

© 2021 by Jennifer Sherman

Library of Congress Cataloging-in-Publication Data

Names: Sherman, Jennifer, author.
  Title: Dividing paradise : rural inequality and the diminishing
American dream / Jennifer Sherman.
  Description: Oakland, California : University of California Press,
[2021] | Includes bibliographical references and index.
  Identifiers: LCCN 2020029258 (print) | LCCN 2020029259 (ebook) |
ISBN 9780520305137 (cloth) | ISBN 9780520305144 (paperback) |
ISBN 9780520973275 (ebook)
  Subjects: LCSH: Equality—Washington (State)—Case studies. |
Washington (State)—Rural conditions—Case studies.
  Classification: LCC HM821 .S544 2021 (print) | LCC HM821 (ebook) |
DDC 307.7209797—dc23
  LC record available at https://lccn.loc.gov/2020029258
  LC ebook record available at https://lccn.loc.gov/2020029259

Manufactured in the United States of America

30 29 28 27 26 25 24 23 22 21
10 9 8 7 6 5 4 3 2 1

Contents

Prologue: Discovering Paradise

I first visited Paradise Valley in the summer of 2009, with my climbing partner Will. I had moved to Eastern Washington the previous summer to begin a tenure-track job at Washington State University. Will, a Washington native, was a knowledgeable guide to the many beautiful outdoor recreation areas of the Pacific Northwest, some well-known, some obscure. He had not told me much about Paradise Valley ahead of time, except that we had to drive through it to access nearby alpine rock-climbing. "You'll love it," he told me, and I trusted him.

As we turned into the valley and crossed over the Paradise River for the first time, I was awestruck. The free-flowing river—a rarity in Washington State, where most rivers are dammed and harnessed for electricity—sparkled like strings of jewels in the late afternoon sunlight. Everything was bathed in the golden light that shone off the water, and it felt ethereal. Tree-covered mountains rose from its sides as we wound upward along the curving road into the valley. The mountains grew larger and the landscape more impressive the further we went. It was higher up, when the valley floor opened up into wide, lush meadows flanked by steep snow-covered peaks, that I first began to sense the significance that this place would have for me.

Five years earlier, I had wrapped up a year spent in another mountain valley: Golden Valley, California—a remote, beautiful, and harsh place. Golden Valley became the subject of my 2009 book, *Those Who Work, Those Who Don't: Poverty, Morality, and Family in Rural America*. The landscape of Paradise Valley evoked the landscape of Golden Valley for me, a similar combination of verdant green valley floor with alpine peaks rising above. Yet as we drove through the main towns of Paradise Valley, I was struck by how different this place felt. While Golden Valley had been a community on the decline, with few services and little public life visible to the outsider, Paradise Valley was a tourist mecca, offering a steady stream of options for lodging, food, and retail. There were art galleries, coffee shops, ice cream parlors, and pizza places as well as restaurants that ranged from brewpubs, to upscale dining, to casual restaurants catering to large families with children. There were stores selling trinkets, high-end clothes, health food, and sports equipment. There were multiple businesses that rented skis in the winter and bicycles in the summer. Everything that tourists might want, regardless of their cultural backgrounds and social class, was available somewhere in the valley. In this way it was nothing at all like Golden Valley and its barren lack of services.

As a sociologist, questions immediately filled my head. What made these two mountain valleys—both in the Pacific Northwest, both quite remote, both once dependent on logging and ranching—so very, very different from one another? The role of amenity tourism was the obvious answer, which seemed to reinforce everything that I knew from the rural sociological literature about the positive impacts of this form of economic development.[1] I was amazed that an area as remote as Paradise Valley had been able to create and sustain amenity tourism on such a scale, and despite a few empty storefronts and FOR SALE signs on run-down motels, for all appearances it seemed as if the region had been incredibly successful at it. But other questions gnawed at me as we drove through the valley: Where do the locals live, work, and spend time? Who are the locals? Are they like the working-class population I knew in Golden Valley? What is the impact of tourism and recreation on their community and sense of themselves? Do the jobs amenity tourism creates sustain a comfortable lifestyle for local families? How do they experience the amenity-tourism economy, and how do they feel about people like Will and me, driving up on a long weekend in cars stuffed to the windows with expensive outdoor gear, to camp, climb, eat a burger, and drink a beer before heading out again without ever getting to know them?

As we headed further up into the Cascade Mountains to find camping for the night, I told Will that I was going to come back and study this place someday. He laughed at me, somewhat baffled as to what I found so interesting. For him, Paradise Valley was an annoyance you had to drive through in order to get higher into the mountains, a place of traffic jams and tourists best avoided unless you needed to stop for supplies. It was merely the gateway to our wilderness weekend, not a goal in and of itself. I returned to Paradise Valley many times in the ensuing five years, to climb, to camp, to ski, and occasionally to just relax in the mountains. I stayed in Forest Service campgrounds, vacation cabins, and hotels depending on the time of year and the purpose of the trip as well as whom I was with and their preferences. I continued to be fascinated by the place and the questions that nagged in the back of my mind on each trip, making me feel slightly uncomfortable with my social location as an amenity tourist in a rural community.

I finally got my chance to study Paradise Valley in 2014, ten years after I'd left that other mountain valley. I was no longer a young, naïve graduate student living hand-to-mouth and wondering if I could pull off a research project of this scale. I was now a tenured professor on sabbatical, driving a Prius instead of a beat-up Subaru, with a salary that was higher than that of most of my interview participants. I had years of experience in qualitative and ethnographic research, had interviewed hundreds of people over the previous decade, and understood the things I would need to do to comprehend the social dynamics of this place. Within ten months in Paradise Valley I was able to do significantly more data collection than I achieved in my twelve months in Golden Valley—fortunately so, because I found Paradise Valley to be much more socially diverse and complicated than Golden Valley was in the early 2000s.

The resulting book is not a sequel to my 2009 one; rather, it has been written in a sort of conversation with it, continuing my in-depth investigation of the dynamics of rural America in the twenty-first century, including the struggles, the rewards, and the cultural discourses that permit its residents to make sense of their lives. In this endeavor it is my intention to shine a light on American culture more generally, including helping to understand the ways in which we as a nation have come to accept and believe in the intense inequality that we are experiencing in the early decades of this century.

Acknowledgments

A project of this size and scope is a massive undertaking, spanning many years and requiring much help. I am so grateful for all of the people who contributed to the creation of this work. It took a virtual village to make this book.

In Paradise Valley this work relied heavily on the assistance of countless people, including each and every participant. Thank you so much for opening your homes and your lives to me and my recorder. Thanks especially to those people who helped me get started in Paradise Valley and make connections, and who continually helped me improve my understandings through hours of conversations that elucidated, confirmed, and challenged my observations: Sarah, Terry, Elana, Sandi, Glen, and Amy. Thank you also to Rita, Carol, and Lloyd for providing me with such a beautiful and supportive living environment. I miss the views, the chickens, and the conversations we shared. And thank you to the friends I made along the way, including those mentioned above, as well as Marianne, Kay, Larry, and Jayne. I miss you and am so grateful for all the ways in which you shared your time, resources, and insights with me.

Thanks also to my amazing writing group of brilliant, talented, and supportive colleagues and friends: I cannot tell you enough how necessary you are to my ability to produce quality work. I have benefited so incredibly from knowing and working with you all. You are vitally important to me as friends, peers, critics, inspirations, and role models. Jennifer Randles, Daisy Rooks, Jennifer Utrata, and Kerry Woodward—thank you so much for the hours you put into reading my drafts and commenting on my work. I value your feedback so much and rely on you perhaps too much to ensure that my work is as good as it can possibly be. Thank you for being so reliable, supportive, insightful, and critical of me and each other for so many years. I could not do this without you and can only hope that I give back as much as I get from this incredible group of brilliant scholars. I am so blessed to work with you all.

I am also grateful for the friendship, support, mentorship, and critical feedback I receive from inspirational rural sociologists Leif Jensen, Kai Schafft, and Ann Tickamyer, who reviewed versions of this manuscript. Kai, I am so grateful that you reached out to me so early in my career, which has always been richer for it. Ann, I am so fortunate to know you, and so thankful that I had the opportunity to work closely with you. All three of you have been such important influences on my career. You are some of the best people I know.

Thank you to Pierce Greenberg, who helped with background data for this project, including tables that appear in Appendix A. It is always a pleasure to work with you, whether as mentor or peer. I feel lucky to have been both.

I am fortunate to have such a supportive department at Washington State University, and thank in particular Lisa McIntyre, Monica Johnson, Alair MacLean, Clay Mosher, and Jennifer Schwartz for their support of me and my career as well as for providing advice over the years as they fly by. I am extremely appreciative for the financial support I received from the Sociology Department at Washington State University, which helped to fund this research.

I received grant funding from the American Sociological Association's Sydney S. Spivack Program in Applied Social Research and its Social Policy Community Action Research Award. I am extremely grateful for this support.

Thank you also to my editor, Naomi Schneider, for believing in this work and holding me to the high standards of the University of California

Press. I am honored to work with you and to benefit from your vast experience and knowledge.

Special thanks to Holly Rydel Kelly, the most amazing transcriptionist in the world. I value our working relationship and friendship so much. One of the hardest things I ever did was share my raw data with another person, and I never anticipated how much I would get out of this relationship beyond incredibly accurate transcripts. Thank you for sharing your thoughts, feedback, and friendship over more than a decade of working together. I am so lucky to have shared a campsite and grilled fruit with you that fateful night in the Cascades.

Thanks also to my Tri-Cities support team, who helped me through so many transitions, including this one, and who shared my love of Paradise Valley: Andrea Aebersold, Vanessa Cozza, Michelle Froh, Jeremiah Newell, Dean Olin, A. J. Rehwalt, Andrea Rehwalt, Mary Seidler, Pat Sullivan, Robin Sullivan, and Spencer Wickler. You are some of the kindest people I have ever known, and I miss you and the community all the time.

Thank you also to my friends in Moscow, who make everyday life livable and are there for me no matter how crazed I get: Alexandra Teague, Chad Burt, Dylan Champagne, Ben James, Erin James, Jennifer Ladino, Tara McDonald, Jodie Nicotra, Ryanne Pilgeram, Rochelle Smith, Melanie Neuilly Wolf, and Toby Wray: I love you guys and am so lucky to have found such an amazing community.

This project would not exist without the influence of John Plotz, legendary mountain man, close friend and climbing partner, and the best rope-gun in the West. Thank you for introducing me to Paradise Valley, and for all the time you spent there with me over years of adventuring together. Thank you for your friendship and love, and for being a sounding board and critic, as well as a source of so much laughter and adventure. Your legend will not be forgotten by me. I appreciate and value all the time we have spent together.

Thank you to my family—Joel, Judy, Ben, and Tanisha Sherman—for supporting me throughout all of my crazy choices and adventures. I wish we all had more time together, but cherish the moments we have.

Huge thanks to my partner, Jeff Hicke, for his love and support. It is not easy to be with an academic, particularly when you are one yourself. There are far too many times when we are both consumed by the pulls of our careers and by the multiple stresses of our lives. Your patience with me has been epic, and your perspective, challenges, and insights invaluable. I love you.

Thanks also to Laurel and Ava Hicke for welcoming me into your lives and accepting me as a friend and member of your family. I am so blessed to know you and to get to witness and share your journeys in life. You inspire me, and I look forward to many great things from you both.

1 Rural Deindustrialization, Decline, and Rebirth

On a frigid, sunny morning in December of 2014, I drove several miles up a steep, winding dirt road above Reliance, Washington, to interview Louise and Roger Clark, a retired couple who had lived in the Paradise Valley region for sixteen years.[1] Despite being narrow and dangerous due to the sharp drop-off on one side, the private road was extremely well maintained. Thankfully it had been plowed to the gravel; otherwise it would have been impassable in the brutal cold, which frequently turned snow into glassy ice. Nonetheless, the drive was frightening in my old Prius, the road so steep at times that I had to downshift to make sure I didn't lose speed. When I finally arrived at the Clark house, a large open-concept ranch with a wraparound porch at the top of the hill, the snow was piled so high on all sides that I could not figure out how to enter it or even where to knock. I had to call the Clarks, who let me in through the garage, which was the only passable entrance.

Inside, I understood why this home was worth the winter hassles. The beautiful interior was constructed of solid wood in the light hue that is common across Paradise Valley. Much of the furniture was made of similar rough-cut wood, a style popular in the area's vacation rentals as well. We sat in a large, airy living room with vast bay windows looking out onto a gorgeous, sprawling view of snow-covered mountains in all directions. As we gazed at the valley below, Louise and Roger described what enticed them from the Seattle area to retire in this remote place where they had no prior social connections. They spoke about having visited the valley on camping and hunting trips when they were younger and of growing tired of the rain after decades on Washington's west side. They talked about the incredible views from their secluded mountain home. The dream to relocate permanently to Paradise Valley really began with an emotional response to witnessing the beauty of the place. The Clarks were struck by the valley's splendor. Louise told me that on her first visit she was awed by "the apple blossoms down south from Eagle Flat coming up valley. It was just so pretty, I never forgot that."

I heard similar tales from recent in-migrants across Paradise Valley during the ten months that I conducted research there. It was a common experience to be astounded by the impressive scale of nature in this place, to be so moved by it as to want to make the valley one's home. With its stunning physical landscape and remote but vibrant community, Paradise Valley perfectly represents what is for many Americans the idyllic image of the rural West. The combination of scale, beauty, and isolation are for many Americans intrinsic parts of idealized visions of rural America. Like generations of white settlers before them, and undoubtedly many still to come, the Clarks succumbed to the call of the rural idyll and decided to make Paradise Valley their retirement home.

What exactly is the rural dream that so many have chased here? Scholars define the rural idyll in multiple ways, most focusing on the romanticized vision of rural life as wholesome, innocent, virtuous, and simple compared to the rapid pace, modern inconveniences, and potential danger and risk of urban places.[2] The imagined rural is often a vision of a lost Eden, of a past perfection now mostly lost to urbanization and industrialization. This imaginary is often "divorced from harsher realities of rural life and masking exploitation and oppression."[3] In this vision of rural perfection, the rougher aspects of modern rural communities are obscured by our longing for utopia coupled with desires for peace, tranquility, and infinite space.[4] As this book illustrates, this powerful albeit somewhat inaccurate and naïve image has held sway since early waves of white settlers first pushed the Native populations from rural America.

This longing for rural utopia continues to inspire both young families and older retirees like Louise and Roger to invest in their own private pieces of paradise. It is a choice made at the individual level for often very personal reasons and seldom with thought regarding the social impacts of this type of movement of people and resources across space and place.

This book is not about the desire to settle in a beautiful location, although these narratives and pull factors are an important part of the story. Rather, it is about the human costs of the commodification of the rural ideal and the underlying assumptions and understandings regarding who does and does not have the right to live in desirable places. Although much recent discussion of rural areas, both in the press and in academic treatments, has focused on decline, destruction, and despair, this book focuses instead on rural success and growth.[5] It is a story about one of rural America's seemingly best options for progress, development, and economic stability. It is also about the tolls this takes on the populations who have lived in rural communities since an earlier time, when rural places were valued more for the resources that could be extracted than for the amenities that could be reserved for elite recreation and enjoyment.

Beyond being a story of rurality itself, however, this book reveals the tension between a leisure class and a working class, illuminating the ways in which Americans' differences divide us and impede our abilities to understand or care about one another. It is a tale of the impacts of the rapid and disastrous growth of inequality in the United States and the resulting loss of access to the iconic American Dream for many, as more and more resources are accumulated by a few.[6] It is also a story of the ways in which loss, anger, and disenfranchisement intersect with privilege, apathy, and denial to divide and undermine a community and a nation. The story of Paradise Valley demonstrates the human impacts of inequality from both sides of the divide, illustrating the mechanisms and processes by which we come to accept such extreme levels of inequality as normal, natural, and deserved. Increasingly divided experiences and perspectives contribute to the alienation, lack of empathy, and dehumanization that drive cycles of increasing social and political polarization in this community, as in the larger nation. The case of Paradise Valley illustrates that as these differences and divisions become more deeply entrenched, we come to believe more and more in the righteousness of those most like us, and the inherent undeservingness of those on the other side of the divide. This book provides a critique of these processes and their inevitable outcomes, offering a window into understanding the experiences, motivations, and challenges faced by well-meaning individuals from both perspectives.

LOSS AND RESILIENCE IN PARADISE VALLEY

In order to understand the larger case, it is necessary first to understand Paradise Valley itself and how it came to be divided. Paradise Valley's history and present trajectory are tied into the history of the rural West more generally. Once seen as an endless frontier, the West was "tamed" through the efforts of Manifest Destiny, the belief that it was God's will that white Americans settle and populate the entire continent of North America. Throughout the nineteenth and into the twentieth centuries, westward expansion relied on small-scale agriculture, later giving way to extractive and land-based industries including mining, logging, oil drilling, and industrial agriculture that came to dominate in the mid-twentieth century.[7] The era of these industries turned out to be short-lived for rural America, however, as global competition combined with neoliberal agendas to move extraction and production overseas in search of cheaper inputs and wages as well as weaker regulations.[8]

Subsequently, as deindustrialization occurred across the United States, these and other natural resource–based economies collapsed and declined, leaving many rural places economically devastated in their wake.[9] The victims of deindustrialization are scattered throughout rural America, visible from coast to coast and throughout the Heartland and the Rust Belt. The loss of manufacturing and extraction jobs during the late twentieth century left much of rural America in economic ruin, and rural communities experienced population loss, declining infrastructure, and high unemployment.[10] Frequently these concerns were compounded by lack of access to high-quality public schools and/or higher education, which helped to fuel cycles of out-migration that further impeded rural communities' chances of competing for new economic opportunities.[11]

The impacts of these trends have been shattering for rural communities across the United States, which were faced with the loss of mainly men's jobs in sectors that had long provided stable, living-wage, union-ized, and full-time and/or year-round work. In many places jobs in such sectors as manufacturing and resource extraction were not replaced, or they were replaced by service-sector jobs that tended to be low-wage, nonunionized, lacking benefits, feminized, insecure, and part-time and/or seasonal.[12] Rural communities that were dominated by single indus-tries had their labor markets ravaged by industrial decline. This shift in the nature of available jobs has resulted in widespread working poverty as well as changes in the gendered nature of rural work.[13] These trends were further exacerbated by national and global economic challenges includ-ing the Great Recession in the early 2000s, which hit rural America par-ticularly hard.[14] Together, these macro trends left many rural American communities hollowed out and struggling to sustain themselves into the twenty-first century.[15]

Despite the historic and cultural ties to land-based industries, the forces of neoliberal global capitalism have been unrelenting, and most rural communities will not see these industries return to their past sig-nificance in terms of either economic activity or job creation. Among the long-standing impacts of economic restructuring in recent decades is that by almost all definitions, poverty and unemployment have been higher in rural than in urban areas.[16] Given the combination of geographic isola-tion, lack of infrastructure (particularly in areas like broadband and other digital technologies), and lack of highly educated workers, many rural communities face extremely limited options for economic development. Even in those places where new resource-based industries are viable, such as areas where natural gas can be extracted through fracking, develop-ment often occurs in boom-and-bust cycles and there is limited job cre-ation for the local workforce.[17]

Accompanying these trends, political and economic winds have shifted away from protecting rural communities. Neoliberal attitudes and agen-das have focused increasingly on deregulation of many spheres of the American economy, resulting in decreasing restrictions on corporations, lower tax burdens on corporations and the wealthy, and fewer protections for both workers and the poor.[18] The results have been a forty-year period of unprecedented growth in American inequality, as corporate profits grew and corporations kept more for themselves, and wages grew quickly for the wealthy but stagnated or fell for less educated and skilled workers.[19] These processes ravaged rural communities, where the losses of unionized jobs in manufacturing and resource extraction have left gaping holes in labor markets, and available service-sector jobs do not support basic survival, let alone upward mobility.[20] New industries increasingly cluster in the nation's booming urban centers, while its hollowed-out rural places become increasingly depressed, impoverished, and viewed as undesirable and expendable.[21] The result has been economic suffering in rural America as well as frustration and anger at liberals, the political machine, and urban Americans more generally.[22]

For decades, one of the few rays of light in the rural economic development landscape has been amenity-based tourism, promoted for its potential to reverse downward trends and replace declining rural industries.[23] This form of development cashes in on privileged urban dwellers' desires to temporarily experience the peace and tranquility of the imagined rural idyll. Research into amenity-based tourism development has suggested it can to contribute to population growth, job growth, higher incomes, and lower poverty rates, while attracting young, educated, highly skilled in-migrants and stemming the flow of out-migration and "brain drain" in rural communities.[24] Although researchers have also identified numerous potential downsides of this form of development—from cost-of-living increases, to decreased community attachment, to culture clashes, to the growth of low-wage employment—building an amenity-tourism economy is still pursued as a goal by rural communities across the nation in the hopes that it can help overturn their economic fortunes.[25] While research suggests that results of this form of development are mixed at best, it represents for many communities their best chance for achieving new prosperity.

Paradise Valley is one of many rural communities that trusted its fortunes and its future to amenity tourism, in the hopes that it could remake itself in the wake of the forest industry's decline in the Pacific Northwest. Situated amid some of the most stunning natural landscapes in the West, within a day's drive of major cities including Seattle and Portland, its chances were good. Although it took decades for the investments into tourism to fully pay off, over time it has caught hold in the region. Modern Paradise Valley is an exemplar of the transition from an extraction-dependent economy to a tourism- and amenity-focused one. The region has been particularly conscious, thoughtful, and critical of this form of development even as it pursued it, with leaders and vocal citizens who made wise choices along the way so as to retain the rural and small-town feel of their community versus seeing it grow into a place they could not recognize. Paradise Valley is an extremely successful rural community both in terms of building a strong economy based in amenity tourism and in-migration as well as in terms of retaining its essential character. Yet as this book describes, even for this rural success story, rebirth comes at a price.

PARADISE VALLEY'S TRIUMPHS AND CHALLENGES

Paradise Valley lies on the eastern slopes of the Cascade Mountains in Washington State. The valley's exact boundaries are unclear, but most locals agree on a roughly sixty-mile area that contains four distinct (but not all incorporated) communities, each with fewer than one thousand residents living within town boundaries. These communities include Outpost, Pinedale, Eagle Flat, and Reliance, the latter two having the largest populations. The school district, which includes this same region and adjacent unincorporated areas, has a population of roughly five thousand year-round residents. The towns differ in the types of tourists, second-home owners, and in-migrants they attract, but all of the communities are economically reliant on amenity-driven tourism and in-migration to some degree.

Like many high-amenity communities in the rural West, Paradise Valley has built its tourism economy around a combination of celebrating its western cultural heritage and commodification of its physical landscape and the myriad outdoor activities that can be pursued in and around the valley. Various promotional websites tout the region's options for outdoor sports, food, arts, and entertainment. As chapter 2 describes in more depth, over time the area has come to rely not just on visiting tourists for its economic base but also on part-time residents with primary homes elsewhere as well as on amenity migrants like Louise and Roger Clark. This combination of visitors and new residents has allowed

Paradise Valley to attain a surprising amount of success in terms of economic growth and development.

However, as this book discusses in detail, these victories are not without their challenges. Although Paradise Valley provides an exemplary case of rural success through amenity development, it is also an exemplary case of the unequal distribution of that success. Paradise Valley was ultimately able to reinvent itself only through sacrificing some of its opportunities for working-class residents' survival.[26] The community's mostly working-class "old-timers," themselves relative newcomers into a land that they settled during its earlier period of resource extraction, have not necessarily been included in the valley's impressive rebirth and reinvention. Among the documented potential downsides of amenity development are issues including gentrification, social and cultural clash, and reorganization of local power structures in favor of better resourced in-migrants—all of which are visible in Paradise Valley.[27]

While previous scholars have uncovered the multiple forms these negative outcomes can take, this book explores the processes by which these types of social inequality are produced and reproduced as well as their impacts on individuals and the larger community and society. Highlighted in this exploration are the roles of real and symbolic resources in creating and sustaining the growth of inequality in this community, illustrating the multiple dimensions along which unequal access to advantage and distribution of privilege occur. As inequality deepens, the impacts of access to both real and symbolic resources are exaggerated, increasing opportunity for some while deepening marginalization for others. These processes, while highly visible in a small rural community, are not unique to it. The story this book tells is a small-scale version of social forces that are playing out across the nation and on a global scale.

Symbolic Resources and Social Boundaries

As Paradise Valley has grown through in-migration of mostly wealthy urbanites, it has experienced many negative impacts alongside the positives. Among the most striking of these impacts is the growth of inequality in the valley along with an accompanying decline of social cohesion as it becomes increasingly split between those who do and those who do not have easy access to social support, economic security, and other important aspects of the American Dream, including stable work and affordable housing. Connected to these issues are the systematic loss of livelihood, sense of community, and hope experienced by those with longer histories in the valley, in contrast to the various ways in which more recent in-migrants access jobs, social connection, and a sense of personal success and satisfaction there. Much of this story is about the vast differences in resources between older and newer generations of Paradise Valley residents, including disparities in both economic and noneconomic resources.

An economic gulf between the populations underlies the most basic divisions between them. Although there are differences in their abilities to compete for better-paid jobs across the valley and thus substantial income disparities, the more significant difference between Paradise Valley's old-timers and newcomers lies in their access to wealth. Sociologists have long pointed out the importance of wealth versus income in terms of structuring life chances and contributing to persistent inequality.[28] Earned income can be cut off easily through the loss of a job, but wealth—meaning ownership of assets including homes, cars, savings, stocks, bonds, and other types of investments—persists and grows over time and can be passed on to subsequent generations. Wealth is also important in that it often can cover large expenses for which income alone may be insufficient, such as a down payment on a home or educational tuition for children. It can also cushion against income shocks, including a seasonal layoff or job loss, providing a safety net that helps many families to afford basic necessities until steady income is reestablished. Thus access to wealth can constitute a major advantage or disadvantage for individuals and families beyond mere income level.

Although economic differences are an important source of division and inequality between social groups, they are not the only ways in which people distinguish between and hierarchically divide themselves. Sociologists also study the overlapping matrices of multiple types of social division, including differences of race, class, gender, and sexual identity.[29] While ostensibly noneconomic in nature, these social divisions correspond to systems of power, privilege, and access—or lack thereof—to multiple other societal resources, both economic and noneconomic in nature. They are based in differences that are more symbolic than real, constructed by societies through the meanings that they attach to variations that may or may not be visible to the eye. While almost all human societies share this tendency to create symbolic boundaries between groups of people, the specific boundaries that are most salient depend on the characteristics and cultural norms of the populations themselves.[30] In-group and out-group statuses can be constructed through boundaries based in race, class, gender, culture, religion, or age, among countless other possibilities.[31] Boundaries that reinforce inequality are maintained through both social institutions and face-to-face interactions on the micro level, in which differences are reified and reinforced.[32]

More homogenous communities like Paradise Valley, with its almost entirely white population (see chapter 2 for more on the demographic makeup), may have limited access to certain forms of distinction, in this case differences by race. However, racial homogeneity does not mean that a population is lacking in ways to differentiate and divide members. Scholars of race point out that although whites are generally privileged relative to other racial groups in the United States, whiteness itself is not monolithic, and there are many variations in the degree of privilege associated with white racial status. Furthermore, the meaning of "whiteness" changes according to social context and reference groups.[33] Within the racial group there are multiple statuses that vary across other axes of privilege and experience, particularly those related to social class and related resources.

These types of class differences form the basis of most of the division discussed in this book. Like other types of difference, social class distinctions both result from and structure differential access to resources, and these distinctions are tied to both economic privilege and cultural understandings regarding the value, moral standing, and deservingness of different social groups.[34] Like other types of inequality, social class is often largely invisible to those who have the most advantage and privilege.[35] Yet despite its relative invisibility, social class is frequently one of the most significant forms of division, particularly in the modern United States.[36] Social class is created and reproduced through multiple mechanisms, including purely economic resources like wealth and income but also through a number of resources known to sociologists as symbolic capital.[37] This concept assumes that social status hierarchies are maintained not just by economic differences but also by resources that are not strictly economic in nature but act in similar ways: most importantly that they can be traded for other real and symbolic resources depending on the social setting.

This book pays close attention to the roles of four symbolic forms of capital in Paradise Valley that significantly structure social life: social, cultural, human, and moral capital. Social capital consists of one's social connections and the resources that can be accessed by those within the social network to procure both economic and in-kind benefits.[38] For the rural poor, social capital often can mean the difference between aid through difficult times or facing them alone.[39] Cultural capital consists of tastes, manners, values, habits, and material objects that help to distinguish groups of people from each other, such as knowledge of, interest in, and preferences for such things as art, music, recreation, and entertainment.[40] In certain circles and social settings, cultural capital may be tradeable for social connections as well as potential job opportunities, as in the case of manners and self-presentation, which can help or hurt a job candidate.[41] Cultural capital is often necessary for making connections and being taken seriously by others in elite settings.[42]

Human capital consists of investments into individual education, training, and job experience, with higher levels generally being converted into higher salaries, labor market opportunities, and job benefits.[43] Education often plays an ambiguous role in rural communities, however, where limited labor markets complicate the returns to human capital and frequently require out-migration to find work that fully rewards education, skills, and training.[44] Moral capital, which has been documented in rural American settings, consists of external exhibitions of one's morality according to locally constructed norms and understandings. It may be such things as outwardly manifesting one's work ethic and family values within a community where these values are considered important. Although morality may not always become a tradeable form of symbolic capital, in my previous rural work I found that moral capital "often becomes a dominant social force and social boundary marker precisely in places ... which are relatively homogenous and lacking in sufficient other sources upon which to base social distinctions."[45] Like other forms of symbolic capital, moral capital can be traded for advantages in social settings as well as in school (where human capital is obtained) and the labor market.[46]

Together, these various forms of real and symbolic capital contribute to a person's social status within a society as well as to life chances, opportunities, and choices. They structure prospects either for amassing more resources or for being shut out of social networks and denied access to both real and symbolic resources. In addition to differences in economic capital, Paradise Valley's newcomers bring to the community significant amounts of symbolic capital, further privileging them relative to the working-class population that predated them. These differences in real and symbolic resources form the basis of the intense inequality that exists within the community and provide numerous mechanisms for its reproduction over time. Differences in symbolic capital are often even less recognized than differences in economic capital, contributing to the tendency for those with privilege to be blind both to their own advantages and to their impacts on less-advantaged populations around them. The unequal distribution of real and symbolic resources underlies inequality throughout modern America; the failure to acknowledge these differences and the unequal access to power and opportunities that they create is a major issue for the larger United States as a whole. This book documents this phenomenon, which I refer to as "class blindness," in depth.

Inequality in Paradise Valley is in many ways a micro version of inequality in the United States in the early twenty-first century. Although the growth of American inequality is well-known and documented, it is rarely acknowledged in everyday life.[47] As with other sources of division, such as racism, there is a growing tendency for those with privilege to abandon offensive terms and open acknowledgment of prejudices, which obscures rather than addresses the underlying feelings, belief systems, and systemic forms of oppression and subjugation.[48] There are numerous ways in which the national conversation and media aid in this obfuscation, purposefully distracting attention away from inequality and the exploitation of the many by a few elite corporate and political interests. Thus the national discourse becomes one of division, anger, and resentment without actively addressing either the sources or the outcomes of inequality, allowing us to dehumanize one another without focusing concern on the actual causes of our struggles.

The case study of Paradise Valley provides a window through which to view these processes as they unfold in the daily life of rural residents across the social class spectrum, chasing their versions of the rural idyll and the American Dream. The insidious growth of class blindness is one of the mechanisms through which Americans in Paradise Valley and beyond come to accept, normalize, and justify privilege and disadvantage on the basis of social class.

RESEARCH METHODS

To learn about these underlying social forces, I moved to Paradise Valley in September 2014, where I lived full-time until July 2015. During my time there, I completed eighty-four open-ended in-depth interviews and ten months of ethnographic observation and participation focused on learning about residents across the class spectrum. The combination of interviews with less structured participant observation allowed me to learn about people in different ways and to see the differences between their self-conscious thoughts and articulated understandings of their situations as well as the unscripted ways in which they navigated and interacted with their community setting and social world. This combination of methods facilitated following individuals over time and witnessing their journeys as they unfolded over the course of different seasons, situations, and life events.

These methods are complementary in that the confidential, recorded interviews often give participants the space to take on private issues and express deeply personal thoughts and understandings as well as the opportunity to consciously censor themselves. The less formal settings often provide less access to private or personal musings but much more access to natural and unedited discussions and insight into everyday actions, behaviors, choices, and opinions. Most of the formal interviews lasted from one to four hours, with the average being about two hours. Primarily participants were interviewed alone, but five couples and one mother-son pair opted to do joint interviews. The majority of interviews took place in participants' homes, which ranged from large, airy, artisan-crafted modern homes like the Clarks', showcasing exposed wooden beams and picture windows with extensive mountain views, to much smaller and more modest rental homes, subsidized apartments, and cramped single-wide and travel trailers in various states of disrepair. Many participants chose not to meet me in their homes, preferring instead to meet in such settings as public parks, cafés and coffee shops, pubs and bars, work offices, the community center, and the deli section of a local grocery store.

I got to know and recruit interview participants through multiple means, including ads I placed periodically on the local electronic bulletin board; through face-to-face recruiting during my volunteer work in settings around the valley; through the recruiting efforts of several key informants with extensive social ties in the valley; and through "snowball sampling," a common technique in which participants are asked to pass along information about the study to eligible individuals within their social networks. Participants were offered incentives of $25 gift cards to a local grocery store or $20 in cash. In recruiting interview participants, I aimed to achieve a diverse sample that drew from varied and unrelated social networks that spanned the class spectrum. Interviewing continued until a saturation point was reached and additional interviews neither produced new analytical themes nor represented new populations or perspectives. Interviewing ceased in June 2015.

The ethnographic research consisted of numerous activities and immersing myself into daily life in Paradise Valley in as many ways as possible. I did approximately twelve hours of regular volunteer work every week between three locations: a public library where I shelved books and helped check them in and out; Angel Food, the local food bank for which I volunteered for weekly food distribution; and Home Front, a family support center for which I volunteered in the front office, helping with small fundraising tasks as well as answering phones and greeting clients. I also volunteered for numerous special events that occurred during my time in Paradise Valley, including working at benefit events for local nonprofit organizations; holiday celebrations for the public; and charity events such as the subsidized gift program for low-income families for the Christmas holiday.

Beyond these structured activities, my ethnographic work also included involvement in the daily life of the community and getting to know as many people as possible from different social strata. I shopped at local stores and frequented local services; regularly attended yoga classes and line dancing; skied, hiked, and rock-climbed with community members; attended parties, plays, films, lectures, church services, concerts, benefits, and gallery openings; and invested as much time and energy as I could into building relationships with residents across the class spectrum. I was open with everyone with whom I worked and interacted regarding my identity and research agenda. I tested my budding understandings of local dynamics against those of Paradise Valley's full-time residents and aimed to be constantly learning about both the community's internal dynamics and the local perceptions and experiences of those dynamics.[49] Ethnographic observations were recorded in hundreds of pages of field notes typed over the course of the year, generally within twenty-four hours of the original observations. More information about data collection and analysis is provided in Appendix A.

As a white, middle-class, well-educated woman, I in many ways fit the profile of a recent in-migrant to the community, although I differed from these residents in my purposeful transience and lack of children. Because children and family were important connectors to Paradise Valley's upper-class social world, I was not immediately recognized or accepted as a desirable member of that community, and early on in my fieldwork I often felt uncomfortable in newcomers' social settings and alienated and/ or excluded from their tight social circles.[50] Over time I gained greater access and acceptance, however, and forged meaningful friendships with a number of newcomers. Yet as a sociologist studying inequality, there was often some degree of unease for me, and I was repeatedly struck by the amount of advantage and privilege that many newcomers uncritically displayed and exercised.[51] I did my best in these moments to keep my reactions to myself and continue to learn about and from those who generously included me in their activities and social lives, although I often talked out my thoughts and impressions with a few key informants from the community who helped me gain additional insight and understanding into these issues and dynamics.

On the other end of the social spectrum, despite my experience in rural settings, my social class, education level, and in-migrant status meant I was not viewed as a local by working-class old-timers, nor did I have easy access to this population at the outset. Thus I worked hard to build trust and create connections to these residents through my volunteer work as well as through providing a sympathetic ear or an extra set of hands to aid in any way I could outside of the formal service setting. It was extremely important to me that I built and maintained connections across the social class and temporal spectrums in Paradise Valley, in order to best understand the ways in which different social groups interacted (or didn't) and experienced and perceived the community. Although it is difficult to ever fully immerse yourself in a social world that you are actively studying, often the moments of discomfort, awkwardness, and self-consciousness are also the ones that elicit real insights into the social processes being observed. Much can be learned from the boundaries and resistance that you encounter, especially from those in positions of power.[52] Nonetheless, despite these difficult moments that are par for the course in field research, I truly enjoyed my time among the residents of Paradise Valley, both longtime and recent, and remain grateful for the warmth, humor, generosity, and kindness that was shown to me across the valley.

OVERVIEW OF THE BOOK

This book tells the story of Paradise Valley in chapters that break down its social class divide to delve into the lives of individuals and families on both sides—the rural working-class "old-timers" and the mostly urban in-migrant "newcomers"—before looking at the ways in which their worlds interact with and influence each other. Chapter 2 introduces the field site in depth, describing the place itself and its economic and social history. It describes the valley's current population and explains how the social divide is observed and experienced by residents on both sides. The chapter explores longtime residents' perceptions of the changes to the place and community, and their positive and negative impressions of these changes. This background sets the stage for understanding the chapters to come, which investigate in greater detail the different experiences of residents across the social spectrum.

Chapter 3 focuses on the newcomers, chronicling their motivations for moving to Paradise Valley and the challenges they face as well as their strategies for addressing them. After looking at the different concerns and interests that bring them to the valley, the chapter describes the economic and career sacrifices that many people make to be there, and the ways in which they adapt to the labor market realities to live comfortably. It also examines the different ways in which newcomers find social support in the community and the ways in which social capital is utilized to fill in gaps in the community's infrastructure and aid with the realities of rural daily life. Newcomers are confronted with many unexpected struggles, and they mobilize their resources in creative ways to address these challenges successfully and create their desired rural utopia. The chapter introduces the concept of class blindness, arguing that newcomers rarely acknowledge or understand their own advantages relative to old-timers. Rather than recognizing differential access to resources or structural disadvantages as the causes of the differences between the populations, newcomers frequently attribute old-timers' struggles to a lack of work ethic or moral virtue.

Chapter 4 takes a similar look at the lives of old-timers, documenting their reasons for living in Paradise Valley and the challenges that they face. After exploring their deep attachments to the place and their roots in the community, the chapter looks in depth at struggles in three important areas of everyday life: work, housing, and family. In contrast to the narratives of newcomers, old-timers describe often insurmountable challenges in each of these areas, beginning with their inabilities to secure full-time, year-round, living-wage work that will adequately support their families. Old-timers face struggles in securing affordable and stable housing in the valley, exacerbated by their lack of wealth to invest and lack of social and moral capital needed to navigate the rental market. Old-timers struggle to secure safe and affordable childcare, which negatively impacts women's work and families' income generation. Finally, the chapter examines old-timers' reluctance to ask for help despite these challenges, elucidating the struggles they face in accessing aid through social networks and the social and personal repercussions of turning to the local social-service sector. Stigma management strategies both assist and undermine low-income residents in their daily survival. Overall, these overlapping areas of struggle mean that old-timers are increasingly unable to achieve basic subsistence, let alone success, and must reduce their expectations of achieving even a diminished version of the American Dream.

Chapter 5 brings the two sides of the story together to illustrate how these very different social, economic, and cultural experiences collide in Paradise Valley. It returns to the concept of symbolic capital, systematically exploring the different ways in which newcomers are able to mobilize symbolic resources that old-timers cannot access. It exposes the degree to which social capital is experienced as waning or lacking for old-timers, who describe isolation and rejection from the larger community. However, newcomers describe high amounts of social support and cohesion within their own networks, where it is exclusively reserved for others who have similar resources to share. Cultural capital contributes to resource differences between the two groups, allowing newcomers to justify excluding old-timers from their social circles because of their differences in interests and leisure preferences. For old-timers, lack of cultural capital translates into feeling judged and left out of many of the most vibrant parts of Paradise Valley's social world and its best resourced social networks.

Chapter 5 also documents the ways in which the social divide is reinforced through the local schools, further entrenching preexisting differences in human capital between the two groups that disadvantage old-timers as they graduate into the local labor market. Also described are old-timers' efforts to make claims to moral capital through words and actions that reference their work ethics and family values. However, these efforts, and this form of symbolic capital, go mostly unrecognized and unrewarded in Paradise Valley, whose powerful newcomer population neither appreciate nor reward it. Thus the one resource that many old-timers might be able to mobilize is of little value in Paradise Valley, where its importance pales in comparison to that of social, cultural, and human capital in structuring life chances and outcomes. Overall, the chapter illuminates the processes of resource hoarding and exclusion that create such different outcomes and experiences for Paradise Valley's social groups, making visible what is often invisible to those on the ground who have many ways to ignore, justify, and reify social class differences. Differential access to these overlapping types of real and symbolic capital contributes to Paradise Valley's ever-deepening social divide.

Chapter 6 looks at the impacts of these social forces, the combination of class blindness with downsized dreams and a deepening divide, on both newcomers' and old-timers' worldviews, concerns, and senses of efficacy. Newcomers rationalize their privilege through impersonal forms of charity and philanthropic financial donations that allow them to feel that they are actively addressing inequality and poverty, without putting a human face to their concerns. This focus on their own altruistic intentions and positive activities facilitates class blindness in their everyday lives, allowing the social divide to continue to deepen unabated. This stance is very much in keeping with the political liberalism that most newcomers embraced, which similarly espouses concern for issues without extending real empathy or understanding to struggling individuals, particularly in one's own community. It is also consistent with more urban forms of charitable giving versus more traditionally rural forms of community concern that often focus on individuals in need rather than larger social issues and categories.

Although old-timers are more likely to focus their support and concern on individual plights, they struggle to make sense of themselves and their declining fortunes in their home community. They expressed a large amount of frustration at times but often were unclear where to focus it. In addition to describing anger at newcomers, many old-timers turned their hostility on community members who struggled even more than themselves, thus further contributing to the degradation of their own social networks and social capital. Old-timers' sense of frustration and disempowerment further translates into specific political and ideological stances, which unlike those of newcomers, focus not on their own positive contributions but on the need to defend themselves from hostile outside forces, including the government itself. The chapter illustrates old-timers' sense of powerlessness in their community, state, and nation, and how this lack of agency was easily harnessed into the right-wing antigovernment anger discourse that was popular at the time. Building upon themes that were widespread in the mainstream media, old-timers were able to relate antigovernment discourse to their own experiences of disempowerment in the rural West. This allowed them to make sense of their situation and to identify a clear enemy force. Yet despite the identification of an enemy, this discourse offered no solutions to old-timers' problems, as it focused on victimhood, anger, and alienation without providing a constructive pathway to improvement. Thus neither group's worldviews or ideologies provided the tools that the fractured community needed to bridge its own gaping social divide and create real connection and understanding across different social locations.

Chapter 7 maintains that despite these dynamics of division, there is hope for this community and America more generally. Social connection can be pursued at the same time as social justice, and differing resources and experiences do not necessarily have to result in failures to know, care about, or understand one another. This final chapter draws parallels between the inequality documented in Paradise Valley and that which is growing across the nation, arguing that the valley represents a microcosm of larger trends and processes occurring across the United States in the late twentieth and early twenty-first centuries. Although the growth in inequality has multifaceted negative outcomes, there are small ways in which communities can begin to bridge their social class divides and create space for social connection despite differences in culture, social networks, and resources.

The chapter highlights several best practices from Paradise Valley's extensive nonprofit and social-services sector, focusing on those that provide necessary services, including educational access, family support, and poverty alleviation. The highlighted organizations are chosen not simply because they provide support, but because of their efforts to build social capital and social connections in the process and to help shrink the distance between the community's most and least resourced residents. Such efforts are necessary but not sufficient to help us overcome class blindness and political frustration, and to improve access to the main tenets of the American Dream for all citizens. I call for both large- and small-scale change to address the multiple economic, social, cultural, and political barriers that keep the dream out of reach for too many Americans, both urban and rural.

2 Changing Times in Paradise

> This is a great place. Don't tell anybody about it. Keep your
> mouth shut. Really, because this is a heaven, and I'm scared
> of too many people trying to get a piece of it, but then
> again, that's what makes it *it*. People have to come in.
> People go, and that's the way of the world.
>
> —Carrie Baker, thirty-six-year-old low-income stay-at-
>   home mother

As a sociologist who studies rural poverty and inequality, it is rare that my research takes me to places as desirable as Paradise Valley. Few people who learned about my work during that year reacted with anything other than envy at my good fortune. I never ceased to feel gratitude for the chance to live among such beauty and so many amenities. Yet modern Paradise Valley has followed a long trajectory to become the place it is today, and was not always a tourism and outdoor recreation mecca. Paradise Valley, like any community, is a living entity that exists in a state of constant motion and adaptation. Much of this book portrays the community in a specific moment in time, and it is important to understand how it got to that moment.

AN INTRODUCTION TO PARADISE

In many ways the towns that make up Paradise Valley feel like other remote rural communities in the rural mountain west. The smallest have just a few services, like a gas station and general store, while the larger towns include other mainstays of rural civic life, such as public libraries;

community centers; restaurants and diners; auto repair shops; specialized businesses like drug, hardware, and feed stores; and churches. However, unlike many remote rural communities, there are also many businesses that provide services beyond these basic necessities, including art galleries, theaters, health food stores, bakeries, breweries, wineries, bike and ski rental shops, souvenir shops, and boutiques. A number of these services cater mostly to short-term visitors and tourists, but many are also patronized regularly by community residents.

My relationship to Paradise Valley began five years before my research did, in the summer of 2009. At the time, the middle of the Great Recession, Eagle Flat in particular felt like a town on the decline.[1] Its small grocery store and gas station felt much like the limited-selection, high-priced services I had encountered in other remote rural places. There were a number of cheap motels lining the road, not all of which looked fully functional. There were a few businesses in Eagle Flat that appeared to cater to outsiders, but otherwise it was a relatively nondescript town—one that most out-of-towners passed through quickly on their way to more tourist-friendly destinations and amenities deeper into the mountains. We did not stop there.

Over the next few years, I visited Paradise Valley on average once or twice a year in order to ski, hike, and rock-climb, just infrequently enough to wonder at each new development. I noticed the expansion of the grocery stores and their services in Eagle Flat, Reliance, and Pinedale. I observed the opening of new coffee shops, bakeries, pubs, restaurants, boutiques, art galleries, and high-end hotels. I noticed the old bars boarded up, the cheap motels abandoned, and the restaurants turning over as the nature of the valley changed. Each time I return now, I see new developments that continue this trajectory and am surprised at how rapidly change is occurring. I am repeatedly surprised at how crowded the valley seems and at the seemingly endless stream of RVs and SUVs that flood the area on weekends and holidays. Like all places, Paradise Valley is in a continual state of flux and change. Unlike many rural communities, however, the change is relatively rapid and mostly consists of growth rather than decline.[2]

I moved to Paradise Valley to begin my research in August of 2014. Although housing was hard to secure there (see chapter 4 for a discussion of my housing search), my advantages in the housing market and short-term tenure allowed me to find an apartment within a larger house on five acres of riverfront land just outside of Eagle Flat. My beautiful yard included a large fenced garden, a chicken coop with a half-dozen chickens, and stunning views of the Cascade Mountains. My first weeks there were the tail end of summer—hot, hazy, and smoke-filled, as is increasingly the "new normal" across the Pacific Northwest.[3] It had been a particularly destructive and ruthless fire season that year, and tourist towns across the region were struggling. The valley felt eerily empty, and the usually crowded restaurants and bars were lifeless, desolate, and abandoned.

The smoky heat receded into fall's golden light, nights going from stifling to chilly in a matter of weeks. The valley filled up again, particularly on weekends. As the fall progressed, with crisp days and clear blue skies, the yellow tinge of larches on the mountainsides was a fleeting wonder to behold. Soon the days turned cloudy and moody as the threat of winter lay ever heavier in the air, and the roads and stores became crowded with large pickup trucks with gun racks and men in camouflage and orange. By November, winter set in. Snow became the modal forecast, and gloves and hats were needed even for brief tasks outdoors. I went through the Eastern Washington ritual of changing from regular to studded tires, as I adjusted to the reality of living with more snow on my gravel driveway than my Prius could clear and frequent near-misses on the valley's poorly maintained back roads. Getting out of the valley became a harrowing adventure, best avoided unless truly necessary. As winter matured across the valley, the tourists turned mostly to snow sports, and now the pickup trucks pulled snowmobiles, while smaller SUVs carried ski gear on rooftop racks and boxes.

By March, winter's grasp was loosening, and the frozen ground gave way to moisture and mud. Businesses around the valley closed for the shoulder season, when tourism slowed to a crawl. It wasn't long until the tourist season began in earnest again, however. As the ground gave way to carpets of brilliant yellow balsamroot flowers, the region filled with vacationers again. The roads into the valley became congested once more, with lines of RVs holding up SUVs loaded down with kayaks and bicycles, and drivers tailing one another in their impatience to begin recreating. The heat once again became oppressive, and both locals and visitors flocked to lakes and rivers to cool down. As I ended my time in Paradise Valley, Eastern Washington was once again ablaze, another stifling smoke season just beginning in the height of the summer tourist season.

PARADISE VALLEY'S ECONOMY THEN AND NOW

When I moved to Paradise Valley in 2014, its economy was still in recovery from the Great Recession, which hit rural Washington and tourism hard.[4] The rise of the tourism industry in Paradise Valley began back in the 1970s, as Washington State's logging industry began to collapse, alongside declines in other resource-based industries including mining and ranching. The recreation and tourism industries now dwarf these land-based industries in their share of the local labor market. During the Recession's recovery period, Paradise Valley did better than many tourism-dependent areas, but employment was below national averages, with labor force participation hovering under 60 percent and unemployment well over the state average. Even by 2015, close to 20 percent of valley residents and nearly a third of children in the valley lived below the poverty line. The region's top industries were mostly tourism-related to some degree, including accommodations and food services, retail, and construction. Accommodations and food services alone provided about a quarter of all employment in the region, but the jobs were low-paying and generated less than a fifth of all local wages. Multiple industries, including accommodations and food services, construction, and agriculture, provided mostly seasonal jobs with employment that peaked in August but declined by 20 percent to 30 percent between then and the low point during the March shoulder season.[5]

Economic instability and marginality are not new in Paradise Valley. The valley's first white settlers, intruders to a place that had long been inhabited by Native Americans, were mostly unsuccessful fur trappers and traders, who were later supplanted by miners looking for gold, silver, copper, and zinc. They pushed out the area's Native populations beginning in the late 1800s, relocating them to more remote reservation lands as miners demanded increasing amounts of valley land. Mining in the region mostly proved to be inconsistent and difficult, and numerous towns in the area came and went with the formation and failures of different mines. The valley was difficult to reach, surrounded by steep mountains, deep canyons, and winding rivers, and the main road into the region wasn't finished until the early 1900s. The early twentieth century also saw multiple attempts at agriculture that produced mixed results, as early orchardists contended with drought and other challenges. Later orchards that relied on irrigation ditches to provide regular water were more successful, and orcharding was an important part of the local economy until technological advances in the industry combined with extreme weather events to put many local growers out of business in the 1960s.

Among the more successful early ventures were sheep, cattle, and hay ranches, some of which are still operated by the descendants of early white settlers. These ranchers took advantage of abundant land and adequate water, which were more reliable than the mines had proved to be. Nonetheless, drought in the early twentieth century chased many away from the valley's arid hills. Throughout much of the century, ranchers took advantage of grazing rights on public lands, a practice that continued for decades until population pressures in the region led to restrictions on public land use. For much of the twentieth century it was common for private land also to be accessible for grazing cattle or horses—a practice whose demise numerous longtime residents lamented.

Logging and sawmills became another successful economic driver in the twentieth century, and multiple small-scale mills operated across the valley. As larger mills opened and logging became a more reliable industry, local men migrated from ranching to forest industry work. This trend accelerated in the middle of the century with the opening of a large, modern mill in Eagle Flat, which drew male laborers from across the valley. The mill became one of the most secure employers in the area, dominating the economy for forty years and employing several hundred workers. Local forests, including many managed by the US Forest Service, provided abundant timber to keep the mills running, and logging roads opened up many previously inaccessible parts of the valley. The Forest Service would become an important employer in the region as well.

The timber industry declined across the Pacific Northwest in the late twentieth century, and the Eagle Flat mill closed for good in the early 1980s.[6] It was during this same period, beginning with logging's decline in the 1970s, that tourism became the region's economic focus. Local efforts were undertaken to make the area more attractive to tourists, particularly those drawn by the area's physical beauty and western culture. Most locals who were there at the time describe having little understanding of the impacts that tourism would have on the valley, nor any inkling of the type of in-migrants that tourism would eventually bring. Early visitors were mostly temporary tourists interested in pursuing a variety of outdoor sports, including hunting, fishing, snowmobiling, horseback riding, camping, hiking, and skiing.

It was only later that Paradise Valley began to attract more permanent amenity migrants, including retirees and second-home owners. Locals describe an influx beginning in the 1990s, when economic shifts including a strong stock market and the dot-com boom contributed to the growth of a new group of middle-class Americans with significant disposable income and interests in outdoor fitness and recreation. Wealthy residents of Washington's urban west side began to invest in second homes in the region, many of which were lavishly custom-built on large acreages but visited only sporadically. These new residents would come to change the economic fortunes, residential patterns, and larger social and cultural worlds of Paradise Valley.

Eventually another shift occurred, beginning in the early 2000s as high-speed Internet became more readily available. Although weekend visitors and second-home owners continue to be mainstays across the valley, a number of both retired and working-age adults began to transition to full-time residency in Paradise Valley.[7] Although they did little to change the mostly white makeup of the valley, many of these in-migrants were distinct from the previous residents in terms of education, wealth, and income—multiple aspects of social class status.[8] Some of these newcomers (i.e., retirees) did not need or want full-time work, and some brought their work with them, often combining telecommuting with periodic trips over the mountains to meet in person with coworkers and clients in bigger cities. Others left their urban careers behind and looked for permanent and stable work in the valley. Some of these in-migrants entered the local labor market and competed for the same jobs as longtime residents; others created new opportunities for themselves by opening businesses, including inns, restaurants, shops, therapeutic practices, and numerous nonprofit organizations.

Their multiple resources—including wealth, education, and professional skills—allowed many of these newcomers the freedom to find or create jobs that they found interesting and enjoyable.[9] They often found that their economic niches were profitable due to the increasingly large pool of well-resourced newcomers available to patronize their businesses.

When asked how long it took to build up a client base, one alternative health-care professional told me that it happened "super-fast. People want it. It's educated women that are already into taking care of themselves and being really informed." Local artists and craftspeople similarly spoke of their reliance on wealthy homeowners and urban visitors who had the disposable income to invest in artwork.

The economic, educational, and social-network resources of these in-migrants allowed them to invest their time and energy into numerous causes around the valley about which they felt strongly, building a complex and wide-reaching charitable sector. The nonprofit sector in Paradise Valley swelled, providing some of the better-paying and most stable jobs in the area.[10] According to locals, there are "more nonprofits here than anywhere," with estimates ranging from 60 to 120 nonprofit organizations across the region. My own census using multiple sources identified more than 70 different local nonprofit organizations or local chapters of national nonprofit organizations in Paradise Valley, including organizations that focused on sports and recreation; community building and support; education; conservation and the environment; the arts; safety and rescue; poverty and social services; and politics.[11] These organizations filled in many of the gaps in services that are common in remote rural areas. They also provided numerous jobs for well-educated adults but often relied heavily on urban connections including the valley's second-home owners to fund them. In-migrant Shawn Murphy explained:

> The dynamic here is that those people [second-home owners] have money. It's like, they're the targets of, you know, people that are really invested, including some of these organizations. They're looking at these people as the cash cows and saying, "OK, how can we take these people's money? How can we convince these people that what we're doing is worthy, get them to write a check, and then apply that towards what is worthy causes?" ... Everyone's trying to raise money in Paradise Valley. There's how many nonprofits, and they're all trying to get you to break out your checkbook. So those second-home owners are hugely important as far as financing the budgets of all these organizations that are working to do good in the valley.

Thus the community came to rely heavily on second-home owners and repeat visitors with strong attachments to the area to help fund its local economy and services. This in turn changed the nature of available jobs in the region, the skills demanded by the labor market, and the interests that could be supported there.

Over time, the labor market became split: on the one hand, there were a limited but significant number of white-collar jobs that required higher education and professional skills, as well as fundraising and networking skills, which were generally stable, decently paid, and year-round. Also at the high end of the wage spectrum were a limited number of jobs for skilled carpenters, which were often well-paid, stable, full-time, and close to year-round. On the other hand, there were a larger number of jobs in retail and food services, construction, and tourism, which required less education and professional experience but were also low-wage, seasonal, and insecure. The bifurcation of the labor market corresponded to a growing divide within the community, between the groups I refer to as newcomers and old-timers (explained in the following section). Lifelong resident Edna Larson explained that these changes made it difficult for local young adults to survive in Paradise Valley:

> It used to be timber and that sort of thing here, and now it's pretty much recreation that supports the valley. Quite a few Forest Service jobs, but not here like they used to be. It's more recreation now. . . . It doesn't usually pay as good, so it's hard for the kids to come back here that love it unless they retire and get back here.

This change happened slowly, however, as some of the earliest waves of in-migrants who arrived in the post-logging era were either more similar to the existing residents in terms of education and class status or were limited in the types of work they could find there. Many earlier in-migrants brought less personal wealth and described finding work as teachers, service workers, and Forest Service employees, and adapting to the social and cultural rhythms of Paradise Valley. For these early in-migrants the valley's economy did not support sustained social class divisions, as there were few opportunities for making higher incomes or finding year-round work. Thus the community continued to have mostly a working-class feel for several decades. Over time, however, social class boundaries shifted and calcified, as more-privileged newcomers began to create opportunities and outlets for themselves and ultimately came to dominate the housing and labor markets as well as other sectors of community life.

Howard Jenkins, a seventy-five-year-old retired teacher, had moved to the valley forty-two years earlier during the first wave of new arrivals. He described his impressions of its residents at that time, as well as his generation of in-migrants and the later waves that followed:

> The only original and most fabulous and colorful people are the ones who grew up here and have lived here their lifetime. Amazingly rough, rugged, tough pioneer types, still here. And then a movement in the early '70s of the back-to-the-land type. . . . And the changes actually have been massive, from a pioneer-type community, really isolated. . . . It really was the Wild West, in almost every way.
>
> Q: When did that start to change?
>
> Um, in the '80s, I think. For about ten or fifteen years, there was no huge obvious change, but as more people started migrating in from the Seattle area, that's when it started changing. . . . A lot of the people coming in have enough money, they don't have to earn a living here, some retirees, people rich enough to build a second home. It takes some ingenuity to earn a living here. . . . Some of those folks do become part of the community, they're wonderful folks, but many of 'em are just invisible.

The most recent waves of in-migrants were different from previous waves in multiple ways, including the amounts of wealth they imported from mostly urban lives and livelihoods. There were also more of them than in previous periods, which allowed them the critical mass necessary to create their own communities and subcultures without integrating into the working-class culture of the preexisting residents as earlier in-migrants had. These dynamics, including differences in resources as well as in opportunities, lifestyles, and cultural understandings, set the stage for the community divisions detailed in the next section.

DIVIDING PARADISE: NEWCOMERS AND OLD-TIMERS

These changes are the backdrop against which this book takes place. They contributed to the current state of the community, in which two groups of people with different histories in Paradise Valley experience it in distinctly different ways. I rely on the ideal-typical terms "newcomer" and "old-timer" to describe these two groups, a distinction that on its face oversimplifies the meanings embedded in the terms. While they are consistent with how Paradise Valley locals described and made sense of their community and its social divisions, these terms represent much more than simply time spent in the valley. The term "newcomer" was commonly used in Paradise Valley to refer to a group of people who were distinct not only because of their shorter time in the valley (typically fewer than twenty years) but because of their real and symbolic resources as well as generally liberal political views.

Louise Clark, the sixty-eight-year-old retiree who had lived in the valley for sixteen years, explained: "You are not considered a local until you have been here about twenty years at least, that's what people tell us. I have had two people tell me that in the last month." Beyond just their shorter time in the valley, however, for Paradise Valley locals the newcomers are "city people" (Gregg Rossi, age fifty-seven, thirty-seven years in Paradise Valley) and "people from the Coast" (Wes Thompson, age forty-five, Paradise Valley native) who "bring money, they bring new ideas . . . more education, more liberal attitudes" (Philip Stevens, age seventy-five, thirty-one years in Paradise Valley). Newcomers are perceived as wanting "to change this to make this like the Coast" (Marc Tate, age forty-two, Paradise Valley native); and "the newbies came in [thinking], 'Not in my backyard. Now that I'm here, we're gonna stop all the logging and keep it pristine'" (Donald Barnett, age fifty-four, twenty-seven years in Paradise Valley).

The newcomers came to the valley for a variety of reasons but often held certain interests, resources, and core values in common. They tended to have higher educational attainment than the local population, more wealth, and higher incomes. This population also included more adults who openly identified as LGBTQ (lesbian, gay, bisexual, transgender, and queer/questioning), including a number of prominent community members who were in same-sex couples and marriages. Politically, most newcomers voted liberally, and their concerns tended to focus on issues like environmental conservation and social justice. Most were interested in the area specifically because of its local environment and outdoor amenities. A large number of newcomers partook in outdoor sports, including hiking, biking, running, camping, backpacking, and both downhill and cross-country skiing. They were often portrayed by old-timers through stereotypes that focused on these sports and the specific clothing brands and styles commonly worn by outdoor endurance athletes.

These images of educated, wealthy, liberal, urban in-migrants were often contrasted against an opposing group, which was referred to through both time in the valley (generally more than twenty years) and a number of images and terms that evoked a working-class and land-based work orientation, lower education, lower cultural capital, and more conservative political ideology.[12] Although this group also loved the outdoors and the local environment, their main interests and hobbies were often different—they preferred activities like hunting, fishing, swimming and floating in rivers, riding ATVs and snowmobiles, and horse packing. Locals regularly used the term "redneck" to describe the older generation of Paradise Valley residents, explaining that the local population "is really redneck. Votes for the NRA and that stuff. Even Tea Party" (Howard Jenkins, age seventy-five, forty-two years in Paradise Valley), and "it was just a redneck logging town [in the past]" (Maria Setzer, age forty, seven years in Paradise Valley). Asa Hobson, a thirty-eight-year-old valley native whose parents were from the previous generation of in-migrants, explained this contrast and how the populations evolved over time:

When my dad and mom got here, it was probably equal parts orchard and logging. . . . It was some of the first real lefties that came into the valley, I guess you would say. And then for a while there it was like 50/50. You know, kind of rednecks and, you know, liberals. And now we have had this big influx of—to where, like, it is obviously tipping the scales because we have a lot of people coming from Seattle too now, and buying a second home or liking the place a lot on vacation and staying.

Donna Cox, a sixty-seven-year-old in-migrant who had lived in Paradise Valley for four years, felt there was a growing divide between the two groups: "There's . . . the old-time people who have been here forever. A lot of them are ranchers or farmers or whatever, and I see that conflict between the newies and the oldies increasing." The "liberal/redneck" divide was characterized in various other words as well, and over my time in Paradise Valley I heard terms including "salt of the earth," "denim," "Carharts," and "redneck" contrasted with "environmentalist," "Lycra," "spandex," "Patagonia," and "trust fund." I have chosen to use the terms

"newcomer" and "old-timer" to represent these various shades of meaning both because they were used repeatedly by locals and because they
represent the poles of this perceived divide without openly disparaging
either group. Nonetheless, this simple binary represents opposing ends
of a continuum, which as the above quotations suggest, is comprised of a
number of factors including time of residence, income, education, cultural
capital, and political stance.

Like any continuum, it includes a number of people who fall somewhere
in the middle. Peter Williams, who had visited Paradise Valley for decades
but lived there full-time for just eight years, described the valley's longtime residents as including "a lot of old-timers, and old-newcomers"—the
latter referring to people who had longer histories in the valley but looked
more like newcomers in terms of education, political stance, income, and
cultural capital. Thirty-three-year-old Sabena Griffin, who had moved to
Paradise Valley as a child and later left to pursue advanced education and
work before moving back, described her friends in the valley as falling
into a group in the middle of the continuum, which she referred to as
"hippie-rednecks":

> So it is like a hippie state of mind, but then they are really into, like, redneck
> sort of things. Like chainsaws and guns and hunting, and drinking beer.
> They got their Rainier [beer] and their monster truck, but then they are
> totally environmentalists at the same time or something. They are wearing
> Carharts and some festival shirt.

Although there were people in the valley who fell somewhere in
between the two poles, most recognized that the extremes did exist, and
they often spoke of the community's social divide in binary ways. Table
B.1 in Appendix B categorizes the interview participants in my research
according to this typology, illustrating the multiple facets of these terms to
clarify the degree to which each person quoted exemplifies the "newcomer"
or "old-timer" position within the community. I use a five-point index
including time in the valley, political leanings, cultural orientations, education, and income to categorize each participant (listed by pseudonym).
As can be seen in the table, not all short-term residents are categorized as
newcomers and not all long-term residents are considered old-timers, as
social class status makes up a significant component of the index and can

trump length of residency in the final classification. Although time in the valley often predicts (or is predicted by) social class, political leaning, and cultural orientation, it is not an exact match for all individuals. Nor are all individuals perfect fits for their final classification, although for most it is consistent with the ways in which they and others view them.

The interview sample was almost evenly split between old-timers and newcomers (forty and forty-three, respectively), with a single unclassifiable participant designated as "old-newcomer." Taken as groups, newcomers and old-timers look different in a number of ways. In terms of the components that make up the classifications, the trends are clear: although the average age of the two groups is similar in the interview sample (forty-nine years for newcomers, fifty-one for old-timers), newcomers, on average, had lived fewer than fifteen years in the valley, while old-timers spent an average of more than thirty years there. Close to three-quarters (74 percent) of newcomers were classified as middle-income, while just 18 percent of old-timers fit into this category.[13] Newcomers mostly had a bachelor's degree or higher (74 percent), while just 8 percent of old-timers did.[14] Newcomers tended to have more educated parents as well: 64 percent of newcomers had college-educated parents, while just 26 percent of old-timers did. Old-timers had also often experienced harder living. More than 38 percent of old-timers discussed having past or current drug or alcohol problems, compared to 7 percent of newcomers.[15] A full 56 percent of old-timers reported having experienced some form of abuse as children or adults, compared to 34 percent of newcomers.

With regard to political views, 69 percent of newcomers reported liberal leanings, and another 26 percent reported no preference or side, while fewer than 5 percent reported conservative preferences. Old-timers were much more likely to be conservative (26 percent) or undecided (59 percent), with just 15 percent reporting liberal leanings. There are other noticeable differences between the two groups. Newcomers were more likely to be employed at the time of interview (60 percent versus 41 percent of old-timers). They were also slightly more likely to be married (67 percent versus 59 percent of old-timers), but old-timers had an average of 2.1 children, while newcomers averaged 1.4. Old-timers were more than twice as likely to attend church regularly (29 percent versus 14 percent of newcomers), although both groups expressed high levels of religious faith when nondenominational religious beliefs were included (52 percent of newcomers and 66 percent of old-timers).

Both groups were mostly white, but newcomers in the sample were slightly more so (95 percent), with just one participant of Asian race and another of Latinx ethnicity. Old-timers were 85 percent white, with one Asian participant, and five reporting some Native American heritage.[16] By and large, race was not an issue that either group acknowledged openly, although as chapters 3 and 4 discuss, both groups discussed issues such as "safety" and other potential code words for racial concerns as among their reasons for choosing to move to or stay in a remote, rural community. As I have found in previous work, white rural populations frequently use terms like "safe" and "family-friendly" to refer obliquely to the ways in which living in rural communities allows them to avoid racialized concerns.[17] Neither old-timers nor newcomers had much interest in racial issues as political concerns, and few discussed race casually either.[18] I noted in particular the absence of discussion around then-current events such as protests related to verdicts in the shooting cases of unarmed Black men Michael Brown and Eric Garner, both of which occurred during my time in Paradise Valley.[19] It seemed that for many residents the lack of ethnic or racial diversity in Paradise Valley allowed them the space to avoid recognizing race much at all.

This pattern is consistent with what sociologist Eduardo Bonilla-Silva has described as "'New Racism' practices" such as color-blind racism "that are subtle, institutional, and apparently nonracial," which allow the dominant race to protect and benefit from the current racial system without admitting to being racist.[20] Newcomers were more likely to bemoan the lack of racial diversity in Paradise Valley, but mostly when either they or their children were members of a racial or ethnic minority group.[21] Rare, but also more common among newcomers, were conscious attempts to demonstrate that they were not racist, such as describing their friendships with persons of color. Old-timers rarely but occasionally did discuss racial issues more overtly, including referencing their own racialized experiences and struggles as minorities in the valley, and openly acknowledging racism there, either past or present. These rare admissions included one elderly Paradise Valley native who confided in her interview that her grandfather was in the Ku Klux Klan. She told me: "I am not proud of that. But it's a fact."

Despite inhabiting the same small community, newcomers and old-timers make up distinct populations within it. In modern-day Paradise Valley, residents from both sides of the divide must find ways to coexist in a rapidly changing social landscape. For old-timers the community was changing in tangible ways that were not always expected or desired, even if they were accepted as necessary, understandable, or even inevitable out-comes of amenity tourism and development.

"YUPPIE WONDERLAND": IMPRESSIONS OF CHANGE

The community's transitions were felt on multiple levels by those who had lived for longer periods in the valley, who spoke at length about both the positive and the negative sides of the changes brought by tourism and amenity development. I heard repeatedly about improvements in the availability of services in the area, and the growth of arts and culture. I also heard much about new struggles, including gentrification and ris-ing housing costs, restricted access to land and water, and what many perceived as a decline in civility or in community itself. Almost no one I met or interviewed ever suggested that the region should not have pur-sued amenity tourism, which was nearly universally recognized as eco-nomically essential, but many still lamented the side effects of this form of development.

Despite its necessity, it was hard to deny that tourism and in-migration had visceral, tangible impacts on the community. Longtime locals often evoked the turnover among valley businesses and landmarks to describe the ways in which the community was morphing during their lifetimes. They talked about the number of new businesses, as well as the chang-ing nature of the services they offered, in answer to my questions about whether the community had changed. Typical responses included:

> It is gentrified. You know, it's—I mean, bakeries were opened. Health food store. Those things came and went over the years, but now they work. Because the clientele is here for it. You can have a bakery in each town, you know? And food—and coffee places—you know, you can just tell that it is,

you know—Seattle has had its influence. And a professional theater? That was unthinkable twenty or thirty years ago.

—Roy Watson, seventy-four-year-old middle-income retired teacher; forty-three years in Paradise Valley

When I moved here, most of the commercial—70 percent of the commercial buildings in Eagle Flat were empty and for sale back in the '80s. It was just emptied out. Maybe not that much, maybe 50 percent, just empty. And of course in the '90s it started pickin' up and people started going, "Wow, I can buy a commercial building for 10 cents on the dollar. I can't build something for that." It got gobbled up and then rented out, and then at one time I think we had five coffee shops. Everybody was gonna run a coffee shop.

—Donald Barnett, fifty-four-year-old low-income carpenter; twenty-seven years in Paradise Valley

[Now there's] nicer restaurants, and um, just you know, and nicer motels. I mean, the new motel here in Eagle Flat . . . I know it's, it's spendy, it's high priced, but it's nice. And it's what all the tourists and people want. And I think you need that. You haveta still have that.

—Audrey Patterson, fifty-nine-year-old poor, Supplemental Security Income–dependent; forty-six years in Paradise Valley[22]

These external and superficial changes were as obvious to old-timers as they were to an occasional visitor like me, but beneath the storefront facades was a complex series of more significant demographic, economic, and social changes. While some changes, like nicer hotels, were of little threat to old-timers, other shifts impacted them more seriously.

Rising housing costs were an issue that affected almost everyone in Paradise Valley in one way or another. Studies of local housing trends described a tight housing market dominated by seasonally occupied second homes, an extremely low vacancy rate, and widespread housing stress. For many homeowners this meant that the values of their homes had risen markedly over time; for some this meant that rising tax rates on those homes would eventually force them out, while others experienced it as rising personal wealth.[23] Early on in my volunteer work, I ate lunch with a coworker who had moved to Paradise Valley in the 1970s. My field notes from the conversation describe this dynamic:

She talked about the people who had moved here with money that they could sink into houses and land, but also of people like her, who moved here at a time when land was cheap, and with working-class jobs they were able to buy modest houses that later ended up being worth so much more than they had paid for them, even adjusting for inflation. She said that they bought their house for $20,000 and sold it for $250,000. She explained that the exponential growth of housing values has made people like her wealthy, while others are kept perpetually out of the community's prosperity.[24]

Changing land values and land uses were among the top concerns of many of the long-term locals I met in Paradise Valley. While my coworker and a number of longtime families with large landholdings became increasingly wealthy through these processes, others experienced them with more ambivalence, strain, and concern.

In addition to rising housing costs, the economic transitions described earlier in this chapter were also a major concern for many old-timers. Thirty-eight-year-old Jessica Wheeler, a waitress in a local restaurant, expressed anxiety about the economic challenges that valley natives like herself faced:

> One of the biggest challenges for Paradise Valley—which I don't want to see happen—is for our economy here to chase the locals out of here. Because there is a lot of people that kind of live here and have their little dream vacation homes and come party here or whatever, but we locals make the wheels go around, and if our economy—if we continue to go at a rate to where we can't survive around here, then they are going to chase a lot of us away, and that's not going to be a good thing. I guess that is one thing that scares me. I just want to be able to stay.

The transition to a mostly service-based economy, combined with rising housing costs, created significant struggles for many of the valley's old-timers. The ability to survive in Paradise Valley was one of the major differences that separated old-timers from newcomers. In addition to different economic opportunities and constraints, the very different lifestyle expectations and orientations toward money and disposable income were stark between the two groups. Even those old-timers who made a living from services they provided to newcomers often could not help but critically note these differences. Longtime local construction worker Donald Barnett commented: "There's a lot of people, myself included, who have over the years gone from workin' for people in my income bracket, just to try to help 'em get into a house and make a living, to workin' for people who are spendin' $6,000 on a shower faucet. Which is kind of absurd."

Alongside concerns regarding rising housing costs and struggles to survive, many old-timers bemoaned changing orientations toward land use as newcomers took control of increasing amounts of valley land. Unlike the previous settlers, who mostly used private land for farming and ranching, many newcomers purchased large tracts of land that were not put into commercial uses, but rather were desired for pristine views and privacy. Between these purchases and the work of local conservation groups, over time larger and larger tracts of valley land were set aside for either private or limited public recreational uses. An acquaintance in Eagle Flat, a long-time rancher, shared his thoughts about these changes:

> He said that he had been here since 1977 and that it had changed so much. He told me that back in those days everyone knew everyone and knew everybody's business, but now he goes into town and he doesn't recognize people anymore. He talked about the old industries, ranching and the mill, which was still running when he moved here. He said that those two industries alone employed about four hundred men back then, but now those jobs are gone. After the jobs left, he explained, people started selling their land to outsiders. He mentioned Pinedale in particular, where he said people started selling a "pile of rocks" for $50,000 an acre, and that wealthy people from the west side were more than willing to pay it. He said the area attracted people from all over the place, including "from New Jersey and other foreign countries." He told me that he clears snow out in Pinedale in the wintertime for money, and that a lot of his clients are these weekender types. He said they're not bad people, but they sure are different, with different attitudes and ideas about things. He half-apologized for the "foreign countries" comment, joking that it made it clear how he felt about things.
>
> He gave an example, explaining that he used to run "about 20 head of cattle" in the hillsides where public land had open grazing rights. He described people who would buy large lots that abutted the public land and wouldn't want to mar their views with fences. But then they would complain when they saw his cattle cross their yards to get to their watering holes and salt licks. He shook his head, wondering aloud why they wouldn't just put up fences if they didn't want cattle in their yards.[25]

Issues regarding fences and NO TRESPASSING signs were common complaints among old-timers, as the valley changed from seemingly infinite public land with open use to a model of mostly private ownership. As I traveled around the region to interview its inhabitants, I encountered many of these signs warning strangers away from its most breathtaking properties, including those that announced entire roads to be private and closed to trespassers.[26] Edna Larson, who had lived most of her seventy-seven years in the valley, had this to say about the region's changes:

> I think what we notice the most is the NO TRESPASSING signs that spring up when we used to be able to just ride from one end of the valley to the other on our horses, and as long as we closed the gates and was respect-ful, there was no problem. But now, uh, the newcomers think that—they like it here because it's so free, but they don't want anybody on their property.

Irene Nelson, a fifty-four-year-old artist who had lived in the valley for thirty-five years, had similar observations:

> Nobody had NO TRESPASSING and all of these things. It was assumed if you needed to go through to get your buck or whatever—if the gate is open, you leave the gate open. If the gate is closed, you close the gate. You don't shoot people's livestock. And the first thing that city folks do when they come in is they put up a great big fence and put NO TRESPASSING. The first thing they do.

For longtime residents there was an obvious tension between restricted land use and the new economic reality of Paradise Valley, in which construction of new homes was a major source of jobs and income, further contributing to land-use pressures of this nature. Chad Lloyd, a twenty-eight-year-old sawmill worker who had lived in the valley since high school, described this conflict as he experienced it:

> We've sold all the lumber that goes into all these houses. So it's kind of bit-tersweet, like, oh, that's great. The company I work for is doin' very good, but I wish that house wasn't there, 'cause I used to like to go hunt there. I used to like to be able to hike through there to go fishing, and now there's houses. It's changed a lot....I don't think it was necessarily public land, but there was nothin' there and you were able to hike through, and nobody was like, "Hey, get off my property!" Or even being able to look out on the side of the mountain and there's five houses whereas five years ago there was nothin'.

In addition to changing uses for private land, the ways in which tourists in particular used public land, and growing pressures on its use by new stakeholders, led to increased enforcement of land use restrictions, which often rubbed old-timers the wrong way. Although they frequently didn't fully understand all of the regulations and their origins, I heard repeatedly that Paradise Valley had gone from basically a lawless western outpost to a much more regulated community. Valley native Wendy Harris, a thirty-seven-year-old stay-at-home mother, explained that when she was young, "I could ride in the back of a pick-up, and you wouldn't have to worry about gettin' pulled over and gettin' a ticket if you were just goin' across the street. You could ride your horses in town. Can't do that anymore." Fifty-five-year-old valley native Owen Roberts complained about new restrictions on hunting and fishing, including catch-and-release require-ments. He said:

> Some of the changes that have happened didn't need to happen. Like fishing regulations and hunting—I don't fish no more. I don't, because of regula-tions. Like I told people—if I catch something, I'm going to eat the damn thing. I am not a person—why turn something away after you have caught it?

Such restrictions had particularly serious impacts on poor residents like Owen, many of whom couldn't afford the license fees and felt shut out of what had been lifelong cultural practices. He expressed concern about the transition away from subsistence-focused hunting:

> I don't catch things for trophy. I catch it to eat it. And I was brought up that way. If you kill something, you are going to eat it. And a lot of people don't see that around here. A lot of people come here for the big antler deer. Just for the antlers.

Longtime local Irene Nelson described a similar sentiment, also com-plaining about the complicated new regulations:

> There is rules everywhere now. Stuff that I used to do as a kid, I'd be consid-ered an absolute outlaw now. . . . They don't want you to go fish—you need an attorney to go fishing. Oh, you can't fish on this part of the river, but you can fish over here. But you can use barbless here, but you can't use—I mean come on. You know? That is crazy. And the same with hunting regs, they are just absolutely bizarre.

Like Owen, Irene expressed frustration with overly restrictive regulations, but also dismay at the forces that made them necessary. She said:

> You never used to see people just slaughtering just to kill. There was always a use for it. Now you hear about these guys leaving headless critters. I mean they are—the game agents are having to do a lot more of this. It used to be considered—if you were subsistence hunting, they would do this [gestures with head to indicate turning the other cheek].... Nobody needed to be on welfare, because you could—and I have done it myself. Especially when I was younger. You didn't make shit for wages. You really don't anymore—even now. If you are a local, you don't make much. But if you are hungry, you go harvest a deer. But you are not stupid about it. You go, Oh, there is a deer and there is a wounded one. You don't take the premium, and—you don't go get them for their antlers. That is just wasteful. And I—do I kill? Yes, I kill. But I have never killed for fun. Anyways, that is kind of some of the difference I see.

The wastefulness of sport hunters was a source of consternation for many old-timers. Martha Crawford, an eighty-year-old valley native, similarly commented: "When I was growing up [everyone] ate venison. Nobody, you know, just shot one and left it lay." The changing practices and regulations made subsistence activities like hunting and fishing increasingly difficult for old-timers and changed the nature of rural life as they had known it. But beyond the loss of these traditions, many old-timers expressed frustration at orientations toward hunting and fishing that contrasted glaringly with the subsistence culture in which they had been raised. Many old-timers similarly struggled to practice subsistence activities like gardening and canning, as they were increasingly squeezed into small and rental housing units with limited storage and little or no access to land, including many old-timers in subsidized apartments and tightly packed trailer parks. They often described childhoods filled with such activities but struggled to engage in them as adults.

Martha Crawford remembered the gendered subsistence activities of her childhood and early adulthood fondly. She recalled:

> My dad and my brother liked to go moose hunting, and that was their trip, I guess you could say, into Canada. And they would do that. And they hunted and fished and everything, you know. So, and then mother got, instead of canning a lot of things, she got really good at freezing a lot of things. And so

she would freeze and put things away, and that's how they ate, really. And she planted a garden. She was a gardener.

These cherished memories often brought into relief how times had changed in Paradise Valley. Greg Rossi, a fifty-seven-year-old, retired US Forest Service employee, described his family's subsistence traditions with a sense of nostalgia and loss:

> Everyone was poorer [then]. Property was dirt-cheap here, but everyone was happy. That's where hunting was more favorable then, 'cause that's how they stuffed the freezers in the winter. They'd harvest stuff in the gardens and stuff. Everyone was more close-knit, and they'd harvest stuff and save it for the winter. My ex-wife, you know, they're a logging-ranching family, and they can all their own stuff. So we'd live in my basement here all winter long off the stuff she grew just right here with just two little gardens.

For those who remained poor, this loss could be both personal and material. Fifty-nine-year-old Audrey Patterson had grown up in the valley, but as a disabled adult with an ailing husband, she found it hard to get by. The couple now lived in a travel trailer on rented land, where gardening wasn't an option. I asked her if they practiced any subsistence activities in order to help augment their meager diet. She replied:

> Nope. We didn't have a place, this year we didn't have a garden spot. I just haven't had the opportunity. When I was growing up, we always had a garden ... we always had our meat, we butchered chickens and stuff. We just haven't had the means to have those. We probably will once we get a better setup and see what we can do there and stuff. I'd like to have, you know, we had our own pigs.

For many Paradise Valley natives, subsistence activities like these were both an important part of daily survival and part of their cultural heritage.[27] Young local couple Emmet and Amy Farley described the excitement of finally being able to practice theses skills after buying their first home:

EMMET: We want to start learning—relearning these skills of—

AMY: Well, we want to teach [our son], you know?

EMMET: You know, gardening and food preservation and stuff like that.

AMY: So that's why we are excited we finally have our own house, because at a rental I'm not going to put a bunch of time and energy into a garden if we are just going to move.

As these quotes suggest, old-timers with long roots in the valley experienced changes in access to land and housing not simply as a frustration but often as threats to their abilities to survive as well as to their culture and way of life.

While changing land use and access jeopardized their subsistence, a number of old-timers told me that other types of changes in Paradise Valley's culture, including more nebulous values and interests, were what concerned them the most. Maura Engle, a forty-nine-year-old in-migrant from a different remote rural community, described her understanding of the cultural divide:

> It does seem like there is more Coast people here. And that—the people— the locals who have been here for a long time are chewing on glass because of that. You know it is one thing to move into a place and assimilate, and it is another thing to come in—"Cows on the road?!" Well, it was a cow's trail before it was a BMW trail. So if you can't handle it, plan your schedule accordingly.

This change in attitudes over time was noticeable to many locals with rural roots, a number of whom found it vexing. When asked how the community had changed over her thirty-eight years in Paradise Valley, sixty-two-year-old Marilyn Edwards sighed audibly and said:

> This place turned into like a yuppie, um, uh, what do you wanna call it, wonderland or something. You know, where everybody wants to go fly fishing and everybody wants to go rafting and everybody wants to own a million dollar home along the backside of Eagle Flat, of Paradise River, going up towards Reliance, and everybody wants to be a skier, and, and they've just put in all these, you know . . . they just changed it. It changed.

Doris Foster, an eighty-year-old farmer who had lived in the valley for forty-nine years, described a similar impression: "Most all of the people that come up here now, they live here just because they like to be close to the skiing and fishing . . . and more of that kind of thing than farming, I guess." For Greg Rossi the cultural difference centered on specific rural experiences that newcomers lacked. "People don't understand why we log or ranching," he told me. "They're more city-orientated, kinda...it's just a different mentality from a farmer to a logger to someone movin' in from Seattle or somethin', and their whole mentality's a little bit different." He explained:

> When I moved here, there was more farm people, people more in—you know, in tune. There was a lot of families that [horse] packed.... So there was a lot more families in tune with horses and mules and goin' packing in the wilderness as a family. There was more ranching, more logging. There was a different style of stuff goin' on.

Beyond simply that newcomers were different from old-timers in their cultural orientations, many old-timers felt a loss of their place in the community as more and more people moved in who didn't share their history and didn't know them well. Valley native Wes Thompson, a forty-five-year-old public employee, described the estrangement he sometimes felt now:

> A lot of—for me personally, just a lot of people I don't know any more and a lot of, you know, I used to be able to walk downtown and knew everybody on the street, and everybody's house, and nowadays, it's like, I don't know half the people that are in [the grocery store], you know.... There's a lot of people I don't know. Like I said, I used to be able to walk this whole town and I could name everybody that lived in every house. And they all knew me and they knew my parents and my brother. Nowadays I can't. It's like, "She used to live there. I don't know who's there now."

Caleb Daniels, who had lived all of his twenty-six years in the valley, similarly explained: "It used to be where you could—you knew everyone. It seems in the past ten years or so it's been a bunch of new faces." For longtime residents of a small, remote place, being confronted by increasing numbers of strangers was disconcerting and alienating. It also meant that beyond a few very successful business leaders and wealthy landowners, old-timers had a diminishing voice in community politics. Martha Crawford, who had lived all of her eighty years in the valley, described what she saw as a distressing change in the nature of local leadership, beginning with a previous mayor who "decided that it was good to have people, uh, from outside of the town" on the local council. A number of the valley's old-timers increasingly felt that their home community no longer welcomed or included them in the ways it once had.

Despite these challenges, however, many old-timers were both positive and hopeful about the valley. Although most longtime residents agreed that the community was changing due to in-migration, many accepted the changes with optimism despite their concerns. Alongside her many worries, Martha accepted the necessity of the tourism industry: "It was no longer a farming, and logging community as it had been. But so they needed—really needed something to draw the people, if they wanted to stay here." Barbara Phillips, a seventy-year-old rancher who had moved to the valley as a young adult, had many concerns but also praise for some of the changes: "I think it's nice to have restaurants—very, very nice. And the art—they do a lot with art, and there is a lot of interesting things going on. And so, I know if you meet nice people and they—there is more positive than negative." For eighty-one-year-old retiree Joyce Morris, who moved to the valley in the 1980s from a city herself, change was only a problem if the past was lost and forgotten. She said:

> In my day, the community was kind of a remote place. It was a little Western town, and what we did in the winter was go to people's houses. It's changed—it's grown, I don't want to say changed. We have that heritage, but it's grown, with people coming in and maybe doing their jobs and their work, they can do it on computers now and have houses all around, so it's a lot different. But I have a strong sense, a lot of people of my day want it to be like it was. But I don't think that. I want it to be kept as it was, as our memories and our heritage, but the people coming in are young people like yourself with wonderful ideas. We have theater, we have music, we have wonderful trails. I think it could be all incorporated in together, but people need to understand.

Old-timers described the region's growing pains as bringing both new opportunities and new struggles. Although few could imagine a future without amenity tourism and in-migration, many old-timers wondered whether that future held a place for them.

EXPLORING PARADISE VALLEY'S DIVIDE

Paradise Valley, as a rural community experiencing both population and economic growth, is somewhat uncommon in the United States, where most rural places are struggling to find their economic hooks in the era of postindustrialization.[28] There are many rural places in which such growth would be welcome, and Paradise Valley residents also recognized the benefits it brought—from arts and services to educational opportunities to infrastructure and jobs. Newcomers brought new energy to the community; real concern about its present and future; and openness to new ideas, lifestyles, and viewpoints.[29] The vibrancy and opportunities they created helped to counteract brain drain and to ensure that there were prospects for well-educated and capable young adults who wanted to live in a beautiful rural setting.[30] Nonetheless, Paradise Valley provides a cautionary case of rural inequality, which while occurring at the local level for this community is also the result of much larger trends in urban-rural inequality occurring across the nation.[31] As such, the story of Paradise Valley allows us to delve inside the processes that result from and sustain American inequality, which are both unmistakable to those experiencing it and often invisible to those perpetuating it.

Amenity tourism and the in-migration of privileged urbanites had many undesirable outcomes for Paradise Valley in addition to the economic and social benefits. As is common across the United States as a whole, increasing economic inequality can also bring a host of social ills. Beyond the changes in culture and lifestyles that this chapter outlined, the growing gap between new and old, rich and poor, and more educated and less, led to differences in access to resources, efficacy within the community, and individual opportunities and outcomes. The rest of this book explores the impacts of inequality on Paradise Valley, elucidating the processes by which it occurs and is reproduced and the consequences of its reproduction. Throughout this book these impacts are described from both sides, with a continuing focus on the adverse impacts for the community's most vulnerable residents, its old-timers. These impacts include not just the changing nature of available jobs but the changing meanings of work and workers, including who is seen as worthy of the jobs that are left and who is seen as expendable in the new economic landscape. Residents' struggles to survive begin with work and jobs but include struggles for housing, childcare, and education. For families, the impacts of these struggles include inabilities to navigate work/family conflicts and the retrenchment of traditional gender roles; mental health impacts of stresses associated with precariousness, inadequate living conditions, and loss of self-respect;

and multiple ways in which anger, frustration, and sense of loss contribute to social isolation, decreasing social capital, and the loss of faith in the political system.

Paradise Valley is a place in which urban and rural cultural norms clash and structure both newcomers' and old-timers' outlooks and interpretations of each other and of their social world. This book presents the story of Paradise Valley itself but also the tale of a divided nation whose hope lies in increased interaction, inclusion, and understanding of one another despite our differences. Despite increasing inequality in this community and in the nation, it is not too late for either Paradise Valley or the country at large to reverse course and find ways in which to heal the divide and to maximize all citizens' chances and opportunities for achieving their versions of the American Dream.

3 Living the Dream

NEWCOMERS MAKING IT WORK IN PARADISE

Despite its surface similarity to other small, remote, western towns, Paradise Valley was distinctly different. It wasn't just the number of motels, inns, and lodges that stood out to me, but the nature of the businesses themselves. Unlike previous small towns where I had lived, I could easily take yoga classes, get vegetarian and gluten-free food, and purchase high-end outdoor gear all within the valley's limits. At the farmers' markets alongside vendors selling local produce, jams, and baked goods were a number selling hand-made pottery and furniture as well as clothing made from alternative fabrics including hemp, organic cotton, and upcycled wool. Paradise Valley's services catered to a much more urbane, middle-class demographic than I had seen in most rural communities, including other communities dependent on tourism. I wondered whether such services were frequented by local residents, guessing initially that they must only attract outside tourists and visitors passing through. Over my time in the valley I learned that in addition to its short-term visitors, many of the valley's permanent residents, particularly its newcomers, used these services heavily. I could often guess the social class status of a prospective interview participant just by the location he or she suggested for the interview, as numerous places catered clearly to the newcomer or old-timer crowd, and few spots were frequented equally by both groups.

Although the valley attracted in-migrants from across the class spectrum, including a number of lower-income individuals and families who were funneled into the bottom rungs of the seasonal and tourism-driven labor market, the bulk of more recent newcomers had substantial resources of either real or symbolic capital. For many the decision to move to Paradise Valley was one with both positive and negative impacts on their own personal trajectories, often including career and income sacrifices alongside the many positive aspects. In a community that lacks infrastructure on multiple levels, newcomers had to be both creative and proactive to live comfortably. In this endeavor they relied heavily upon informal support and social networks to provide what the public sphere did not. Although the community and social setting were seldom the first motivations newcomers provided to explain the decision to move to Paradise Valley, they often proved to be among the most important to newcomers' long-term happiness and survival in the valley. Newcomers were drawn to the valley's unique physical and recreational attributes and both consciously and unconsciously contributed to remaking its social world to ensure that it fit their needs and visions of what rural life and rural community should entail.

"OUT OF THE RAT RACE": MOTIVATIONS FOR THE MOVE

> What brought us here was the beauty of the mountains and
> accessibility of them also. And there is this image of going
> from Reliance to Pinedale that is so gorgeous in the fall. So
> that was the first image, and it is golden fields and these
> mountains. . . . Subsequent to that, we started learning about
> the community and how rich it is.
> —Dennis Wright, seventy-five-year-old married, middle-income
>   retiree

As I learned about newcomers of varying ages and life histories, I discovered that their stories mostly contained a few common elements that motivated the choice to give up urban amenities and incomes to move to a remote rural place. More-advantaged newcomers came there for reasons including the desire for an idealized rural lifestyle, often combined with the draw of Paradise Valley's stunning physical landscape and the affordability of land and homes there, as well as specific interests in outdoor sports and agrarian pursuits like gardening or small-scale farming. Their conceptions of rurality often focused around understandings of rural communities as safe, easy, supportive, and family-friendly. Many newcomers talked about wanting a slower-paced lifestyle, to get out of the "rat race," and to escape the alienation they experienced in cities and suburbs.

Although some newcomers had visited the community repeatedly prior to the decision to move there, and others had been part-time residents for extended periods of time before permanently relocating, most were following steadfast dreams of an improved life in a rural community. The dream was often built on a scaffolding of idealized images of rural communities that have long held sway in the American psyche. These images, along with the physical grandeur of high-amenity places like Paradise Valley, have proved to be an important draw in many similar rural communities.[1] Although these images are powerful across the class spectrum, it was their combination with privilege in terms of wealth, human capital, and cultural capital that allowed most newcomers to realize this dream and make new lives in a place where they frequently had few previous ties and only limited job prospects.[2] The idea of Paradise Valley as promising a slower-paced, more peaceful, and safer lifestyle had drawn newcomers for generations, including many of the parents of the community's current native-born young adults. Howard Jenkins, one of the rare longer-term "newcomers" explained his decision to move to Paradise Valley in the 1970s this way:

> We moved here partly to get away from—to get out of the fast lane, to get out of the rat race, to live. We bought a small ranch up at the Eagle River, 80 acres. What did I think? We didn't know a single person and didn't want to know a single person [laughs]. We were just moving out into the country, the edge of the wilderness.

The desire for a slower-paced lifestyle and the safety it theoretically provided continued to inspire more recent waves of newcomers. They often spoke in these types of terms, which explicitly avoided any discussion of race or social class, despite potentially being code words for both.[3]

We were living in Seattle and really had grown tired of the anonymous
nature of Seattle. . . . I don't know, there was just too many transient people.
It didn't feel close anymore, so we wanted to move to a smaller community
for a slower, simpler lifestyle.

—Matt Graham, forty-three-year-old married, middle-income business owner

I love it here. . . . I like how much nature there is. I like that it's small, it feels
like a safe place to raise a kid.

—Maria Setzer, forty-year-old married, low-income substitute teacher

By and large we live here partly because it is very safe, it is very wholesome,
it is very healthy.

—Andrew Bowden, forty-six-year-old married, middle-income carpenter

The pull of the rural idyll has a long history in the United States, and
this image of rural communities as slower-paced, safer, and more
family-friendly continues to both justify the decision to live in rural communities and draw new generations of in-migrants to them.[4] The fact that
vast tracts of land could be purchased and inhabited by single families
in Paradise Valley helped to make the rural dream a reality for urban in-
migrants.

Access to large parcels of relatively untouched land where homes
could be purchased or built was key to achieving this rural lifestyle for
many newcomers. As I visited with newcomers around the valley, I witnessed firsthand the grandeur of many of these spaces, including a number of beautifully crafted houses built from rough-hewn timber with
shiny modern appliances and hardwood floors, with ample windows that
looked out onto large expanses of private property, usually encompassing
stunning views of mountains, rivers, and forests. For many of these in-
migrants the housing market was relatively easy to enter and navigate, as
valley prices were considerably lower than in the inflated urban housing
markets they were exiting. Within the interview sample, 73 percent of
newcomers were homeowners, and several current renters were planning
to buy in the near future.[5] Wealth from landholdings and inheritances
allowed retired teacher Roger Clark, introduced in chapter 1, to afford his
large, artisan-crafted home on an open hillside with 360-degree views.
He explained:

We inherited some money from my folks, and that helped buy this property. Along with my aunt, I got money from my aunt. Not a ton, but I did get some from her . . . and so that helped us, I think all in all with her and my mom and dad's inheritance. And we bought this piece of land. Plus we sold our home. We sold the 10 acres [near Seattle]. So all of that accumulated and helped us buy this place and have money to build this home. So things worked out well for us in that respect.

For carpenter Shawn Murphy, a forty-three-year-old divorced father of two, the wealth he accrued in his previous professional career similarly allowed him to invest in land in Paradise Valley. He told me:

I came here with a nest egg. . . . But that was also the culmination of a lot of years of working toward that goal of building my own house, buying property, and so it's like, I worked and I bought and sold a few things . . . all with the goal of getting to a place where I didn't have to—it's not like I'm retired, I'm nowhere near retired, but I wanted to get to a place where I didn't have to kill myself with a huge mortgage and force myself in that situation to work all the time.

The relative abundance and affordability of homes, land, and/or open space was an important part of the initial draw into Paradise Valley, allowing newcomers to live comfortably while surrounded by the physical beauty that they associated with rural areas.[6] The sheer amount of physical space that most newcomers' homes occupied contributed to their senses of peace, quiet, safety, and slow-paced lifestyles that were among their main motivations for moving there.

The rural ideals of safety and a slower-paced lifestyle alone did not explain the amount of in-migration the valley had experienced, however. Paradise Valley's draw lay not simply in its rurality but also its amenities, particularly the physical environment. Equal in importance for many newcomers were specific lifestyle preferences, particularly those for outdoor sports and agrarian pursuits. As is the case with many high-amenity communities in the West, the promise of access to a plethora of outdoor opportunities often played an important role in newcomers' decisions to move there, frequently being mentioned alongside family and safety issues.[7]

We just wanted to live in a small town where you could drive for a half an hour and be at a great trailhead and get above tree line. We didn't want to have to—I lived in the Seattle area for a bunch of years, and you could drive for three hours and get to a good trailhead. We wanted to be closer than that.

—Hannah Lowry, forty-five-year-old married, middle-income consultant

My youngest was in kindergarten when we moved. And we kind of wanted to move—we liked this community as a place to raise kids as well. I like to ski.

—William Turner, sixty-two-year-old married, middle-income retiree

I was looking for a place that wasn't too crowded and I could ski at. And [my wife] was looking for a place that had some trees and she could farm. And this is sort of where they overlap.

—Todd Stewart, thirty-eight-year-old married, middle-income field scientist

For these newcomers, Paradise Valley was unique not simply because of its beauty and access to affordable land, but because of its trail systems, rivers, mountains, and proximity to hiking, skiing, and other outdoor activities. Particularly in the upper end of the valley, it was uncommon to meet in-migrants who did not cite outdoor sports as among their main motivations for moving there. Thus for many newcomers the move to Paradise Valley represented both a push away from a fast-paced, cramped, anonymous urban lifestyle and a pull toward living closer to nature and having constant rather than occasional chances to recreate outdoors.

In addition to being drawn by the physical amenities, many of Paradise Valley's newcomers were also attracted by the uniqueness of the community, which was known for being more liberal than most other small towns in Washington. Over time, as the community enticed increasing numbers of politically liberal, culturally sophisticated urbanites to move there, it became even more attractive to others like them. The combination of the idealized rural lifestyle with its physical amenities, services, and socially liberal environment contributed heavily to their decisions to move to Paradise Valley as well as to their loyalty to and appreciation of the place once they arrived. For many in-migrants the valley was not interchangeable for other high-amenity rural communities that might have similar physical attractions but a different social milieu. Maya Ferrer, a thirty-four-year-old massage therapist, had moved to the valley from a Portland, Oregon, suburb after visiting a number of times. She explained that initially she and her husband had expected to be occasional visitors, "but then we just kinda fell in love with the place, and so decided to move here." She elaborated:

> It's like paradise. Yeah. I can't imagine living somewhere else. Just has every-thing here, it's just exactly what we're looking for. Um, the rural component is very important, being close to wilderness is really important, but also that we have a progressive community here and a tight community is also really important. And so often in rural communities it's very conservative, and, um. And then also just all of the influx of tourist money and second-homers brings so many benefits, like having a cool bakery, and a pub, and art gallery, and library system, and everything. So it, it's kind of, it's like the best things of the city in my mind, but a more rural aspect. So it's pretty special.

For many newcomers, the valley was attractive both for its rurality, exemplified by physical beauty and slow-paced lifestyle, as well as for its urban-style services and attitudes. In addition to its more tangible ameni-ties, many newcomers talked specifically about the community itself as one of the most important assets they found there. "Community" had mul-tiple aspects for newcomers, who emphasized different issues depending on their own interests and preferences. Often their ideas of what rural community should be were constructed from the same types of rural ideal-izations that they cited as primary motivations for moving there. Included in these rural-centric images of "community" were homogeneity and tight social connections. Shawn Murphy commented: "There's a lot of beautiful places. But I did find really a place that had the mix of, you know, kind of the recreational activities that I liked, but also a really solid sense of com-munity." Lisa Banks, a thirty-eight-year-old hairstylist, similarly focused on this sense of rural community cohesion in explaining her decision to remain there. She said:

> There is something intangible. There is a closeness to spirit here. I think everyone feels that. I feel like you have to want to live here, because we are [so isolated]. So people that live here want to be here, so that like-minded-ness kind of filters through everyone, so you get that sense of community. And something intangible, though. I feel like there is an energetic pull here. I don't know what it is. It's magical.

For newcomers like these the term "community" was tied into rural-ity in many ways, and they came there searching for social interconnection, regardless of its specific content. But for others the specific cultural makeup of the community mattered as much as, if not more than, cohesion itself, and Paradise Valley's *difference* from their common associations with rurality was an equally important aspect. Although they rarely explicitly discussed social class in this context, it was clear through their descriptions that the rural community experience they sought had a specific class character, which differentiated it from most other types of rural places.

Many newcomers explained that what made Paradise Valley special was not simply that it was a small community but also that it was known to be socially and politically progressive and that it lacked many of the social and cultural norms that they associated with other, more conservative, rural communities. They frequently portrayed the valley as an oasis of liberalism in the midst of rural conservatism, often explicitly comparing it against other parts of Eastern Washington, or even the eastern part of its own county. Gary Wolfe, a fifty-eight-year-old park ranger asserted that "people have preconceived notions of a small, rural community just because it's east of the mountains. And it's gonna be ultra-conservative and you know, and you've come to learn probably actually this is a little blue dot in a 75 percent red county." Technology consultant Hannah Lowry explained that for her Paradise Valley was unique in that "it's a lot of great, educated, progressive people in a small area, if you just stay in the valley." Brooke Gilbert, a stay-at-home mother who had been in the area for two years, contrasted Paradise Valley with a more typical rural Eastern Washington town where they had lived briefly before moving there. She recalled:

> We didn't do well there. It was an interesting experiment in Middle America. Super-conservative, super-religious, super-white, super-small. Huge adjustment. So then we looked at other options that were within a commutable distance. We moved here for the school, but also for the diversity of thought that's in the valley, not necessarily ethnic diversity, but it's something.

As newcomers like Gary, Hannah, and Brooke explained it, Paradise Valley was stereotypically rural in its small size and its social cohesion, but importantly different from most rural western towns with regard to its cultural norms and values, which they described as more politically liberal and culturally sophisticated than other nearby communities.

This combination of rural setting with urban sensibilities was among Paradise Valley's most important selling points for many of its recent in-migrants. Katrina Graham, a forty-six-year-old married stay-at-home mother, had moved to Paradise Valley in the wake of the Great Recession as part of a plan to financially downsize. Originally their Paradise Valley home was seen as a remote getaway for weekends and vacations. Eventually, however, they came to view moving there as a possibility. Katrina explained:

> We built it as a vacation home when the economy was robust, and we loved it just because of the scenery and, you know, the way it made us feel. And then the economy hit the skids, and we couldn't afford two homes, and where did we want to live? Seattle or here? So we chose here.

Although it was Paradise Valley's physical amenities that originally inspired them to purchase a second-home there, she explained that the community itself, and particularly the cultural norms they shared with many other newcomers, were now their main reasons for staying:

> I like the quietness, and I like the privacy. I love the community, which, the community is pretty long and mile-wise it stretches, but it feels small. I love that things that are important to us are generally felt by most of the community, and we feel like we fit, whereas in some place like Seattle, what is Seattle? You know, it's a million different types of things, and—so I think that's important. I like the outside [laughs]. . . . We enjoy being outside and we—things that are important to us, like eating organic and local food, that's important in our community. Doing things more simply and having less—I don't know, less of a consumer-based lifestyle, that's here, and that's how we feel.

Claire Woods, a forty-two-year-old nonprofit consultant, had a similar set of reasons for moving to Paradise Valley, initially citing rural lifestyle issues including the desire "to have the ability to live off the grid." But as she mused more about her decision, she explained: "You know, a big part of my draw here had to do with the environmentalist nature of the community and their activism, and I got drawn right into that community." The liberal nature of the community was not Claire's first motivation for being there, but an important contributor to her decision to stay long-term. Newcomers were drawn to Paradise Valley because it exemplified certain aspects of the rural imaginary and simultaneously replaced conservative rural attitudes with more urban-based, progressive ones. While many came there because they craved the beauty, safety, and slow-paced lifestyle they associated with the rural idyll, they also sought to avoid many of the more socially conservative and working-class aspects of rurality, and to replace them with more upper-class norms and liberal cultural and political preferences.

As the number of newcomers with wealth, education, and cultural capital increased and spread across the valley, so too did these types of attitudes and services that catered to those who desired a specific lifestyle. By 2014, Paradise Valley offered numerous options for these types of services, which borrowed heavily from urban trends, while often presenting them with a self-consciously rural bent. For most newcomers the combination of rural and urban struck the right balance, and they generally believed that the community met the bulk of their basic needs. Nonetheless, several newcomers still felt that improvements could be made and that even more urban influence and ambiance would be necessary to entice them to put down more permanent roots. As fifty-three-year-old entrepreneur Frank Brooks told me:

> The tipping point is almost there. We need another thousand people here, probably, to get it to be livable. We have no movies, no culture at all. We go to all the local plays, but it's like herding cats. It's rural theater. It's fine, it's fun to go to, but if you want to do anything, you have to go to Seattle, and Seattle's a smaller city by city standards. And like I said, if it wasn't for doing sports, I don't know why people live here. But it's OK.

Despite occasional complaints like this, Paradise Valley's unusual combination of amenities continued to attract a particular demographic of outdoorsy, ex-urbanites with the means and opportunity to trade in urban real estate for their own pieces of physical and social utopia. Once there, the ones that stayed often found even more to love about the community, which catered to urban-based tastes and interests while still preserving its distinctly rural character. But, as the following section illustrates, for many this rural dream came at a cost.

SURVIVING IN PARADISE: CAREER SACRIFICES AND LABOR MARKET SUCCESSES

> I met a middle-aged woman who had moved to Paradise Valley a couple of years earlier from Seattle. Like many others, she had been a weekend warrior who thought it would be great to move there permanently. She said that

they had taken a big pay cut to do it, and now they just sort of scrape by, like everybody else. "There sure isn't a lot of money to be made in the valley," she said.[8]

Conspicuously missing from most newcomers' origin stories were mentions of job opportunities as reasons for moving to Paradise Valley. Some, like Katrina Graham, moved to their second-homes in the valley as part of a process of downsizing to a single house in the wake of the Great Recession, choosing to work remotely in order to survive. It was rare for newcomers to move there specifically for labor market prospects, however.[9] Most acknowledged that the move to Paradise Valley was financially difficult for them. Phillip Stevens, a seventy-five-year-old retired ski instructor, told me: "The local joke is, you have to have three or four different W2s to make it in the valley. And the other joke is, if you want to be a millionaire in the valley, come here with two million." In a conversation with a local leader who worked on economic development issues, I was told that there really weren't many viable businesses in Paradise Valley, and that many of the local businesses were just hobbies for wealthy in-migrants who "buy themselves a job" that doesn't have to support them or even sustain itself.[10] Although only a few interview participants admitted to being comfortable without some source of income (including retirement income), a number who were local business owners did disclose that they barely made a profit.[11]

Most newcomers felt that their personal incomes had taken a major hit when they moved to Paradise Valley, despite mostly expressing satisfaction with their employment outcomes. Newcomers who worked locally were frequently employed in such areas as teaching, construction/carpentry, nonprofit organizations, and medical professions, while several were engaged mainly in subsistence activities that did not bring in earned income. A number of retirees did not work locally for income but relied on retirement and investment incomes instead.[12]

For carpenter Shawn Murphy, career sacrifice was factored into the decision to move to Paradise Valley after decades of working in high-paid jobs in cities like San Francisco and Salt Lake City. The wealth he accrued in his previous career allowed him to invest in land in Paradise Valley and to choose part-time work that didn't use his college degree but allowed him the freedom to pursue outside interests. Shawn had worked in a number of professional and service jobs in the valley and was thinking about leaving his current job soon, although he appreciated its flexible schedule. He told me that since coming to Paradise Valley:

> I've always felt capable enough of doing whatever that I've never had to worry about getting a job. It's like, I'm happy to go do some physical labor thing. I can do construction. I have those tools. And there's construction here, no problem, I can do that. I didn't move here with any sort of plan on what I was gonna do.

Shawn's attitude—a combination of sacrifice, resignation, and optimism—was similar to that of many in-migrants who left more lucrative careers to move to Paradise Valley. Although most openly acknowledged that they could have higher incomes if they lived somewhere else, they were often willing to make a number of career sacrifices to live in the valley, and few struggled for long to find work. Newcomers experienced a relative advantage within the local labor market, where their combinations of education, skills, and professionalism were highly valued and often placed them ahead of old-timer job-seekers who were widely believed to lack these forms of human capital as well as work ethics.

Although they might acknowledge the problems with old-timers as workers, newcomers seldom saw themselves as being privileged in the local labor market, particularly given the career sacrifices that they made and the various struggles they encountered. Kate Poole, a thirty-three-year-old nurse, commuted more than an hour to work. She felt that the commute, the salary, and even the career itself all represented sacrifices. Originally trained to work with hearing-impaired children, she quickly realized she would need to change careers to survive in the valley. She said:

> When I came here, I did think initially about trying to find something like that to do here, and there just wasn't the population naturally, you know? Because the school that I worked at was like the hub for the Seattle area for programs like that. And of course they don't have it here. So I felt like it was something I was sort of sacrificing to live here, and I did so happily, but it's something I still miss a little bit.

After trying several other jobs, Kate finally settled on nursing as a field that would be both fulfilling and available in the region, but she nonetheless faced a long commute over treacherous mountain passes to get to work each day. She also lived with a lower level of financial security than she had in her previous career:

> When I lived in Seattle, even though the cost of living was more, like I was able, just because of my job I had benefits, I had paid holidays, and paid vacation and all that kind of stuff, so I was able to have a nest egg. When I moved here it was like, forget it. No more nest egg. It is just a sacrifice.

For Anya Wilburn, also a nurse, it was not the career choice but potential benefits and advancement that were curtailed by the decision to remain in Paradise Valley. The forty-two-year-old mother of one had worked in multiple jobs in the tourism industry in Paradise Valley, before seeking additional training to improve her career prospects. "Waitressing is just so unreliable because of the tourist season," she explained, "there's so many months when there's not a lot of tourists. . . . My husband was a carpenter back then, and he had no work in the winter. Most of the carpenters didn't work in the winter back then." The career change had made year-round work available, but Anya still didn't have the same opportunities that she might in a larger community. She explained:

> You have to be willing to accept less pay, to not have full benefits, to work way harder, versus in the city I could go and get triple the money, double the money at least, and have set call days. It's a totally different work environment in terms of a provider. It's rough out here. I think that's one of the main differences. I mean, I love that I get so close with—I'm doing all the care of all these people for so many years, that I get so close with them. . . . But it's definitely exhausting, and I don't know many people who do it for that long.

Newcomers' stories were rife with these kinds of sacrifices and statements of resignation, justification, or acceptance. Almost every newcomer I interviewed mentioned underemployment in terms of hours, salary, or prestige as the trade-off for living in the valley.[13] The following quotes represent just a few of these discussions:

> You know, certainly I cut my salary in half, and I turned down a job that was going to pay me a couple hundred grand, more than that. That was hard. But we made that decision.
>
> —Frank Brooks, fifty-three-year-old married, middle-income entrepreneur

I had planned on working part-time when I retired, and there's just not the options here.... I'd have to be going to Seattle, and I don't know my way around Seattle very well.... So financially it has been—I have to die sooner than I planned to.

—Donna Cox, sixty-seven-year-old divorced, middle-income retiree

Well, we came initially, [my wife] was interviewing for a position and that was a—you know, this would be perfect. And I was going to be primarily the dad and maybe working carpentry and that was going to be awesome, and she didn't get that [job]. And then we decided, you know what? We want to come here anyway. We've got to do this. And so all of a sudden it became more, you know, the onus on me to be the primary wage earner.

—Andrew Bowden, forty-six-year-old married, middle-income carpenter

For newcomers, underemployment was generally accepted as part of the equation, a necessary evil that they agreed to tolerate when they made the decision to move to Paradise Valley. Most of them seemed relatively content with their choices, despite these wistful discussions of what they had given up. Although Paradise Valley's restricted labor market imposed limits on their salaries, benefits, and ambitions, generally newcomers found the jobs and incomes they needed to survive there. Underemployment and early retirement were common among newcomers, but unemployment was rare. Critically, most newcomers were able to find some work locally that they enjoyed, and they often felt that in terms of flexibility and freedom they had improved their quality of life, if not their incomes, by moving to Paradise Valley.

Thus the job search was often disappointing, but the challenges were not insurmountable. To find work, newcomers generally relied on their personal resources, including human capital in the forms of education, job skills, and experience; cultural capital in the forms of "soft skills," professionalism, and knowledge about the arts; and social capital in the form of connections to other community members who worked locally and could help them network for jobs.[14] For many, wealth also aided in their work choices, allowing them to live comfortably on lower incomes and still be able to afford housing, leisure activities, and investments into children's futures. Wealth also meant that these newcomers could afford the costs of job training outside the valley as well as reliable vehicles that allowed them a greater geographic range within which to find work. They frequently commuted very long distances to their jobs, including several who worked as teachers and medical professionals outside of the valley as well as a number who combined telecommuting with periodic trips to larger cities.

A number of male in-migrants, like Shawn Murphy and Andrew Bowden, gave up higher-prestige careers to work in construction and carpentry, finding the higher-end jobs in this sector to be well-paid despite their seasonality. This sector was a common standby when other jobs ended, as short-term work was often easy to come by for newcomers whose friends worked in the industry. Newcomers of both genders also frequently found work in the nonprofit sector, which although large given the small size of the community was nonetheless small enough that word quickly spread about a skilled employee or contractor from one organization to the next. Field scientist Todd Stewart found a job soon after arriving in Paradise Valley and moved with ease from positions in nonprofits, construction, and the government sector as old jobs concluded and new opportunities arose. He recalled:

So we moved in, in January, with neither of us having a job, or career, or place to live, or really anything. And I think that summer I ended up putting together a bunch of odd jobs. . . . I started doing some odd jobs with the fish restoration organization, and I ended up working for the next four years and becoming year-round. And then that company kind of dissolved. . . . And then I worked for—I pounded nails for a summer, and then worked for the USFS [US Forest Service] for four years.

Claire Woods, who currently worked as a nonprofit consultant, found that having the resources to start her own small nonprofit led her into new job opportunities. As her story illustrates, establishing herself as competent in one area was key to opening new doors. She explained:

Everybody who comes here starts a nonprofit. So I started a nonprofit. Never tried that before. . . . We got that going. I don't remember when I started the forestry thing. It was probably a couple of years later. And that attracted the attention of another nonprofit that was working on forestry and fire prevention. And they wanted me to work for them. So I got a better paying job for them, and that just kept leading to other things.

On the other end of the spectrum, Kevin Martin, a twenty-six-year-old cohabiter, relied on personal wealth to avoid steady work altogether and live very simply on next-to-no earned income through subsistence activities and trades with friends and acquaintances. He explained that despite his financial stability, he still did odd jobs for his own satisfaction:

> I have this pile of money now, and still, I'm getting paid $10 an hour in an orchard to pick apples, and still I work on farms and trade for food, and where I live I don't pay rent. I trade my work for rent, because that money's not for just living off of. I mean, we used it to buy our yurt, that's for sure. And I bought some really nice tools, that will serve me my whole life with, but I'm not trying to just be like, "Well I don't need to work anymore." I think that's really unhealthy, for the brain to be on vacation.

For these and other newcomers, real and symbolic resources allowed them to navigate the local labor market in ways that while not necessarily providing significant job prestige, benefits, or income, at least allowed them to survive comfortably and happily.

This set of resources was often invisible to the newcomers who possessed them, however, existing as a form of privilege that they seldom acknowledged. Although the proximity of the social divide in Paradise Valley meant that few could completely ignore social inequality, privileged newcomers seldom saw themselves as actively contributing to the divide through their own advantaged positions. In much the same way that "color blindness" allows those with racial privilege to ignore or negate the existence of racial inequality while still benefitting from a racist system, a sort of "class blindness" allowed many of Paradise Valley's newcomers to ignore—yet maintain—their own advantages in the local labor market and beyond.[15] Thus without knowing many unemployed adults in the valley, newcomers tended to assume that such people were individually responsible for their own lack of work and that personal failures and bad choices, versus structural inequalities and differences in resources, impeded others' labor market success. The construction of these types of symbolic boundaries between newcomers and old-timers allowed newcomers to draw on familiar American cultural ideologies such as individualism to justify their own privileged positions, while also explaining the struggles of the less fortunate as deserved and self-imposed.[16]

According to Shawn Murphy, who claimed to never have trouble find-ing work locally, it was not the labor market that was flawed but individu-als who were unwilling to take available jobs. Although he acknowledged that many low-wage positions wouldn't allow someone without wealth to become a homeowner like himself, he still believed that individuals should accept low-wage work regardless of whether they could survive comfort-ably with it. He explained his understanding of unemployed locals, whom he felt were personally responsible for their troubles due to their own poor work ethics and lack of social connections:

> People who say they can't find a job, like, I—you know, that doesn't ring true to me. Finding a job that pays you enough to, say, buy land or a house, that's a different thing. So there's jobs available. [Local restaurants] constantly have a hard time filling positions. So you have these jobs that people find, like, is it really worth making $10 or $12 an hour? So I think there's a lot of people in the valley who choose not to work those low-level jobs and instead choose to rely on assistance.... I feel like there's—if you have the initiative, and then the human connections, the personal relationships that come with being here for a while, there's never a shortage of work to be done or found or created. But it does take initiative and somebody actually who's willing to bust ass and work hard. And so I feel like there are those opportunities, and sometimes there's a dearth of character as it relates to people willing to do those things.

As Shawn described it, finding a job in Paradise Valley was easy for those with sufficient personal connections and strong work ethics. The roles of education, job experience, and wealth were missing from this assessment, however, which ignored the struggles that the nonwealthy faced in finding work locally and making ends meet through low-wage work.

Toby Cook, a thirty-two-year-old valley native, similarly took his labor-market privilege for granted and judged those who lacked it as morally deficient. His well-educated parents had moved to the valley before he was born, establishing themselves as teachers in the local high school and pil-lars of the community. After returning to the community with his college degree, Toby chose to work in construction and carpentry, which he pre-ferred to other local options. He described the ease with which he found work in Paradise Valley:

> Construction was the first thing I really got into, started working for lots of different contractors around the valley and learned a ton, and then also

it feels good to put a lot of energy into something and actually see it go somewhere. Uh, whereas being a waiter or being in the Forest Service you don't get that. And then construction is also a seasonal thing where I could take the winters off and go traveling, um, ski bum trips, whatever. It just fell in perfectly with my lifestyle.... It must be my reputation around, but um, people know that I'm a good carpenter and I get calls and I have to turn down work, like at least, well in the spring, it's almost every week.

Like Shawn, Toby believed that anyone could find work in Paradise Valley, and those who could not had only themselves to blame. He similarly made no connection between structural inequalities and labor market successes in Paradise Valley. He said:

If you grew up here and you can't find work, there's a problem with the person, not, not the uh, not the economy. 'Cause people are always wanting work done around here.

Q: So who are the people that can't find work?

I would say people that don't know a lotta people. Or if you actually grew up here and you can't find work, then you're a drug addict or, um, you have a reputation of, um, not being a good worker.

This failure to acknowledge one's own labor market privilege or others' disadvantage was common among newcomers and facilitated the belief that the difference between the groups had to do with a lack of moral character versus differential access to resources. The blindness toward social class issues and structural inequalities, and the explanation of class differences through claims to individual moral virtue or vice, allowed newcomers to rationalize their positions and deflect responsibility for their impacts on the local labor market.[17]

Despite these kinds of claims that anyone who wanted a job could find one in the valley, most newcomers did acknowledge the limitations of Paradise Valley's labor market, and most had stories of personal sacrifices that they made to survive there. Newcomers' resources aided them in multiple ways that allowed them to find and keep the best jobs that Paradise Valley had to offer, despite the challenges that the labor market posed for them. Although many accepted downgrades in their salaries, career trajectories, working hours, or travel times to work, they did generally manage to find acceptable and fulfilling work that enabled them to survive in

Paradise Valley. However, few were conscious of the ways in which their personal resources and class privileges made local jobs more obtainable, and more sustainable for them than they were for the valley's old-timers. Real and symbolic resources not only facilitated their successes in competing for local jobs and surviving on lower incomes, but also helped them to navigate challenges to work-family balance that the community's infrastructure (or lack thereof) created. These differences in resources nonetheless remained unacknowledged by most newcomers.

"EVERYBODY HELPS WITH EVERYTHING": GIVING AND RECEIVING SOCIAL SUPPORT

> I think by and large most people that come here try to give back and be involved and help out the community to be a better place.
> —Anya Wilburn, forty-two-year-old married, middle-income nurse

Despite their likelihood of finding work in Paradise Valley, newcomers were seldom completely self-sufficient there, nor was life easy. Although they came with expectations of a slower-paced, calmer life, they frequently found themselves harried, having to make multiple sacrifices in terms of time and work activity to navigate Paradise Valley's structural lacks. Adaptations to life in Paradise Valley had results that disrupted gender norms within many families, with women and men facing unexpected challenges to maintaining egalitarian gender relations that had worked in their urban-based lives.[18] Although couples and families adapted in order to navigate Paradise Valley's challenges, newcomers also relied heavily on their social networks to address challenges endemic to rural living, including a lack of available childcare; a lack of infrastructure including public transportation and road maintenance; a lack of access to health care, particularly specialists and emergency care; and a lack of cultural and educational opportunities for children.

While not all of these challenges were equally salient for all residents, for those that were, their abilities to cope with them depended on their individual resources, social connections, and social standing within the community. Newcomers often pooled their resources, drawing on human, cultural, and social capital to address the community's deficiencies. They shared their own skills with each other and with children through offering a plethora of classes in art, music, dance, and therapeutic activities like yoga and meditation. They provided rides to hospitals and medical appointments for close friends and loved ones, hosted one another when natural disasters threatened homes, and provided financial help for those facing medical crises. And most important for daily life, newcomers created complex exchange networks to help each other with childcare, and with many of the large and small chores that rural life required.

Newcomers created intricate trade webs that in many ways simulated the desired rural idyll but that generally existed separately from old-timers. Participation in informal exchange networks, while not universal among newcomers, was practiced to some degree by most. Although exchange activities often added extra duties to already hectic lives, these trades generally directly benefited most participants. Participation in exchange networks was assumed by many to be an important part of rural life and the creation of rural community. In addition to participation in informal exchanges, many newcomers participated in more formal acts of charity and volunteerism, most commonly through giving money and/or time to local nonprofit organizations. Like informal exchange networks, philanthropy and volunteering built social connections, while allowing participants to give back to the community. Newcomers mostly felt a strong sense of commitment to constructing the type of cohesive, supportive rural community that they had hoped to find in Paradise Valley. Together, these acts of community-level support both mitigated Paradise Valley's challenges and created additional ones for newcomers, adding further levels of responsibility and obligation to those already stretched thin by the choice to move there and the realities of rural life.

"There's This Big Safety Net Here": Childcare Challenges and Social Support

Work-family balance and access to childcare were among the most commonly discussed problems in the community, and the lack of childcare was acknowledged by community leaders as well.[19] It was unusual for a parent of young children not to mention struggles to find affordable, reliable, and trustworthy childcare in the region. In discussing her childcare challenge, Anya Wilburn explained: "Yeah, [for] any working mom I think it's tough around here. There's not a lot of options." Anya felt extremely fortunate to have found someone she trusted, but "she's not licensed. . . . which kind of sucks, but she's very affordable and very flexible, and she'll take 'em early in the morning and late at night." Many other parents were not able to find providers with similar levels of flexibility and availability, or they were unwilling to trust their children to unlicensed providers, and few had good options for after-school care for older children.

For parents who couldn't find full-time regular care, one common strategy was to adjust their jobs and work schedules to accommodate their parenting responsibilities. Generally in heterosexual-couple households it was women who sought jobs with this kind of flexibility, while their husbands tended to have more rigid and regular work schedules.[20] Hannah Lowry had a full-time career in high-tech before moving to Paradise Valley, but now she held several part-time computer consulting jobs with different local businesses. She explained that after the move and having children, she and her husband "switched roles and he became the major wage-earner." While his job was full-time and had regular hours, she opted for multiple jobs with more flexibility. She explained:

I have a bunch of different jobs, so if you add 'em all up, it's a full-time job.

Q: It sounds like that would be more than full-time.

Well, a lot of 'em are just a couple hours a month.

Q: Are you happy with your work situation?

I am, because it means that I can pick up the kids and get 'em to their sports. With the kids being young still, it works really well.

This shifting of gender roles and responsibilities was common for newcomers with children, although not all of them experienced it as easily as Hannah described. Hairstylist Lisa Banks similarly recalled choosing her career in part because it allowed her the flexibility she needed to care for young children:

So in the beginning I worked evenings and weekends. I knew doing hair I could kind of make my own schedule, which is super important because there is not daycare here. You know, daycare is really hard—it was really hard. So we just kind of worked around my husband's schedule. Like I would go in for a few hours in the evening, or I worked weekends—Saturday and Sunday, which was great with people. You know, when he wasn't working. So whenever he wasn't working, I was.

Although her flexible work schedule allowed Lisa and her husband to navigate the childcare challenge, it took a toll on their marriage.

Honestly, it was really hard the first few years because we just didn't see each other. He was working or I was working. And that's just kind of what it was. . . . It was horrible. I mean, it really was—and looking back—when you are in it, I think you just do—like I said, you just do what the next thing is. Tomorrow I have to do A, B, and C. So I think you just kind of get through it. And I really was. Those first years when my daughter was small, and my son was small, and we were newly married and I had a new business and we just moved here—we just got through life. That is what we were doing. Of course, now I don't want to get through it anymore. I want to enjoy it. My children are older. Thank god that all is done. . . . [It was] very difficult for our relationship.

Shifting work schedules to ensure that someone was always home with children could exact a harsh toll on relationships and careers, undermining the simplicity and peace that newcomers sought in Paradise Valley. Nonetheless, this type of flexibility with regard to work and work schedules allowed many to navigate work-family challenges.

Flexible schedules were not necessarily easy to come by in Paradise Valley's labor market, but newcomers were much more likely than oldtimers to have control in terms of setting their own work schedules and hours. Also common among newcomers was women choosing not to work while their children were young, opting out of the labor market until they felt they could better navigate the work-family conflict.[21] Many newcomer women who chose this strategy commented that they had never expected to be stay-at-home mothers. Most were content with the role change and the freedom it allowed them to invest in children, volunteer work, and activities like gardening and self-provisioning, although women occasionally discussed frustration and resentment toward their partners with regard to their career sacrifices.[22] Even with job flexibility or a stay-at-home parent, however, there were still numerous gaps in childcare coverage for most parents of younger children. When newcomers needed child-care beyond what they and their paid providers could manage, they relied heavily on their social networks to help.

For those newcomers who had family locally, parents and siblings were heavily relied on to help with childcare and provide occasional time off from parenting responsibilities.[23] Also very common among newcomers with children were childcare swaps with friends. For busy parents there were often conflicts that prevented them from caring for, picking up their children, or shuttling them to after-school activities like dance and music lessons, and in these cases they relied heavily on friend networks for help. At times I helped in this capacity myself, being called upon on occasion to pick up a working friend's children after school and drop them off at home, activities, or other friends' houses. For divorced father Shawn Murphy, such trades were vital to his ability to survive in Paradise Valley. He explained:

> I think that's one of the wonderful things about living in a small community, is that when it comes to my childcare challenge, it's like, yeah, on a large sale, there's a need and a challenge in childcare still. But on a small scale, there's a network of friends that you can always pretty much say, "Hey, you know, can you step in for two hours or whatever? And I'll help you out." There's this whole informal network of tangible support when it comes to some of those—being in a big city, what are you gonna do?

Hannah Lowry talked at length about the importance of these childcare trades to her:

> I've been amazed at how much everybody helps with everything. Like, just—it feels like parents keep an eye on kids that aren't their own kids. Like, if, you know, if my kids were down there scratching on a sign, which they wouldn't do, but if they did, another mom would probably see 'em and say, "What are you guys doing?" It does feel like there's this big safety net here.... Kids are always going home with another parent. We do trades all the time. There isn't really childcare for eight-year-olds, but you can't just send an eight-year-old home on the bus alone. So people— I mean, [gesturing to a woman who passes by] that lady's got two other kids with her that aren't hers. Two of them are hers and two of them aren't. And I know Daphne, the mom, is probably at [a] meeting right now.

For newcomers, many of whom didn't have family locally, such swaps were an important component of work-family balance, which helped to mitigate the valley's childcare shortage. Social networks of newcomers with similar responsibilities and challenges pooled time and resources to provide parents with the flexibility that their jobs and other commitments denied them. These childcare swaps, combined with women's flexible work schedules and opting out of the labor market, allowed newcomers to ensure that their children were well supervised by trustworthy adults in ways that Paradise Valley's infrastructure could not guarantee.

"When You Get Down to Rural Living": Daily Chores, Challenges, and Gender Roles

Beyond childcare, newcomers were frequently navigating a number of tasks that were either unfamiliar to those with more urban backgrounds or simply too large for a single adult or couple to complete on their own. Newcomers often owned large tracts of private land that needed cultivating, controlling, and winter maintenance.[24] Maria Setzer described a number of challenges inherent to living remotely. "Just the amount of work," she said, "going out and getting firewood and getting ready for winter. It's a place that takes a lot of labor, a lot of labor, whereas in other places you don't deal with that and maybe have more free time to go have more leisure activities and stuff." In these cases, newcomers frequently combined social network help with rewriting of gender scripts. Many relied on their friend networks for occasional aid with labor and equipment.

Over my time in Paradise Valley, I observed newcomers sharing homegrown produce, tools and equipment, and even clothing with others in their social networks.[25] In addition to the childcare swaps she described, Hannah Lowry's friends helped "frequently with, like, borrowing a tractor or helping replace a light bulb in a barn or picking up the mail or letting the dog in and out." For Max Brunet, a thirty-eight-year-old subsistence farmer whose wife had a full-time job, social networks helped with tasks necessary for survival. For him this sort of aid was taken for granted as part of rural life. He told me:

> When we got here, it's like, oh, if you need work on your house you have a
> work party, and have like thirty people show up to your house, and that kind

of stuff. But when you farm just veggies, you know, there's always like twenty people there that just kinda help out. So it's more like the rural consciousness, you know, like on the west side it's more like yuppie consciousness. But here it's more like, oh, we have work to do. Let's get together and get the work done.

In these ways, social capital was mobilized by newcomers to make daily life easier in Paradise Valley. The realities of rural living often forced them to learn new skills and take on new tasks, which for many did not come easily or naturally. Those with more experience, skills, and equipment were generally quite generous within their social networks, ensuring that these resources were available to those who lacked them.

While social networks were able to pitch in and offer help with more occasional needs, however, daily chores often also required flexibility with regard to newcomers' gender scripts and understandings. A number of women across the valley described having "honey-do" lists that they kept for their husbands and male partners, who were expected to take care of a number of more physically demanding tasks. Tracy Douglas, a divorced nonprofit employee, described the ways in which her relationship with her ex-husband changed after moving to Paradise Valley. She said that when they had lived in the city, they were an egalitarian couple: both worked full-time and they shared household chores, doing equal amounts of cooking and cleaning. She blamed herself for the changes that occurred after they moved to Paradise Valley, explaining that she didn't want to do a lot of the difficult manual labor that came with rural living. Tracy didn't learn to run a plow, or split wood, or perform other physically demanding chores—she relied on her husband to do these tasks. She described how over time they turned into a couple with a much more "traditional" gendered division of labor, and she focused more on raising their children and taking care of the household, while her husband did the more physically taxing chores. Tracy described mutual frustration with this arrangement that grew over time, ultimately contributing to the relationship's demise.[26]

Although most didn't describe this level of tension over "second shift" chores, it was common for newcomer couples to describe having relatively egalitarian relationships before moving to Paradise Valley, which transitioned to more traditional divisions of labor over time.[27] Like Tracy, many couples found that daily life in a rural community challenged and changed their previous norms, testing the limits of their socialization into egalitarian roles. Subsistence farmer Kevin Martin gave the following response in answer to a question regarding how he and his partner, Aspen, split up their voluminous list of chores:

> Feminism has done a lot of things in this culture, and I think it's so sweet. And then, when you actually get down to rural living, which is what we're talking about, most women opt for—it's like, "Yeah, I'll cook. Um, yeah, I'd rather actually be inside in the warmth doing this thing."

With regard to the specific breakdown of chores in his household, Kevin explained: "My agreement is that I will always bring up the water, chop the wood, get the wood in the fall—like, that's my job right now—and take out the compost. It's all the heavy lifting." In a separate interview, Aspen gave a very similar description of their division of labor, explaining her understanding of why it made sense for Kevin do more of the "heavy lifting":

> I don't know really what to do with myself in a lot of situations. He has been more inclined towards physical labor and has learned a lot more and came with a little bit more knowledge about building and hammering and stuff. So our horses need a fence built. I don't know how to dig fence posts. Sometimes he'll say, "You just learn by doing." But clearly it is easier if the person who knows how and likes to do physical labor ends up doing it, rather than me being like, I want to be helpful, so I'll get out there and spend three hours learning how deep and how you put just one in.

After moving to Paradise Valley, many newcomers discovered that rural living required skills and proficiencies that urbanites lacked. Men, whose socialization and previous experiences were more likely to include exposure to manual labor, often expressed greater pleasure and interest in tackling these traditionally masculine tasks.[28] Women, however, were often more comfortable taking responsibility for daily "indoor" chores for which their own prior experiences and socialization had better prepared them.[29] In US culture the image of the "rural man" exemplified in physical and outdoor activities, including farming, hunting, and logging, is a powerful symbol of masculinity.[30] The claim to a specific form of rugged masculinity made this sort of physical labor appealing to many newcomer men, most of whom previously had little occasion to practice or perform their masculinity in this way.[31]

Yet because gender is relational in nature, their newfound gender roles also resulted in women focusing on or taking on different tasks and identities, which tended to be associated with traditionally feminine roles of homemaker and mother.[32] Their new dynamics differed from many more traditionally gendered urban and suburban families, however, in that the inside/outside divide did not necessarily mean that women did more home-related chores than men.[33] In Paradise Valley "outside" chores were often similarly demanding and as constant as the indoor chores done by women, requiring significant skills and knowledge as well as physical strength.

Newcomers generally described their changing gender roles, like Kevin and Aspen did, as arising organically from need and pragmatism rather than from ideology or changing gender beliefs. This was the case for Todd Stewart and his wife, Molly, whose gender roles changed to accommodate the nature of their daily chores as well as their decision for Molly to stay home with their young children. According to Todd:

> The distribution of labor changed when she stopped working. But it wasn't—it's been an evolution and it's been more of an evolution and less—I don't know that it had such clear boundaries. But at some point we realized that a distribution of labor is helpful. Like there is reason that different roles develop, because having everybody—developing the skills necessary for everybody to do every possible task—I don't think that is the best way of doing things.... Like right now, we are remodeling the house and Molly has very little interest in learning any of those skills. And so that's completely—that is pretty much falling to me. Whereas there are definitely other things that are—you know, Molly has decided she wants to bake all the bread.... and especially in those periods when I am busy at work and have a project at home that's hungry for time, then it means that Molly ends up picking up more of the—I would say at this point she is probably doing 90 percent of the cooking or something, and 70 percent of the cleaning. And all of the laundry. But at different times, it has been different.

Molly, unlike Aspen, was somewhat ambivalent about these changes, although she did her best to address her own needs. She explained in a separate interview that she took on volunteer work in the community because "I needed to get out of the house in a different way. I needed there to be something that wasn't oriented to my family." Addressing the house-hold division of labor was somewhat more difficult, however:

> I would like Todd to do more. He is getting there. It is not something I spend a lot of time thinking about. But my house also isn't spotless.... I don't have the energy to put into that. I don't want to put my energy into conflict about household chores. But I'm not stifling it either.

For many newcomers the daily challenges of living in a rural area required numerous changes to their lifestyles, social lives, and even family roles. Faced with shortages of childcare, as well as the manifold chores required by rural living, newcomers offered help and support to those within their social networks, in ways that most assumed were common within rural communities. These informal exchanges were vital to most newcomers, who expressed gratitude for their social networks and the support they received. Nonetheless, social networks alone were unable to address all of the challenges that rural living created, which required flexibility in terms of gender roles and understandings within families. While both men and women tended to make career sacrifices in order to live in Paradise Valley, for women the move also frequently meant changing their expectations in terms of working full-time, working outside the home, or equally sharing household chores. Many women expressed contentment with their choices, although a number of others expressed some amount of frustration and resentment, which often came out in more casual settings or in conversation with friends.[34] Previous research suggests that women tend to be more flexible than men in terms of gender roles and to be more likely to make sacrifices needed to ensure family stability.[35] The combination of daily labor that many rural homesteads required, along with the lack of childcare options in the valley, meant that women in particular often found themselves putting career and work aspirations on hold in Paradise Valley, while their husbands became more traditional breadwinners.

Thus, in contrast with previous research from rural areas, in Paradise Valley newcomer families often found themselves transitioning from more egalitarian gender roles to more traditional ones, with men and women taking on more separate and distinct roles to adapt to daily needs and challenges they faced there.[36] While few newcomer couples had anticipated this sort of transition as part of their idealized visions of rural life, most accepted changing gender norms as just one more aspect of the choice to relocate to a rural community. Nonetheless, for women these arrangements were sometimes personally difficult, and a number of educated newcomer women whom I met during my year there left the valley within a few years of my exit from the field, citing desires for more access to career opportunities, friends and family, and larger dating pools for those who were divorced and/or single.

"A Community Is as Strong as Its Volunteers": Giving Back to Paradise Valley

In Paradise Valley pooled resources shared within social networks helped to close the gap between newcomers' needs and what their incomes and the community's services could provide. On the flip side, however, most felt strong obligations to give back to the community in larger ways to help provide vital services or contribute to programs, causes, and activities of interest to them. Volunteer work was extremely common among this group, who gave generously of their time and skills across the valley. Responsibility to the community was a source of pride for many, often presented as evidence of how vibrant the community was. The need to give to the community in terms of both time and money could exact a serious toll on newcomers, however, demanding much of their already limited free time. They were regularly called upon to volunteer for local community groups, organizations, and services; public and private schools; churches; and most commonly, nonprofit organizations.

Paradise Valley sustained a plethora of nonprofit organizations that focused on improving the community from a variety of perspectives. These organizations mostly relied extremely heavily upon donations that came from wealthy patrons, particularly in the Seattle area, calling on second-home owners and frequent visitors with wealth to help invest in the community in a multitude of ways.[37] Most of these organizations employed small paid staffs of local workers but also needed local residents to serve on their boards and volunteer with local events and activities. Newcomers, particularly women, were heavily recruited for these positions, and most felt some combination of honor, obligation, and excitement about these opportunities to help sustain Paradise Valley.[38] Brooke Gilbert, who had been approached by multiple organizations about volunteering, commented: "There's a board for everything, a committee for everything here. People are more proactive than any place I've ever been." Over my time in Paradise Valley, I was told on numerous occasions that I was "lucky" that I wasn't staying long-term in the valley, or I would have already been asked to join the boards of multiple nonprofit organizations.[39]

Once someone was recognized as being an asset to a local organization, these obligations became difficult to avoid. Hannah Lowry had served on several nonprofit boards during her decade in Paradise Valley. She explained how the process worked:

> People just ask you to be on boards. There's sixty-some nonprofits here. There's a lot of boards, and you've got to be on one or else the next board is gonna get you to be on theirs. So you've got to line up your next board before you get off your old board.

Park ranger Gary Wolfe, who was very active with numerous local organizations, described a similar process with regard to juggling these responsibilities. He described stepping down from one board to focus attention on another cause about which he felt strongly but being quickly recruited back into leadership as soon as this second commitment ended. He explained:

> I said, "I gotta go do this." And so I was through with the [nonprofit] board.... It was time to take a break. I told them, I said, "When [my daughter] graduates, then I'll consider getting re-involved with that." It took about a year, and now I'm back on the board. The first board meeting I got elected chairman. That's how it goes.

Not only were newcomers often inundated with requests to join nonprofit boards, but in many cases they were thrust quickly into leadership roles. For Gary the expectation that he would quickly become board chairman was not new. He had a similar experience with a different nonprofit organization, for which he had volunteered when he first arrived in Paradise Valley. He described:

> They did a volunteer recognition dinner, a number of years back. And I had gone, I started volunteering, was down in the basement doing stocking. And

within a year and a half I was on the board and been elected chairman. . . . I said, "I'm like the modern-day American success story, to go from stockboy to chairman of the board in a year and a half!" [laughs]

Rachel Wilson was a thirty-seven-year-old stay-at-home mother who took on volunteer work once her children were in school full-time. She had a similar experience with her volunteer work, in which she was quickly elected president of the board she joined. She told me:

> I'd only been on the board for six months. They said, "Well, that's OK." I still don't really know all of the programs that well. But I can lead a meeting. So that works well. You don't have to know all the programs if you can tell people when to stop talking.

The pressure on newcomers to become active members of the volunteer community was high and often overwhelming. After listing multiple volunteer commitments to local organizations, substitute teacher Maria Setzer commented: "I wouldn't say—I mean, I don't do everything, 'cause I realize that then it just swallows you up." As a local volunteer with a known interest in helping with community events, I was constantly being called upon to help during my time in valley (and even years later). I worked at countless community fundraising events during my time there, many of which were set up to be fun and festive and to attract outsiders, and most of which were focused around raising money to help the organizations themselves, versus providing services directly to individuals.[40] A month seldom went by in which I didn't receive a request to volunteer for at least one such charitable event.

Even for those who were not called upon by so many different organizations, the needs of the local nonprofit and charity sector often weighed heavily upon them and competed with jobs, families, and leisure interests for newcomers' time and other resources. For newcomers on tight budgets the expectation that they give back to the community through attendance at charitable events could be a source of stress, as it was for thirty-three-year-old nurse Sabena Griffin. She explained:

> I try to go to every single thing I can possibly go to. I feel like a lot of money I shouldn't spend goes to that kind of thing. But at the same time I am like, it's supporting a good cause. It is like arts in the schools and stuff like that.

But it's like, oh, there went 50 bucks. I should have paid that electric bill. But it's like, what else am I going to show my kid? I feel like it is very important.

Likewise, the pressure to volunteer for charitable, religious, and nonprofit organizations could also create stress for those with limited time. Occasionally a newcomer would confess to me that she avoided these types of commitments, but for most working-age women in particular, as well as many men and retirees of both genders, volunteering for local organizations was expected and often helped provide entrée to social networks for those who were new to the community.

Retiree Donna Cox, when asked how she met friends after moving to the valley, discussed the importance of volunteer work: "If you want to meet people, you need to volunteer for something." Volunteering and getting involved in local charity activities were important first steps for in-migrants entering the valley, helping to quickly funnel them into social networks of like-minded newcomers. They also helped provide entrée into the nonprofit sector and other professional realms. For parents like Rachel Wilson, who left the workforce to care for children, volunteer positions were critical to maintaining human capital and connections to the local labor market, often paying off later in terms of job-related networking potential when they were ready to reenter the labor force. For newcomers, volunteer obligations could be both burden and privilege.

In most cases the volunteer staffs of nonprofit organizations were made up almost entirely of newcomers, yet the class bias inherent in who was sought for board memberships and other volunteer activities was generally invisible to those participating and rarely discussed.[41] Newcomers described their motivations for participation mostly in terms of being good rural citizens, seldom recognizing that they were privileged through these activities and the access they provided to leadership roles and decisions in Paradise Valley. Nonetheless, volunteer undertakings were an essential part of the creation and sustenance of the ideal rural community that newcomers sought in Paradise Valley and which would not exist without their efforts. For most who took part in volunteer activities and responsibilities, giving back to the community was necessary to create and sustain the rural utopia that they wanted Paradise Valley to be. Gary Wolfe, who did more volunteer work than any other single individual I interviewed, explained:

It's just, my underlying, you know, living in a small community like this, you come to the realization that a community is really as strong as its volunteers are. You know, a community's only as big as the volunteers behind it, which is a real motivating factor for me in getting involved in so many things. Um, without getting totally overextended. You know, there are things that are important to me, as you can tell. Most of 'em have to do with direct service to people.... Those are all entities that make our community better. And that's important to me.

Despite all of the ways in which the move to Paradise Valley challenged newcomers' employment, family, and other trajectories, most were genuinely concerned about giving back to the community and contributing actively to making it a better place. Their sincere desires to share time, money, and other skills and resources with each other and with the organizations that formed the backbone of the community's service sector contributed heavily to making Paradise Valley the unique community that attracted many newcomers in the first place. Newcomers chose to volunteer and share resources with each other for multiple reasons, including altruistic intentions, desires to become socially integrated, needs to keep occupied and busy, and a sense of social obligation. These efforts paid off in multiple ways, sustaining a vibrant community that was proactive in addressing its needs. Helping others and volunteering also provided entrance into social networks with real and symbolic resources to share as well as pathways into work, leadership, and power positions throughout the community. Although these commitments took time from newcomers' already hectic schedules, they generally paid off in terms of the creation of social connections and increased senses of personal efficacy as well as sustaining crucial community organizations and social institutions that might not otherwise be viable in a community of its size and isolation.

CONSTRUCTING AND MAINTAINING PARADISE

For newcomers the move to Paradise Valley was seldom entirely easy, nor did reality exactly meet expectations. They moved there for its rural advantages as well as its uniqueness and difference from other rural communities. However, moving to Paradise Valley also meant that most had

to give up numerous other urban amenities, including career and employment options as well as social and cultural opportunities. It meant often
living with lower incomes, fewer childcare options, and more daily and
seasonal chores, many of which were quite labor-intensive. It also meant
fewer cultural and educational opportunities for children, and greater
travel distances to access basic needs from retail to health care. It was a
decision that few made lightly and that for most required major adjust-
ments in terms of spending choices, career trajectories, family structures,
luxuries, and leisure time. The outcome was seldom the peaceful, easy
existence that most had envisioned when they first decided to move to
Paradise Valley. Yet most newcomers spoke positively about the benefits of
life in the valley, focusing on the advantages that they experienced and the
ways in which they came together to address the community's challenges.

For the majority of the newcomers in this research, the challenges that
they faced in Paradise Valley were mitigated by their personal and social
advantages in the community, which allowed them to flourish there. Most
newcomers were distinct from the community's old-timers in terms of
resources, both real and symbolic. Wealth and income (past as well as present) provided significant benefits to many newcomers, including being
able to afford housing and to live comfortably while owning large plots of
land that included some of the valley's best locations and views, as well as
to buy, build, and rent the largest and best-appointed homes around the
valley. Wealth facilitated ownership of reliable vehicles that allowed them
to commute to work outside of the valley and to live in remote places,
including many homes accessible only by steep, often unpaved roads.
Wealth and income also paid for the specialized equipment and clothing
needed to partake in numerous outdoor activities, including snow sports,
mountain and road biking, hiking, rock-climbing, hunting, fishing, horseback riding, and trail running. And wealth and income made accessible
the many cultural events and activities that occurred around the valley,
including plays, concerts, community dinners, and fundraisers as well as
yoga, meditation, art, dance, and music classes—all of which helped newcomers and their children build and maintain cultural capital.

Beyond the advantages and access that money provided, newcomers
also benefited from a number of noneconomic resources. Rich in symbolic
capital as well as real capital, they often traded symbolic resources for real

advantages. Newcomers generally came to the valley with high amounts of human capital in the forms of education, advanced job skills, and long work histories; and cultural capital in the forms of professionalism and soft skills, as well as knowledge about art, music, dance, spiritual interests, and leisure activities.[42] These resources gave them advantages in the labor market that helped ensure that they were able to procure the best jobs that Paradise Valley had to offer and that they were seldom out of work for long. It also meant that newcomers had options in choosing how and when to work, including the opportunity to choose work with flexible hours and that they found interesting and enjoyable.

In addition, newcomers were generally rich in social capital, including ties to family members outside of the valley who often had resources to share, as well as being part of strong social networks within the valley that allowed them to share resources and benefits with others like themselves.[43] Newcomers relied heavily upon their social networks of like-minded, similarly resourced individuals and families to procure jobs, share childcare responsibilities, help with large and small chores, and lead the community's many civic and socially minded organizations. These sources of social support contributed to the informal safety net that newcomers gratefully acknowledged existed for them in Paradise Valley. Social capital was exchanged within networks and built for newcomers through their involvement in the greater community, including both informal exchange activities and their participation in local organizations, including the volunteer work that many did around the valley. Social capital was a key part of survival in Paradise Valley.

Although it was common for newcomers to be somewhat "class blind" when it came to their advantages in the labor market and other areas in the community, this did not mean that they were apathetic regarding the needs of the greater community. Newcomers were active in numerous types of civic activities, and women and retirees in particular often gave extremely generously of their time in volunteering for local organizations across the community. Their altruistic work did contribute to the building of their social networks, but it also was an enormous part of the community's ability to address its own problems, support its residents, and make informed and thoughtful decisions regarding future projects and endeavors. It also meant that newcomers, despite often short tenures in the community, played outsized roles in deciding the community's concerns and priorities. Newcomers generally were very dedicated to creating and sustaining the ideal rural community they dreamt of when they decided to move to Paradise Valley. Nonetheless, their visions for the community's future did not always match well with the desires, needs, and political preferences of the valley's old-timers.

4 Trouble in Paradise

On my first few trips through Paradise Valley, I was not only struck by the multitude of services that appeared to cater to an upper class, urban crowd, but as a rural sociologist I was also struck by what I didn't see. In my early travels through the valley I observed little sign of the kinds of dwellings and services I had come to associate with remote places in the rural West. I wondered why there weren't more signs of rural hardship, of long-term habitation, and of businesses that cater to more working-class interests, budgets, and cultural norms. The valley's magnificent roadside vistas effectively concealed signs of this kind of life, which nonetheless weren't far away. Just a few turns off of the main highway brought these other types of dwellings and services into view: the dark, old bars where tourists wouldn't feel welcome; the trailer parks; and the run-down cabins tucked away in the valley's sparsely populated drainages. In these places one could find old-timers clustered, as well as in the few public housing complexes and some small homes closer to town. They were often on low-lying land, with cramped, small lots and without impressive views. In these rougher corners of the valley its less-fortunate inhabitants resided, living lives that paralleled but often remained mostly disconnected from those of its newcomers.

I initially got to know the diverse group I call old-timers, the ones who had generally lived in Paradise Valley longer, who fit a more traditionally working-class economic, political, educational, and cultural profile, through the community's social services and my volunteer work with its food bank, family support center, and public library. It was also through word-of-mouth, personal introductions, and participation in inclusive events and celebrations. I worked hard to ensure that my research across the valley included a variety of social networks and social spheres, and that I got to know and speak with this second group of people, with fewer resources, who struggled more but loved their community no less. I was startled at times by the bitterness that came across in their interviews, but more often I was surprised by the lack thereof and the grace with which most old-timers accepted the changes that they and their community had experienced.

Old-timers are tied deeply to Paradise Valley but face a complex set of issues there. Unlike newcomers, who often have multiple types of economic and symbolic capital to help them navigate the challenges of rural life, old-timers generally have fewer resources to aid them in securing even basic necessities, including work, housing, and childcare, as well as food and utilities. Thus while newcomers struggled with some aspects of rural life, but ultimately prevailed and reported feeling successful in Paradise Valley, old-timers expressed senses of loss, frustration, and ineffectiveness at meeting their own needs. The changing nature of the labor market and the community itself have diminished old-timers' power and integration in the valley. These conditions have undermined old-timers' abilities to survive. Most still clung to the ideologies associated with the American Dream, including hopes of economic success and upward mobility achieved through individual effort, ability, and perseverance.[1] For Paradise Valley's old-timers, however, this ideal is becoming increasingly elusive. They struggled to accept their new realities and downsize their dreams, focusing their expectations less on getting ahead and more on basic survival and preserving dignity.

Old-timers frequently conveyed marginalization, resentment, and a sense that the future they had expected or hoped for in Paradise Valley had been stolen from them. Most could not expect to inherit the valley's bounty, nor earn it through their own labor. Instead, facing increasing challenges and diminished dreams, they fought to survive and make sense of their marginalization. They searched for self-respect through individualized efforts and displays of worthiness that did little to alter the structural realities of modern Paradise Valley. Their struggles, which mirror those of many rural Americans as well as much of America's working class, left them with little hope for the future and little voice in the community that they had long called home. Their disenfranchisement was intricately interwoven with newcomers' successes, as old-timers were pushed to the margins of a community that newcomers increasingly dominated.

"IT'S HOME": OLD-TIMERS' ATTACHMENT TO PARADISE VALLEY

Not all old-timers had lived in the valley for their whole lives, but most had been there for at least twenty years. For some, Paradise Valley had been their family's home for generations. For others it was an adopted home, but adopted at a different time in its economic history, when jobs were clustered in natural resource–based industries versus tourism-dependent entertainment and recreation services. Some old-timers had very comfortable working-class backgrounds and upbringings; others had always struggled to survive there. The economic world of Paradise Valley had changed around its old-timers, devaluing their skills and limiting the jobs available to them. Despite the decline in working-class and unionized jobs, old-timers remained in the valley for many of the same reasons that newcomers moved there: they loved the rural lifestyle and sense of peace as well as the valley's physical beauty. Their understanding of the rural idyll looked in many ways similar to that of newcomers, although old-timers often used different language and expressions to describe it and held different orientations toward land use.[2] Despite having fewer chances for success there, most old-timers believed strongly in the value of rural life and of Paradise Valley as a home community, and they wanted to remain there long term.[3] For them, it epitomized "home":

> We're home here. We have our trailer here. We live in a, uh, small trailer, and we found a really good place for it, and my son and his girlfriend and her two

daughters live right next door. We love it. It's home. It's home. It's, you know, I don't know, I just like it here.

—Audrey Patterson, fifty-nine-year-old married, poor, SSI-reliant

I grew up here. This is my home. I know all the backcountry and everything up here. I've hunted and fished all my life, hiked and everything else. This is my area. I know it.

—Wes Thompson, forty-five-year-old married, low-income municipal employee

As with newcomers, old-timers focused on several themes as key reasons for staying in Paradise Valley, including a similar understanding of rural places—and this particular rural place—as safer, calmer, and quieter than urban areas. Wendy Harris, a thirty-seven-year-old valley native explained: "I choose to raise my son here versus going over to the Coast or anything... because just—oh, my God, you talk about somebody gettin' murdered, and it'd be like—you know, it's a common thing over there. Somebody gets murdered here and people are flippin' out!" Although Wendy and her husband struggled to find steady work and make ends meet, she told me: "I'll be here probably till the day I die. [laughs] It's just—it's home." "It's home" was a common refrain for old-timers in explaining their choices to stay in Paradise Valley, but most had many reasons for living there beyond simply that it was their default. Comments that evoked rural images of safety, cohesion, family-friendliness, and a slower pace were even more ubiquitous for old-timers than they were for newcomers:

It's a great place to raise kids really. That's probably the biggest thing that I love about it, is I can... You know what's going on with your kids. It's a good place to raise them. Um, I don't have to worry about all the little things. Like, for instance, my kids, we ride bikes out here and they don't wear their helmets. They should, but I know that there's no traffic coming down here.

—Allison Lloyd, twenty-eight-year-old married, low-income stay-at-home mother

It's more of a tight-knit community. There's a lot more family involvement. It's not—I call it the rat race, but it's not wake up, go to work, it's not that routine of, every day you are surviving to make more money. That's what— being a parent now, that's what I really enjoy. It's not live every day to make more money.

—Chad Lloyd, twenty-eight-year-old married, low-income sawmill worker

I've always liked being part of the rural community. I don't like the big cities.... Too much chaos. I don't like a lot of chaos. It's just chaos. People are always moving a hundred miles an hour, just driving from point A to point B. A friend of mine works about the same distance from his work as I do, and he says it takes him forty-five minutes to get to work in the morning. I'm like, "Really?" "Oh, yeah, traffic jams are just nasty." I go, "I grab my cup of coffee in the morning and my traffic jam's a couple deer crossin' the road, and it takes me ten minutes to get to work if I'm takin' my time lookin' at the scenery."... It might take me an hour to get home, but I stopped and did some fishin' along the way.

—Wes Thompson, forty-five-year-old married, low-income municipal employee

You hear gunshots pretty much all the time, but it's people target practicing. It's not people shooting other people.... You don't gotta worry about people walkin' around at night. A lot of people around here still leave their doors unlocked at night. Over there [in the city], it's like, no. That's somethin' I'd have to get used to.

—Caleb Daniels, twenty-six-year-old single, poor, unemployed

As these comments illustrate, often old-timers had very concrete issues that to them exemplified the benefits of their home community in terms of its quiet, slowness, and safety. While parents often explicitly linked these issues to the family-friendliness of Paradise Valley, old-timers with and without children were equally likely to bring up these themes in discussing their favorite things about the valley and reasons for staying there. As is the case for many white rural populations, terms like "safety" often stood in explicit contrast to urban concerns including crime, chaos, and crowding, and also possibly referenced fears regarding racial diversity.[4]

Like newcomers, old-timers also commonly focused on the rural amenities that they valued in Paradise Valley, although their preferred outdoor activities and orientations were generally different. Edna Larson had lived all but two of her seventy-seven years in Paradise Valley. She described her reasons for being there as "my horse and my snowmobile." Owen Roberts, a fifty-five-year-old valley native, told me proudly that he was "born and raised [here]—I did leave the valley once and moved away for a month. I came back here." When asked what kept him there, he replied: "I am an avid hunter. I like the outdoors. Snowmobiling. I don't ski. I tried that once. Not for this guy. But I love the winters. I love the four changes of the year."

Similar to newcomers, old-timers often spoke of the community itself, its slow pace, and its physical beauty concurrently when talking about their decisions to return or stay there. Valley native Asa Hobson, a thirty-eight-year-old field scientist, mentioned these issues when explaining his decision to return to the valley after ten years away: "Just for the most part you can trust most people. The pace of life. And outdoors. You know, having a beautiful place to live in, and having just grown up here, I always knew I wanted to come back." Sixty-two-year-old Marilyn Edwards similarly hit upon multiple themes as she described her reasons for staying in the community despite poverty, a recent divorce, and estrangement from her children: "This is where I raised my babies. This is where I met my husband. This is where I know every inch of every hill around here, and it's not, it doesn't have, you know, I don't think we have a stoplight yet."

Where old-timers differed from newcomers was in their sense, repeated throughout many of the previous quotes, of a deep-rootedness in the valley. Old-timers spoke of familiarity and the sense of being known, they spoke of their families as major draws, and they repeatedly described the valley as home. This sense of Paradise Valley as where home and family came together was paramount in their explanations for why they stayed there. Caleb Daniels struggled to survive in Paradise Valley but explained his deep ties to the place: "My mom's family, they have founder roots, they're that rooted in." He described his connection to the valley as "sentimental" and told me: "I can still name most of the places where I've lived and where my family before me has lived." Valley natives and young married couple Emmet and Amy Farley had lived elsewhere for several years as adults but returned before becoming parents. Emmet explained: "We both felt like this is where we want to raise a family and be, if we could make it happen." Amy followed up: "All our friends and family are here and it's easy. It's what I know."

For these and many old-timers, Paradise Valley was unique not simply for physical amenities and rural lifestyle but, more important, because it was where they had roots, family, and a sense of home. Even for those who had considered leaving, home and family often kept them in Paradise Valley, as was the case for eighty-year-old valley native Martha Crawford:

I don't know why we didn't leave—well, because at one time my parents were still living here. And then they left, and then there was my mother-in-law and my grandmother-in-law that were living here, and my husband was an only child and so that kind of gets that going, you know? And I would have—I think I would have moved someplace else. We had a couple, three, opportunities and he just didn't want to, so that's that. But it was, at the time, a very good place to raise a family.

Although family played a much larger role in their descriptions of Paradise Valley's advantages than it did for newcomers, old-timers differed from newcomers in their discussions of the community itself. Many spoke of local family and friends, and the friendliness or trustworthiness of local people, but they did not tend to speak in terms of community more generally in the same way that newcomers did. Largely missing from old-timers' descriptions was the "sense of community" that newcomers frequently evoked. Old-timers rarely talked about either the like-mindedness of Paradise Valley as a whole or the specific political orientation of the community. They were also less likely to discuss the ways in which the community itself fit their personal needs, desires, and belief systems, or to describe a sense of feeling supported or integrated into the larger community. Old-timers generally focused much less on this "community" aspect of rurality as a reason for being in Paradise Valley.

Nonetheless, they had many very conscious and concrete examples of the ways in which Paradise Valley symbolized home for them. In general, old-timers were less likely than newcomers to express a desire to leave the valley, with most struggling to imagine themselves living anywhere else.[5] Yet despite this strong attachment, old-timers were more likely to express dissatisfaction with day-to-day challenges in Paradise Valley. Their difficulties stemmed from multiple areas, with financial and employment concerns usually dominating. In addition to struggles with the labor market, the majority of old-timers also contended with perpetual problems in finding and securing housing in the valley. Unlike newcomers, they were often accustomed to rural lifestyles and chores, and struggled with procuring land and homes in which to practice these well-worn skills. For old-timers, labor market concerns often were less manageable than they were for newcomers, and these concerns combined with challenges in finding affordable housing and childcare to make life in the valley much harder for them. Their deep ties to place bound them to the valley and discouraged many from out-migration to places that might have better opportunities. But their lack of connections to those with resources to share, coupled with a cultural focus on independence and self-sufficiency common to rural populations, critically undermined old-timers' abilities to survive in Paradise Valley.[6] These multiple challenges converged to create uncertain and insecure futures for many of those with the deepest roots in Paradise Valley, undercutting old-timers' abilities to achieve even a modest version of the American Dream.

DIMINISHED DREAMS: STRUGGLES TO SURVIVE IN PARADISE VALLEY

> There are just so many jobs. And in my thinking, the housing that we need, it's probably service industry housing, and that's where it falls short, where people are having to come over—live over in Goldenrod in order to work here. That's not right. Something is going to have to change if the valley is going to keep growing in population. But I don't think that there's enough—and thirty years' worth of watching the businesses in Reliance shut down in the wintertime—is there enough business to keep a business open all wintertime and support these people? I don't—it hasn't proven itself yet.
> —Ruth Cooper, seventy-year-old married, low-income Social
>   Security–reliant retiree

Old-timers almost universally lamented the limitations of the labor market in Paradise Valley. They discussed at length their struggles to survive there, citing problems with unemployment and underemployment, seasonal work and layoffs, and the inability to make ends meet on the low wages that both seasonal work and service work provided.[7] Unlike newcomers, most old-timers were not ultimately satisfied with their outcomes in terms of job security, wages, hours, flexibility, or the nature of work itself. While some expressed satisfaction with one facet of their work lives and choices, most struggled with other aspects, and few felt comfortable in their abilities to survive there. Old-timers frequently talked about money as a daily challenge that impacted their survival options, relationships, and ability to partake in social and civic life. Low income was connected to social exclusion for many old-timers, and they frequently discussed financial strain as limiting their abilities to engage in social activities in Paradise Valley.[8]

"It Is Way Hand-to-Mouth": Low-Wage and Seasonal Work

Old-timers generally had less education, income, wealth, and social and cultural capital than newcomers, all of which hurt them in the labor market. They seldom made the kinds of comments that newcomers made regarding ease in finding jobs locally. Most old-timers instead described a lack of available jobs and struggles to find work that was full-time, year-round, and paid living wages. With fewer personal resources, old-timers could not as easily survive on low wages and seasonal work as newcomers, particularly given that most did not have homes that were paid off. They also seldom had reliable vehicles and money for gas that would allow them to seek employment opportunities outside of the valley.[9] Valley native Owen Roberts succinctly described the challenge: "It is really hard to find jobs here in the valley. Especially full-time jobs, year around." Income shortfalls plagued even the more fortunate of old-timers, who rarely had enough family help or personal wealth to support them through leaner times. They spoke repeatedly of struggles to get by with low wages and limited options:

> It is way hand-to-mouth. It is not so good here. I am reluctant to make any changes, even though I feel like I don't earn much more than a basic living wage. And I am fifty-seven. So you know what that's going to look like when you try to retire. I mean, I'll have Social Security. End of story, right? No savings. If I keep at this job. But right now I would never dare to change.
>
> —Pam Rhodes, fifty-seven-year-old cohabiting, low-income service worker

> At one point I had five jobs. Between training horses, washing dishes in the evenings. I was cleaning motel rooms at one place. I was doing a couple of other little jobs for different things. Making ends meet here is really challenging. I have a friend who used to joke—she was like, "Well, I hope you like it because after three years, poverty will keep you here."
>
> —Jody Hammond, forty-five-year-old single, low-income small business owner

> We are struggling but we have got tourism. But unless you have a business that is kind of related to that or has some kind of facet to that, you are strug-

gling. There is many people here that I know that have not just one good job,
but they have like three or four jobs just to make ends meet, you know. . . .
The jobs are seasonal and some just don't pay well.
—Marc Tate, forty-two-year-old single, middle-income retail worker

As these comments illustrate, Paradise Valley's labor market presented
immense challenges for old-timers in making ends meet. Julie Long was
luckier than most in these regards. The forty-five-year-old mother of
four had lived in the valley for all but three years of her life, rent-free in
a house that her parents owned. She and her husband were comparative
success stories among Paradise Valley's old-timers, both having relatively
secure jobs. Julie worked part-time in the school district, and her husband
worked in construction. Nonetheless, they lived below 200 percent of the
poverty line for their family size, in part because of the lack of year-round
work. With regard to their annual income, Julie explained:

In this valley you tend to go—like, I will work in the wintertime because I'm
in the school system, but I only pull in about $1,200 every month, some-
where in that ballpark. [My husband] works—gets laid off for two months
in the wintertime, because he's a builder, so it just all—yeah. And then I
don't work in the summertime.

Even for those with reliable work, the combination of seasonality and low
wages made survival difficult. Julie expressed relative satisfaction with
her family's diminished dream of almost making it on their own. She was
proud of the fact that they rarely relied on outside sources of aid, but, as
she explained: "We are in debt, always."

Low income was a struggle for most old-timers, and few had the kind
of job security that Julie and her husband had. Women in particular frequently listed a string of short-term jobs in the service sector that they
left or from which they were let go for various reasons, often complaining
about the working conditions and the lack of childcare. Men often struggled to find jobs that could support a family. Most felt they could not make
enough money in service jobs and preferred more traditionally rural-mas-
culine jobs that were physical and/or outdoors.[10] Thus they found themselves competing for a shrinking pool of mostly nonunion manual labor
positions in construction, maintenance, and forest and wildlife sectors.[11]
Some families navigated these challenges more successfully than others,

but few old-timers felt entirely happy about their financial situations and job prospects.

Like Julie Long, municipal employee Wes Thompson had relatively good luck in Paradise Valley's labor market and rarely had experienced troubles finding or keeping jobs. Nonetheless, the low-income valley native still struggled to support his family and keep up with the payments on their single-wide trailer in a mobile home park. He had held a number of jobs in the valley: "I worked a ditch for years, and then I did construction, and then I worked for Cascade Logging for years, and then finally ended up with the job in Reliance." He explained that he had enjoyed working for Cascade Logging the most, but left the job because it wasn't sufficient in terms of pay or benefits. Wes told me:

> It was one of those jobs, I drove a dump truck for 'em most of the time. I'd deliver a couple of loads of sand or somethin', next thing I know I'm in the ditch gluing pipe together, or maybe I'm on an excavator or backhoe pushin' stuff in or rollin', movin' equipment around. It was adventure all the time. You weren't doin' the same thing every day. That's what I like. That was the main thing. The only problem was, in the wintertime you pretty much get laid off, like everybody else in this valley. That's the reason I took this job in Reliance, because it's year-round and it's got the medical insurance for the wife and the kid.

For Wes, whose wife was currently out of the workforce, providing for his family took priority over work that he enjoyed:

> Doin' jobs where they were fun, like the ditch, I did that for years, but it's only in the spring and the summertime, and in the fall you shut down and you're done for the year. Which, when I was single, that was fine. Gettin' Unemployment for a few months and then back to work.[12] That didn't bother me too much. But you've got a wife and a family and stuff like that, you've gotta—you can't really afford that. OK, which bill will we be payin' this month?

Although he enjoyed it less, Wes was grateful for his municipal job's benefits and reliability. Yet despite finding year-round work, the family still went without a number of extras. He explained:

> Yeah, it's tight, but we can [survive]. Once in a while we'll have to go without the Internet for a month or two, maybe a couple weeks. We'll hold off on

that one. We had an extra expense we didn't catch. But we got rid of a lot of stuff. We don't have satellite [TV] anymore. We just run local stations. We just don't really go outside of our area. We budget tight. My wife's really good about doin' the budgets, figuring out what we need to do. We always have enough food to keep us goin'.

For Wes, full-time, year-round work only provided for a minimalist existence, and the family nonetheless relied regularly on the food bank as well as receiving occasional aid with utilities. Even so, they contended with periodic lack of access to the Internet, cutting them off from social life within and outside of the valley.[13] Wes acknowledged his choices and constraints but focused on succeeding in his diminished version of the American Dream, in which basic survival was the goal instead of upward mobility, homeownership, or disposable income.

In addition to the problems old-timers faced with low incomes, for a number of them keeping jobs was difficult. There were multiple reasons for this, including in many cases individuals' behaviors and failures to get along with coworkers and supervisors. But often insecurity was part of the job description and the contingent nature of much local work, leading to a constant need to find new jobs and failures to receive raises and promotions. Newcomers might rely on wealth to carry them through seasonal layoffs, but most old-timers could not afford to go without income for months between jobs. Both men and women thus described long histories of moving from low-wage job to low-wage job as the economy ebbed and flowed.

Tilda Conner and her fiancé had encountered these sorts of issues. The thirty-six-year-old had lived in the valley since she was a child and had held a number of jobs in the service and care work sectors. Despite Tilda and her fiancé both currently working, the family relied on SNAP food assistance and the local food bank, and they felt cramped for space in their rented single-wide trailer. Tilda began her local career as a caretaker for a disabled uncle when she was a new single mother: "I would just sit up at the house and take care of him. It was nice, 'cause I could take my daughter with me." Over the years she took on more and more service work to augment her low wages and sporadic hours as a care worker. Luckily for Tilda, she no longer needed full-time childcare. "So now I'm workin' as a housekeeper," she said. "My daughter's old enough where she can be home for, like, a half hour."

Between this job and her partner's retail job, the family was just scraping by. Tilda explained that things would get more difficult soon, because her housekeeping job was insecure. "During the summer," she said, "it was five or six [days of work per week]. During the winter it will slow down." She planned to respond as she always did to these seasonal fluctuations, by taking on additional work: "I'm a caregiver, so I can always get a second job as a caregiver if I need to." Like many old-timers, Tilda was used to working multiple jobs that waxed and waned with the seasons and never quite provided financial security. Few old-timers were strangers to working multiple jobs at once, and even those with the best jobs regularly contended with seasonality and low wages that created significant stress for individuals and families.

For old-timers, work was an area of constant struggle, with good jobs hard to find and harder to keep. Unlike newcomers, they often did not feel that their local connections or work histories helped them much in finding work there, and most felt that they needed to take whatever opportunities they found. Old-timers were often aware of the ways in which their social status negatively impacted their employment trajectories. Maintenance worker Owen Roberts, who lived below the poverty line and was particularly frustrated with his labor market challenges, said this about finding work locally:

> What there is here—it would be nice if people—if they started something—if they brought—if they would hire people from the valley and not people from outside in here to work—because that does happen. It happens a lot. And it shouldn't. They should hire people from the valley first, and then look elsewhere. But I don't know why it doesn't seem to happen that way.

Although many old-timers had long-standing social ties in the valley, they often were not well connected to those in positions of power or with jobs to offer and had fewer opportunities to make these connections.[14] They seldom were approached to volunteer for local organizations, and the few who did described a very different evolution, by which they offered to volunteer after receiving support services, a process that was unlikely to lead to leadership positions within organizations.[15] Old-timers thus had far fewer opportunities for job networking through their social ties than did newcomers.

Old-timers on average also had significantly less education than newcomers and much less experience in professional jobs. Chad Lloyd, a twenty-eight-year-old sawmill worker who dropped out of high school and later earned his GED, believed that lacking a high school diploma had resulted in his having to work his way up from sweeping floors:

> I strongly believe that if an employer sees that you got your GED, either he thinks that (a) you're a quitter, you decided you didn't want to do it, or (b) you had something major come up in your life and you weren't able to finish school. And I think that (a) is a big part of it. "You didn't even finish high school. Why should I hire you?"

In Chad's case he was able to slowly gain skills on the job and rise through the ranks, investing into human capital through experience. But the years he spent working for poverty-level wages put his family at a financial disadvantage, and he still struggled to support his wife and children.

In addition to lack of human capital in the forms of education, job experience, and skills, old-timers with longer histories in the valley that included their own teenage years and early adulthood were more likely to have made mistakes that were remembered locally, which stained their reputations with local employers.[16] A coworker at the food bank once recounted to me the backstory of a young man who had been a client that day. As I wrote in my field notes:

> She told me that he had worked locally [for a while], that he liked the outdoors and the mountains. But while working in construction he'd made a mistake: he'd shot a deer without a license, sharing the meat with friends who needed the food. His boss found out about it and after the seasonal layoff everyone knew what he'd done, and now he was having a very hard time finding work.[17]

It wasn't uncommon for local men in particular to have their mistakes follow them throughout their careers in Paradise Valley. As I found in my previous work, in Paradise Valley a moral stain like drug use, criminal activity, or welfare receipt could negatively impact both an individual's reputation in the community and his or her success in the labor market.[18] For example, stay-at-home father Ryan Boyle, a thirty-nine-year-old cohabiting Paradise Valley native, struggled to find and keep work locally. He had worked for a number of employers around the valley when he was younger and had been fired multiple times for drug use, although he strongly denied having used drugs while employed. In the time that I knew Ryan he was unable to find a job, although he repeatedly said he was looking. His partner, Jessica, explained that Ryan had a bad reputation among some local employers because "he ruined his first couple of real jobs around here by partying too much and being a party kid." Ryan described the community's collective surveillance and memory this way:

> Here, you gotta worry about the person who is sitting behind the coffee counter who is looking out the corner of their eye and saw you do that one little thing, and put this, this, and that together that they heard from Bob. It's just, it's oddly, you know, before you even do something you're guilty and everyone knows. You know, I was still thinking about whether I wanted to do that, and uh, and I did it twice, huh? That's what you heard? [Sighs] And the funny thing is, everyone who lives here knows that the most inaccurate thing you can hear about anything is what somebody said about what somebody said. Yet the next time it comes around, there they are listening to that one again, falling for that one again.

For longtime and native Paradise Valley residents, a few well-known moral slips could translate into a lifetime of labor market struggles.

Caleb Daniels believed that it wasn't his own actions but his family's bad reputation as drug users that haunted him in Paradise Valley. He told me that he had trouble finding and keeping work there, and that local employers wouldn't hire him:

> Apparently I've gotten a reputation around the valley, I'm not sure how, as a drug dealer, a troublemaker. I look at 'em and I'm like, "Really? I'll take a drug test right now. I don't do drugs." . . . It's like, my dad was friends with a couple of drug dealers, and apparently they connected dots. I'm like, you can connect all the dots you want. It's not gonna add up.

For Caleb, social networks with low moral capital were an obstacle in the labor market, exacerbated by his own lack of human capital.[19] He had struggled in school with unsupported learning disabilities and barely finished high school. He told me that he regretted his lack of skills now:

> There's still stuff I don't really understand, but I kinda really need to know in today's work force. I got doomed to be low-level employment. . . . There's been a lot of job opportunities that if I would've known just a little bit more back then, I would have better luck now.

Given their disadvantages in terms of real and symbolic capital, old-timers often faced serious challenges in the labor market, both with regard to finding and keeping jobs and with regard to surviving on the low incomes that local work provided. With relatively little power to address these issues, and few strong ties to those with power in the labor market, old-timers were forced to downsize their expectations, focusing on minimal goals of stable work and basic survival versus dreams of economic success and material comfort. They were often forced by need to rely heavily on formal services to make up the shortfalls between income and expenses. However, these services were limited in the help they could provide and often left families struggling to survive. In addition, while locally accessible aid often helped with specific needs like food, clothes, and utilities, there was little help available for two of the other most common difficulties that old-timers regularly faced: lack of affordable housing and childcare.

"Not Allowed to Inherit My Kingdom": Housing Insecurity in Paradise Valley

> There is the bad of people, like, raising rents, in an already very limited real estate market, and the war profiteers, as I call them, who have taken advantage of the need for housing and profited off of it, which I think is disgusting.... I know of a few cases of that. So yeah, and just young families finding it hard to find housing and to be able to really stay here. And they are the life's blood. They are the people who do the jobs and build the houses for the part-timers and keep this place chugging. So without them, you know, it would be a retirement community, basically. So you kind of need to find that fine line.
> —Carrie Baker, thirty-six-year-old married, low-income stay-at-home mother

In contrast to newcomers, old-timers did not generally feel that housing in Paradise Valley was affordable, nor did they easily navigate the housing market. My visits with old-timers led me into some of the most dilapidated housing conditions I had ever seen, including a number of single-wide trailers with rotting walls and floors; spaces so cramped that there was barely room to walk, sit, or eat; and ventilation so poor that smells lingered and festered. I visited homes in which flies circled and swarmed, and dampness, heat, or cold was amplified by lack of insulation as well as door and window sealant. I visited travel trailers without plumbing hookups, inhabited year-round by residents who used hoses and buckets for sanitary purposes. The difficulty that old-timers faced in finding and keeping safe, secure, and affordable housing was a recurrent theme throughout their interviews and my interactions with them, and even those who were lucky enough to have found stable homes generally acknowledged the widespread housing shortage in the valley.

Old-timers were significantly less likely than newcomers to be homeowners, with just 47 percent owning their own homes, many of which were either single-wide trailers (generally on rented land) or older homes that were often in need of repairs and maintenance.[20] Most old-timers expressed frustration with barriers to affordable housing and homeownership in the valley. They commented:

> I'm always worried about the future! I didn't plan on spending almost eighteen years in a single-wide trailer. I wanted a house before I was forty. It never happened.
> —Adeline Thompson, forty-year-old married, low-income stay-at-home mother

> That's one of the things that I find, you know, really sad about here is it is so hard for young families to find affordable housing. It really sucks to grow up in an area and by the time you are old enough and raising your own family, you can't do the same work that your parents did and still get by. You know? And I know a lot of people in that situation. It's really common, and a rental comes up—like the house you are living in sold. You have to move out, and there is nothing—everything is way overpriced, and it's gone in a day.
> —Emmet Farley, thirty-three-year-old married, low-income construction worker

> I feel like I wasn't allowed to inherit my kingdom. You know, like, I grew up here, I paid my dues. . . . I thought everybody at least should get their acre, their house . . . you know, just your chunk to make it.
> —Ryan Boyle, thirty-nine-year-old cohabiting, poor stay-at-home father

The low incomes and seasonal work that many old-timers experienced were mismatches for rising housing costs in Paradise Valley, which were exacerbated as in-migration intensified and drove ever-increasing demand. Even those old-timers who had managed to find steady, stable work often bemoaned their inabilities to purchase homes and the frustration of never graduating out of the rental market. Unlike earlier generations of less-educated workers, who often managed to eventually buy modest homes, younger old-timers often had to downsize their expectations to let go of homeownership, long an essential component of the American Dream.[21]

For many old-timers, just securing affordable rental housing was difficult, and hopes of ever buying a home were slim. Newcomers relied heavily on reserves of wealth to invest in the housing market, but old-timers rarely had sufficient wealth to buy homes, and many lacked adequate income to cover rising rents. They also frequently lacked the social networks that might provide them with inside information regarding the best rental units and opportunities, as many local landlords were newcomers whose social circles didn't overlap with those of old-timers. Thus, while newcomers lauded the affordability of land and homes in Paradise Valley, old-timers often contended with severe housing stress, insecurity, and instability.[22]

Through my volunteer work at the valley's food bank and family support center, I was exposed repeatedly to individuals' troubles with obtaining affordable housing—or at times, even temporary accommodations. As I worked with the low-income community, I learned of people camping long-term, and living permanently in nonwinterized travel trailers, primitive cabins, and squatters' camps, as well as residing semipermanently at an abandoned motel where the utilities had been turned off. Subsidized public housing in the valley was scarce, and the few existing units had long waitlists, preferences for the elderly and disabled, and high levels of surveillance including periodic cleanliness inspections.[23] While gentrification and rising housing costs impacted residents across the class spectrum, their impacts were particularly damaging to those at the bottom of the labor and housing markets. Emmet and Amy Farley explained this problem in answer to the question, "What do you think are the biggest challenges facing Paradise Valley?" They made explicit reference to newcomers:

EMMET: Affordable housing for the youth—for the younger people around here. Because there is a big disparity between income levels and it makes it hard to live here.

AMY: Well, there is the people that have their second home here that sits empty forty-nine weeks out of the year. And these people come and want to go out to eat and go to the local grocery store and rent bicycles from the bike shop. But the people that work at all those places can't find a place to live, and that person has a house that's getting wasted.

As Amy argued, wealthy outsiders' successful dreams of second-home ownership contributed to housing dynamics that undermined old-timers' abilities to buy their own primary homes in Paradise Valley.

The acuteness of the housing problem fluctuated over the course of the year, intensifying in the spring as low-wage workers flooded the area in search of seasonal jobs, and landlords evicted tenants in anticipation of the higher rents that summer visitors would be willing to pay.[24] Many of the food bank's repeat clients were local workers who could not find permanent housing, often living short-term in informal camping situations on friends' or US Forest Service land, or doubling up with family, friends, and acquaintances. Women admitted to being or remaining in relationships with men because of housing needs. These various types of "disposable ties" were often short-lived, and it was common for informal situations to fall apart.[25] Camping was also impractical in the long-term, and in the late fall people in these precarious conditions often left the valley due to lack of winterized housing options.[26]

In addition to the shortage of affordable rental housing, low-income tenants were often unaware of available units, many of which were not openly advertised. My own search for housing in the valley was illustrative of this issue. In the local want ads in early May, only a single, extremely expensive home was listed for rent. When I called a local realtor to ask how to find rental housing, I was advised to post my own "looking for housing" ad. My ad gave my temporary timeframe, profession and university affiliation, and said I had no children or pets. Within a week, I received more than ten inquiries from local landlords who were interested in showing their homes to me, none of which was advertised openly as an available rental unit. I was offered all of the units I viewed, including one whose absentee landlord texted me the keycode to allow me to view the place on my own after I had spoken to him only by phone.[27] When I asked a local property owner about this tendency to not advertise available rental units, she explained that she would rather find the right tenant informally through word-of-mouth than to advertise publicly and have to "let people down," particularly given the valley's small size and likelihood that she might have to face rejected tenants later in public settings.[28] Those who lacked access to social networks that included landlords, and who lacked significant income, wealth, or symbolic capital, often found that their housing options were extremely limited.

Navigating these multiple challenges required a combination of perseverance, resources, and luck. Such was the case for forty-six-year-old Janice Carter, a part-time bookkeeper who had been in the valley for two years. She spent her first year and a half in the valley living with a sister who had a small guest wing. "Every one of the siblings has lived in it," Janice said, "and none of us has ever survived the winter. I made it the longest." For Janice the arrangement ended badly, leaving her homeless for the summer. As she recounted:

> I, she was being such a jerk that I just grabbed a tent. And I met this guy, who I ended up calling my camping buddy, 'cause he was in one spot and I was in the next one, and then I didn't have to be scared, you know, like of strangers or bears. I mean, I'm no, I'm no girl. I mean, I'm a girl scout and I can take care of myself totally, and I have a gun, you know, but I still didn't like being in the wilderness by myself.

Janice's bout of homelessness lasted six weeks, by which time she was beginning to panic, with fall approaching. She explained that she was lucky to discover an available trailer for rent:

> [A friend's] babysitter was staying with her. She was just finishing shampooing carpets and moving out, and she, and I heard, I was like, "Are you moving?" And she's like, "Yeah." And I was like, "Where? Where did you live?" And she's like, "Well," and I was like, "Is it still open?!" And she was like, "It might be. Go talk to her right now." And I did! And that was awesome. Yeah, praise the lord for that moment. So, it's, and the highway's kinda loud but it's, it's fine.

Janice ascribed this experience to luck and faith, but in securing both this situation and her previous one, social capital played a vital role.

When old-timers didn't have sufficient social capital or other resources, housing concerns could derail their life trajectories. For instance, Caleb Daniels experienced multiple disadvantages in his struggles to find secure housing. The twenty-six-year-old had grown up "hand-to-mouth," moving frequently around the valley. As mentioned earlier, he had a difficult time in school and struggled to find and keep work as an adult. Caleb's extended family lived in the region, and he relied heavily on them for help. Despite their efforts, however, Caleb was often homeless and had spent time couch surfing with family and living outdoors, sometimes sleeping on park benches.[29] We met for his interview in his cousin's cramped, single-wide trailer, because Caleb felt that his current living quarters weren't suitable for guests. He described:

> It's a [travel] trailer that's smaller than this living room. . . . I was homeless before that because . . . the apartment we were living in got condemned, and then to add another kick to the thing, I got fired two days later. I didn't have a place to live. . . . Finally my aunt was like, "I ain't gonna have this," and she gave me the little trailer to live in.

In return for the unit, Caleb was expected to help his aging great-aunt with chores. The situation was insecure for Caleb, who suspected that she didn't really need him there, and he worried about being kicked out. I asked if he thought an eviction was likely, and he paused and responded, "I hope not, but I'm not entirely sure." Caleb expressed anxiety, with no concrete plan for this possibility. He worried that his brother, his closest family member who lived in one of the valley's trailer parks, would not be able to help him. "I can't move down to my brother's because of, they have to sign a contract to live in there that says that only certain people can live there, right down to the number of animals you can have."[30]

While Caleb was lucky to have a web of social ties within the valley, his family's poverty meant that they were limited in their ability to aid him in his housing struggles. Although he relied on his extended family to help house him, given their own lack of resources, the result was intense housing stress and insecurity, including periods of homelessness and substandard housing. Without hope for a higher salary or more consistent work, Caleb had little chance of securing more stable housing, and thus it was unlikely that his prospects would improve in the near future. Employment and housing insecurity had long-term impacts for Caleb, including hesitation with regard to future romantic and family engagements. As he put it:

I want to get in a better living arrangement. But if I get in a better living arrangement, yes, I'd love to have a family.

Q: What kind of living arrangement would you imagine for yourself and your family?

Bein' able to take care of myself without having financial aid from anyone, having a nice stable job, a place I don't have to worry about getting kicked out of at any minute.

Ryan Boyle, introduced earlier, had a similarly difficult time with housing in Paradise Valley, exacerbated by his struggles to find and keep stable work and his reputation for problem behaviors. He had moved frequently as an adult, at times living with his mother, which he described as personally difficult and leading him into downward spirals of depression and drinking. Things improved somewhat when he coupled with his partner, Jessica, who had a year-round job in a local restaurant. Her more consistent income allowed them to move out of his mother's house, but their living conditions were substandard at first. Ryan told me:

> We had our trailer we were living in for two years, because we just couldn't find a place.... It was a travel trailer, and uh, eventually I gave that away just 'cause I don't think anyone with the case work of CPS's [Child Protective Services] interests . . . looking at us raising that kid in that trailer would, you know, vote that we should keep our kid.

The couple briefly and disastrously moved back in with Ryan's mother with their new baby, a tumultuous time during which Ryan lost his job and decided to stay home to provide childcare. Eventually they found the single-wide trailer where I interviewed them separately, in a multiuse trailer park that catered to tourists in the summertime but also had limited year-round housing. On the winter day when I first met Ryan there, the home was cluttered but clean. He expressed a sincere desire to remain there, despite struggling to cover the rent each month:

> We tend to like, bump right up to the edge of paying late. You know, like on the 19th when it's due on the 20th and stuff like that. But barring that and their getting irritated about it enough to make us, to ask us to leave, I want to and hope to stay here 'til [my son's] graduated from high school. You know, like I'm done moving if I can possibly be. This is enough for me, I don't want anything better, and thank you very much, please don't take this.

I interviewed Jessica in the trailer five months later, as spring was deepening across the valley and the tourist season was ramping up. The trailer was cluttered with toys, and now the kitchen was stacked with dirty dishes, and there was a bad smell, a combination of pet odors, rotting food, and dirty diapers. Jessica told me that the electricity had been turned off recently, and they were struggling to find the money to get it turned back on. She said:

> There was a nagging voice telling me to call the PUD [Public Utilities District] and if I would've called them, I would've gotten that ten-day extension and I would've been fine. And now I'm burned because I owe them another extra hundred bucks now. That pisses me off. When they shut you off, you automatically have to pay them a hundred bucks just to turn you on.

In the dim kitchen a single-burner camp stove perched on top of the electric range, and a cooler filled with ice kept milk for their son cold. Jessica assured me that Ryan's grandmother was going to help pay for the electricity to get turned back on soon. In both interviews they told me that they had already exhausted formal utilities aid for the calendar year. Jessica explained that things were tight lately, and that this year's tourist season was off to a slow start, negatively impacting their income. Ryan had been looking for work for over a month, but with no luck so far. At this time, however, Jessica was optimistic that things would turn around for them.

Another month later, Ryan told me that they had been evicted from the trailer. He was vague as to why, saying he didn't really know, but later suggesting that it might have something to do with Jessica's dogs, which barked loudly and might be bothering tourists staying in the park. I asked where they would go and he said he didn't know, that he couldn't turn to his family, and that he didn't think anyone else would rent to them locally. My coworkers at the food bank concurred on this latter point, telling me that when Ryan was younger he got caught up with the wrong people and did some bad things, and people still remembered. At the same time, it was clear that neither Ryan nor Jessica had any intention of leaving Paradise Valley, where both had lived for most of their lives.[31] For Ryan and Jessica their long history in Paradise Valley provided a strong incentive to stay, even as the community's unforgiving memory branded them as lacking moral capital and thus unworthy of its scarce housing.

The final time I saw Ryan, a year and a half later, he was living separately from Jessica and their son, Elliot. He told me that the stress of being unable to secure housing for his family had exacerbated mental and emotional problems for him, and he spoke of anger issues and violence that had led him to serve jail time in the past year. Now Jessica and Elliot lived with Jessica's mother, and Ryan lived forty-five minutes away across the valley with extended family members. He described separation anxiety that led him into rages when he had to say goodbye to his family after a visit, which were sometimes only monthly. Given Ryan's anger issues and criminal record, Jessica's mother would not let him stay with them, or even visit the family at her house. Ryan talked about hoping to reunite with his family and find a home for the three of them someday. But, he explained, his recent felony conviction made him ineligible for subsidized housing for the next three years, and the waitlist was longer than that.[32] For now, Ryan's dreams of homeownership and inheriting his kingdom were on hold, diminished to hopes of someday having a rented apartment where his whole family could live on their own together. Ryan, like Caleb, found that the combination of limited income and low social and moral capital contributed to housing struggles that undermined work life, personal relationships, and mental health.

For old-timers like these, Paradise Valley's limited labor market, along with their own impoverished social networks, produced a toxic combination of financial and housing strain that reinforced each other. Many low-income residents' lack of social capital resulted in a dearth of information regarding available units, while lack of moral capital contributed to additional difficulties in securing safe and affordable housing as well as finding stable work. Financial stress further limited options for finding housing and contributed to housing instability for those who struggled to keep up with rent and other housing-related expenses. In Paradise Valley financial and housing stresses were often interwoven for old-timers, with low, seasonal, and sporadic incomes increasing the likelihood of evictions, and evictions negatively impacting emotional, financial, and labor market stability.[33]

These destabilizing impacts on work, romantic, and emotional lives further impeded chances of finding either secure housing or steady jobs in the future. Although some low-income residents with weaker ties to place and community left the valley, old-timers with stronger ties often stayed but were frequently vulnerable to depression, alcoholism, violence, and drug use.[34] These distress responses decreased their moral capital in the eyes of those with property to rent, further entrenching the downward spirals. Although those with higher and more stable incomes were less prone to eviction, they still encountered housing stress and instability as well as barriers to homeownership. Generally, old-timers were much less likely than newcomers to have significant family support, wealth, or social networks to rely on in navigating housing challenges. Furthermore, housing was not the only challenge that undermined old-timers' abilities to thrive in the sometimes competing realms of work and family lives.

Gruesome Options: Lack of Childcare and Work-Family Trade-Offs

> I would work nights, and he worked days. So we very rarely
> had to do childcare. Childcare, as you know, I'm sure it will
> be a big part of this study—it is a real deal breaker. You know,
> people move. They can't afford childcare. And the childcare
> options sometimes are gruesome.
> —Pam Rhodes, fifty-seven-year-old cohabiting, low-income
>   service worker

In addition to struggles to find and keep secure, safe, and affordable housing, old-timers struggled to overcome the valley's childcare shortage. Unlike newcomers, they seldom had job flexibility or social networks with the capacity to step in and help regularly with childcare provision. Newcomer Hannah Lowry, who in chapter 3 discussed the ways in which her social networks helped her with childcare, had this to say regarding the less-fortunate residents of Paradise Valley:

> Everybody's got other people's kids a lot. Well, I don't think *everybody* does.
> I think there are a lot of parents who go to work at the grocery store or
> whatever from 7:00 to 4:00, and all they can deal with is to go home to their
> own kids who have taken the bus home alone. But for the parents who either
> don't work, of which there are many, or like me, who have one parent with a
> flexible work schedule, we always have each other's kids.

Without the same resources as newcomers, old-timers often were unable to find or afford sufficient childcare and instead frequently made sacrifices to income in order to keep one parent at home with children. The decision to have one parent stay home was significantly more common among old-timers than newcomers and generally described as a necessity rather than a choice.[35] Compared to newcomers, old-timers saw themselves as having fewer choices and less efficacy when it came to making labor market decisions. Women were more likely to opt out of the workforce to provide childcare, but it was also common to find families like Ryan Boyle's, in which a man stayed home because the woman had the more stable job.

Old-timers discussed problems in finding childcare of all kinds, particularly daycare, after-school care, and summer care for older children. Penny Carpenter, a forty-year-old hairstylist, complained about difficulties in finding care for older children: "There isn't anywhere for older kids too during the summer. That is a huge problem here. It is a major, major issue." Not only was affordable childcare difficult to find, but many old-timers had horror stories of valley childcare gone wrong. They often told me that they didn't trust any of the local options that they could afford, as was the case for Allison Lloyd. The twenty-eight-year-old low-income mother had four young children and had given up working after a string of bad experiences. In the following quote, she describes just one of them:

> Childcare is outrageous. And we've had horrible, horrible experiences with childcare. Um, when I did work and I did try to get childcare.... I took [my son] to a lady, locally, that watches a lot of kids. Um, and I would send snacks with him, and I would send diapers. Not one of the diapers got put on him. He would come home with bruises on his legs from sitting in a bouncy chair. I'd come in and he had been sitting in a bouncy chair all day long, and none of his snacks would've been eaten, and he'd have crusty diapers, and it was like, what?! And I'm paying for that, for somebody to put him downstairs in their basement with the other kids. I come to find out, a friend of mine now...she used to date her son, the lady I used to have watch him, and she said, "Yeah, we used to go over there and she'd be upstairs cooking and she'd leave the kids downstairs for hours by themselves." Um, so, that happened...I quit working because of that.

Old-timers who had local family were generally better off when it came to childcare choices, but still frequently complained that family members were unavailable or unwilling to provide as much steady care as they needed. Without the options for flexible work hours that newcomers often had, old-timers' needs for childcare could be more difficult to address within their social networks. Amy Farley explained that both her own and Emmet's mothers were happy to look after their son, but that both women worked full-time:

> I know I can always call them if I needed to, but I am kind of like, I keep telling Emmet we need to find a babysitter that is just someone that Theo knows and I can have to call, because I can't call either of them during the week, basically. So it is like if I need a sitter for some reason, I kind of—I mean, I can call a couple of my girlfriends and they have little kids, but I wouldn't expect them to do that for long periods of time or often.

Amy, like many old-timers with young children, decided that the easiest solution to the childcare problem was to remain at home with her son. But the couple struggled financially, particularly given Emmet's seasonal layoffs.

Wendy Harris, introduced earlier, had also experienced this type of conundrum. The Paradise Valley native had worked a number of service jobs as a young adult, including waiting tables and cleaning hotel rooms, both of which she described as "horrible." With regard to cleaning rooms, she explained: "There were times I was workin' six days a week. We were gettin' there early and not leavin' till after 5:00 p.m." I asked if the money she made at the hotel had been sufficient, and she replied, "I was makin' minimum wage. That's probably why I couldn't cover day care." Wendy relied at first on local family to provide childcare, but after her mother passed away, the conflict pushed Wendy out of the workforce for good. She explained:

> I think [my son] was about four years old, and I'm like, OK. Mom's not here. Don't have a babysitter anymore. My sister's gone. I'm gonna have to think about day care. Went to day care, and it would have cost me almost $500 at the time for him to be in day care for five days a week. And that's not including the gas, 'cause we were living here in Eagle Flat, for me to go to work and back in Reliance. It would have been over the amount of what my paycheck would have been. I'm like, "Are you serious? I'm gonna lose money goin' to work." So Ted was all, "No, then you can be a stay-at-home mom and save us money." That's how I became a basically housewife.

Although dropping out of the labor force solved Wendy and Ted's childcare dilemma, it also made their financial situation precarious, and in the years since the decision they struggled to survive. She explained that things had been stable for a time, but since the Great Recession Ted had struggled to find work locally and without her bringing in income, the family's finances became so tight that they had to "borrow money for food, we lived off of credit cards." Wendy also regularly visited the food bank, a practice that she began during this time. Despite a long history of working in the industry locally, Ted was unable to find construction work again. Wendy said:

> We had to come up with a second job for him. For almost a year we were livin' off the credit cards and Unemployment, and Unemployment was runnin' out, and finally Ted went to his old boss and said, "Look, can I get a loan to go to trucking school?"... And right now he's long-haulin'. He hates it, and I hate it, 'cause we see him three days out of the month.

Their financial struggles were eased somewhat by Ted's new job, but the grueling schedule was hard on the family, and Wendy described stress caused by Ted's long absences, which negatively impacted both their relationship and her health.

The valley's lack of affordable childcare posed an enormous problem for old-timers, which was greatly exacerbated by their lack of good jobs, living wages, job security, and job flexibility. Unlike newcomers, old-timers rarely had jobs with flexible hours that would be consistent with childcare and school schedules, nor were they likely to have strong social ties to others who did. Without this type of social capital or sufficient income to cover the costs of daycare, old-timers were frequently faced with a choice between work and family. Given that women in particular—who mainly worked in the least desirable service-sector jobs—often didn't enjoy the work they did, dropping out of the labor force was frequently a preferable option to paying for questionable childcare. But as their stories illustrate, most experienced this decision as coerced, rather than a choice or preference. In addition to reinforcing traditional gender roles for many old-timer families, it also effectively curtailed women's human capital investment, leaving them with long gaps in their work histories and lack of access to the rare promotional ladders that might exist in the valley's labor market, making it more difficult for them to find work again later. Thus the overlapping struggles with work, income, housing, and childcare reinforced each other, resulting in both material and emotional hardships as well as cycles of dispossession that further separated the fortunes of old-timers from those of better-resourced newcomers.

"YOU DON'T ASK FOR OUTSIDE HELP": SURVIVAL, AID, AND SELF-DENIAL

Given the multiple challenges that old-timers faced, they were often in need of help with basic survival in Paradise Valley. In urban areas, economic need and lack of resources have long been found to encourage heavy reliance on one's social networks, and generations of poverty researchers have documented social support networks as vital sources of housing, childcare, goods, and cash that facilitate survival.[36] In rural communities social support also plays an extremely important role for the poor, who frequently rely on friends and family to make ends meet as part of a patchwork of survival strategies.[37] Although recently researchers have questioned whether social support is universally available to or utilized equally by poor populations, it is still commonly found to be an integral part of poverty survival strategies.[38] In Paradise Valley, however, social support was increasingly the purview of well-resourced newcomers, not the old-timers who faced the most intense need. The general impoverishment of their social networks, the time constraints that most low-income workers faced, and rural cultural norms that prize self-sufficiency and stigmatize aid combined to undermine their abilities to create and maintain social support in this community.[39]

Instead of relying on social networks to provide support in addressing multiple areas of challenge, old-timers often turned to Paradise Valley's well-developed service sector, which depended heavily on financial donations and volunteers. Through its formal sector, they could access food aid, utilities aid, mental health support, aid with clothing and children's toys, and help with signing up for state and federal social services such as health care and food stamps. Although many old-timers also relied on friends and family for aid through leaner times, they generally described this help as very limited, stressful for all parties involved, and requiring payback in a relatively short timeframe.[40] Maggie Chambers, who struggled to make ends meet on her SSI check alone, said that when faced with shortfalls between income and expenses, "I tell a friend who has insisted upon knowing, and she helps me out. But no one is supposed to know about that." Ryan Boyle also relied heavily on family but found the support insecure. "I've been relying on Mom," he said. "Yeah, Mom's had enough of her leftover pension money from Dad dying and stuff to still help us. But according to her, it's tapped out basically." Given the limited help that old-timers were willing or able to procure from within their often disadvantaged social networks, they more often combined this form of help with that offered by formal services. Wes Thompson, who sometimes faced shortfalls despite his full-time job, used both of these strategies when needed. "Angel Food helped us for electricity one month, back when I was laid off, it was one of those things," he told me. "And family, of course, once in a great while."

Old-timers frequently relied on formal services, including local charities and state and federal programs, to help make up the gaps between income and expenses. Subsidized medical care (including Medicare and Medicaid) and subsidized insurance through the Affordable Care Act were the most commonly received form of aid: 81 percent of old-timers received some type of subsidized health insurance. Food bank usage was the next most common form of aid they reported, with 40 percent patronizing Angel Food with some frequency. Utilities aid and SNAP (Supplemental Nutrition Assistance Program, formerly known as food stamps) were the next most commonly received, at 31 percent and 27 percent.[41] Only one old-timer currently received TANF (Temporary Aid to Needy Families, the cash aid program commonly known as welfare), although five others reported receiving it at some previous time period.[42] These formal types of aid helped with basic survival; however, they were highly stigmatized within the community, as is common in both rural and urban settings.[43] Receipt of formal aid fed into newcomers' negative views of old-timers, whom they often portrayed as lazy and unwilling to work.[44] The choice to seek formal aid, while necessary to survival for many, further diminished many old-timers' moral standings within the community.

For old-timers themselves the stigma associated with aid receipt was also strong, and they thus devoted much energy to assertions of moral values and work ethic, to counter the shame or stigma that they felt or feared that others might apply to them. These assertions were both declarative and performative in different settings.[45] Pam Rhodes was one of many who spoke at length of her own hard work, emphasizing the ties between her work ethic and traditional understandings of masculinity. She explained:

> [For years] I had two jobs. And I just, like, worked like a man. I lost a lot of weight. . . . I did waitressing at night, and then in the day I did construction. So I did like, you know, siding and—mostly siding and sanding and finish work. . . . I did some fill-in jobs here and there because it's—it is fun, actually. In the wintertime when the waitressing isn't that demanding, it is not that big of a deal, and you can put in a six-hour day or so, and then go and get washed up and go back to work, and that's another, you know, six-hour day.

In addition to these types of declarations, often old-timers focused on demonstrating through actions and behaviors that they were hard workers or self-reliant, to demonstrate their morality and self-worth to others. These performances took several common forms, including specific behavioral scripts among those who actively sought aid. My field notes from my experiences volunteering at the food bank noted many ways in which old-timers in need took advantage of the open, flexible environment of the service to situate themselves as workers there and to diminish the degree to which they were perceived as dependent.[46] The following passages describe typical displays, which were often gendered, with men performing manual labor and women offering donations or socializing with volunteers. Both types of performances allowed them to blur the lines between workers and clients:

> There was a middle-aged man in a muscle T-shirt and jeans with a loud voice, who while he waited for his groceries insisted on carrying out as many people's as possible. Anyone who might need a carry-out, he grabbed their bags with or without their consent. He was very loud and showy about it, aggressively displaying his usefulness.[47]

> There was one woman who came in today whom I'd not seen before, but whom others seemed to know. She was my age or a bit younger, with clean, well-fitting, stylish clothes and long, nicely styled blonde hair. She showed a lack of deference to the staff, treating them as equals and friends rather than authority figures. She carried a toddler dressed in a clean, striped polo

shirt and jeans. She hung around for quite a while talking to everyone, and like a number of people who come in this way, it wasn't clear to me whether she was worker, donor, or client. She turned out to be a client, and got food like others eventually.[48]

Along with blurring the lines between worker and aid recipient, refusal of aid was another common way in which to assert one's moral worth amid economic need. Allison Lloyd, whose sunny disposition and well-behaved children made her a staff favorite at the food bank, abruptly stopped visiting just a few months into my time there. In her interview, Allison had expressed ambivalence about using the service, explaining that her husband made too much money for them to qualify for food stamps but that given their family size, the food aid was "really helpful." After a few months of her absence, I asked a fellow volunteer if the family had moved away and was told that they were still in the community but had decided to stop accepting help from Angel Food, which they found shameful.[49] Allison reappeared at the food bank from time to time, at one point bringing the staff homemade treats as a thank-you and another time bringing clothing to donate but refusing food.[50] She had explained in her interview that avoiding handouts was an important point of pride that she and her husband worked hard to earn. She said:

> I mean, we'll go to Angel Food for help with food sometimes. Um, we don't, we've never really asked to borrow money from anybody. Like, every once in a while, "Hey, Dad, can I borrow $100 for a week?" you know, and pay it back, but we've never really borrowed money. We've always just kind of made it work, kind of—like I said, I call myself a scrapper. "Oh, let's go pawn one of your guns, and we'll get it back when we have money." Or Chad will pick up a side job or I'll pick up a side job and make it work. We've never really asked for help from anybody really.

Allison was not alone in these kinds of declarations, which were very common among old-timers, including a number who did accept some types of aid when in dire need, but who preferred to cut back or go without when possible:

> I kind of grew up knowing that—or feeling like you don't ask for outside help.
>
> —Adeline Thompson, forty-year-old married, low-income stay-at-home mother

I tried Unemployment once and I just couldn't do it. I was like, "I can get another job."

—Donald Barnett, fifty-four-year-old married, low-income carpenter

I like less government involvement. The more help you get from them, the more they poke into your life anyway.

—Jessica Wheeler, thirty-eight-year-old cohabiting, poor waitress

I just got super frugal. I ate food out of my freezer, I grew food—yeah, I don't—I don't go to the food bank or anything like that. Got really smart. I don't buy anything. I don't buy anything.

—Pam Rhodes, fifty-seven-year-old cohabiting, low-income service worker

I probably could be eligible for food stamps, I'm sure. Oh, I am on state health care. I did get on state health care this year ... and like I said, I probably could get on food stamps. [But] I don't eat that much.

—Jody Hammond, forty-five-year-old single, low-income small business owner

Refusals of aid allowed old-timers to position themselves as adhering to a strict moral code. These claims to morality provided those in need with access to dignity despite their struggles, in a context that allowed them few other avenues to self-respect.

Previous researchers have explored the importance of moral concerns like these to populations living on the margins, and the importance of morality as a symbolic boundary marker that allows those of lower social status to lay claim to some sense of success according to their own cultural norms and standards.[51] For Paradise Valley's old-timers these types of moral assertions played a similar role, allowing people who were marginalized in the labor market and local community to make claims to their own moral worth despite positions of need. Such declarations and outward displays demonstrated to others, including friends, family, service providers, and occasionally an outsider such as myself, that the individual or family had a valid claim to morality. In this way, as for many low-status populations, claims to different types of moral values allowed old-timers to make peace with stigma, low social status, and economic and labor market struggles. It allowed them to claim some amount of personal success, despite the various ways in which structural constraints forced them to downsize their expectations and aspirations. What claims to moral worth failed to do, however, was address larger structural constraints such as the labor and housing markets and the lack of family support options, in constructive or tangible ways. To the contrary, demonstrating one's morality in these ways had few tangible benefits in terms of improving social and economic status for Paradise Valley's old-timers and resulted instead in self-denial of necessary services with little material payoff.

ENDURING PARADISE AND DOWNSIZING DREAMS

For Paradise Valley's old-timers the valley's changing demographic, social, economic, and labor market realities resulted in numerous daily and long-term struggles. Despite their generally longer histories in the valley, old-timers lacked many of the resources that allowed newcomers to create secure and comfortable lives there. The bulk of old-timers, whether valley natives or in-migrants, had strong ties to the place and felt deep attachment to Paradise Valley. They were tied there by many of the same interests that brought newcomers to the valley, including deep appreciation for the beauty, peacefulness, safety, and calm of rural life. In addition, for many old-timers Paradise Valley was the only home they knew.

However, as the social and economic landscape of Paradise Valley changed, it became increasingly difficult for most of its old-timers to survive there. As their stories attest, they struggled to adjust to the rise of the service sector and the decline of working-class and unionized jobs in resource extraction and related industries. For most old-timers the previous generation's dream of jobs that provided reliable living wages and a secure existence in the valley was mostly unrealistic, if not entirely forgotten. Particularly given the current labor market, and the need to compete for jobs against newcomers with higher levels of education, professional experience, soft skills, and social capital, it was increasingly difficult for old-timers to find work that was full-time, year-round, and paid a living wage. Compared to newcomers, old-timers were more likely to complain of struggles to find and keep jobs. With few resources to support them through seasonal layoffs and part-time work, many faced serious challenges in making ends meet. Unlike newcomers, few old-timers had reserves of wealth to cushion against labor market shocks, and even fewer had wealthy family members to whom they could turn for help.[52] They thus tended to only ask for help when already facing serious crisis, such as bouts of homelessness or the loss of vital services.

Old-timers' lack of wealth and precarious labor market positions also left them much more vulnerable in terms of facing the community's other challenges, including those related to housing and childcare. Despite their higher likelihood of having local relatives with long histories in the valley, old-timers were not advantaged in the housing market, as their social networks were less likely to include landlords, and landlords who did know them often did not view them as desirable tenants. Old-timers who owned homes were generally more secure but frequently complained about issues such as rising property taxes and other expenses that created financial stress and threatened to force them out of their homes.[53] Thus old-timers mostly saw housing as a source of stress, rather than an incentive to live in the valley. Many better-off old-timers viewed housing as a growing concern, source of frustration, and source of community division, while less-fortunate old-timers often experienced housing as a current or looming crisis that threatened to undermine their fragile economic, emotional, and relational stability. Most old-timers still hoped to achieve homeownership someday and thus acutely felt the loss of this symbol of American success as they struggled to navigate evictions, homelessness, and substandard living conditions.

Childcare was a similar challenge for most old-timers, for whom social networks could rarely be counted on to provide routine, flexible, and dependable care, and incomes seldom covered the cost of trustworthy and certified local providers. Without the labor market advantages to compete for jobs with flexibility and autonomy, old-timers were unable to concoct creative childcare solutions and instead were often forced to choose between working and spending time with spouses and partners. The unforgiving realms of work and childcare pitted jobs and family against each other for this population, resulting often in decisions to rely on a single income despite the economic and family hardship this created. The decision for one parent to stay at home with children was generally not experienced as a personal preference or choice and often resulted in long-term financial strain and truncated career options and trajectories.

Thus, while newcomers described survival in Paradise Valley as a series of challenges to which they responded with creative solutions, old-timers were much more likely to describe a series of difficult choices and personal, economic, and labor market sacrifices over which they had little agency. They discussed dissatisfaction with jobs, housing, childcare, and financial survival, to which they responded with resignation and downsizing expectations versus a sense of efficacy. They described reluctantly turning to friends and family as well as to private and public aid programs for support, and they demonstrated shame and discomfort with these choices. They reacted to these negative feelings by attempting to assert dignity and morality through both words and actions, which helped them to manage shame and stigma, and gave many a sense of self-respect, but simultaneously created additional hardships and privations that further undermined their precarious existences.

The combined pressures old-timers faced created problems for individuals and families that caused them stress and frustration, at times damaging mental health and relationship stability. The ways in which they responded to these challenges often also resulted in either real or perceived judgment from others in the community, including employers, landlords, newcomers, and other old-timers, entrenching the cycles of marginalization and dispossession. These multiple struggles and disadvantages resulted in old-timers being much less secure in Paradise Valley, both in terms of everyday survival and in terms of being supported and accepted by their home community. Although most could not imagine life elsewhere, they repeatedly voiced frustration and alienation that spoke to the insecurity they felt there. They did not portray themselves as community leaders, nor did they talk about active participation in cultural activities or leadership opportunities to enrich their lives. In general, they had neither time nor resources to devote to volunteerism, nor skills that were sought by local organizations. They thus spoke of Paradise Valley as a physical place and rural lifestyle more often than as a social community, reflecting the growing sense that they were not well integrated into the community itself and that they did not hold power there.

In addition to these economic, labor market, housing, and childcare challenges, old-timers faced an increasing marginalization from Paradise Valley's social world. Their alienation, coupled with newcomers' integration, contributed to a growing social, economic, and ideological divide that grew and intensified over time. Instead of inheriting the kingdom of Paradise Valley and becoming its leaders, the majority of old-timers were left with uncertain futures and ever-diminishing versions of the American Dream, in which they hoped to find success not through financial stability, homeownership, or civic engagement but simply through surviving with as much dignity as they could attain. Their struggles reflect those of many low-income and working-class Americans, particularly those living in areas experiencing in-migration and rapid community change. Their story is not simply about having to adjust to the diminished dream, but to accept it alongside the deepening divide in which their losses are the direct impacts of more advantaged Americans' gains.

5 "Certain Circles"

THE DEEPENING DIVIDE

Just income doesn't tell the story at all around here, you
know? Or anywhere probably, but. There's another divide
here. It's people who chose to live here and people who
didn't choose to live here.

Q: Who were born here?

Yeah. Those are two communities here.

—Peter Williams, sixty-eight-year-old married, middle-
income retiree

As a newcomer myself to Paradise Valley, I found its social world somewhat
baffling at first. I was accustomed to rural communities being difficult
places to gain entrée as a researcher, and to encountering suspicion and
hesitancy from locals who were wary of new people.[1] In rural fieldwork it
had often been necessary to have local informants within the community
vouch for me and my work and provide initial introductions and help getting started on the ground. Paradise Valley was different from these earlier field sites, both easier and more difficult for gaining entrée in its own
unique ways. Compared to many rural communities of its size, Paradise
Valley had a large number of public spaces and events, which meant that
an outsider could easily interact with residents in casual settings. I eagerly
took advantage of these opportunities from the start of my fieldwork.
My early impression of Paradise Valley was, on the one hand, that it was
extraordinarily civic- and community-oriented, with significantly more
opportunities for socializing publicly than many rural communities of its

size. On the other hand, I realized that in most public spaces and activities I was interacting with a rarified sector of the community. In my early field notes I wrote with regard to the participants at these community-focused events that I was "aware that it is a small and elite cast of players and that it is very easy to feel either left out or unwelcome."[2] Once I began to interact more with Paradise Valley's low-income residents through my volunteer work, I became even more cognizant of their absences from these types of community events and activities.

I learned over time that whether a resident experienced Paradise Valley as an inviting, interconnected, and cohesive community versus an exclusionary, unwelcoming, and fractured one depended less on a person's time in the community and much more on his or her social position there. In Paradise Valley, newcomers and old-timers had very different interactions within the same social structures. In addition to their unequal capacities to navigate housing, labor, and childcare markets, newcomers and old-timers lived separate social lives that overlapped only minimally. Although both groups tended to idealize rural communities as cohesive and interconnected, they did not have equal access to this quintessentially rural experience. Newcomers commonly described Paradise Valley as a tightly knit social environment in which they were integrated and supported, while less-privileged old-timers more often depicted alienation, marginalization, and a sense of judgment or exclusion from the larger community. Newcomers frequently portrayed dense social networks, while old-timers, who typically had much longer ties in the valley, nonetheless tended to depict social networks that were thin, fragile, and unreliable. Differential access to real and symbolic resources heavily impacted the treatment that they received from others and their abilities to engage in social and civic life within the community.

In Paradise Valley, social worlds coexist without comingling, due to the creation and maintenance of separate and unequal networks that support or forsake residents. Old-timers regularly struggle to make their voices heard and get their needs met within the rapidly changing social landscape. Newcomers, meanwhile, gain and retain power in the community by building, collecting, and sharing social and cultural capital among themselves, in addition to the human capital, income, and wealth that many bring with them to the community.[3] The one resource that many old-timers have long possessed and valued—moral capital in the forms of work ethics, family values, and rugged independence—is devalued by newcomers.[4] Newcomers both question old-timers' claims to moral capital and downplay its importance relative to the other resources that they possess in abundance. With the community's power brokers unwilling to trade real and symbolic resources for moral capital, its importance and relevance wanes there.

Through these processes, old-timers experience growing struggles to attain, build, or reproduce social, cultural, and human capitals that are increasingly necessary for success in the valley. At the same time, moral capital is declining as a tradeable resource, diminishing into a less effective symbolic boundary marker, of importance and significance to many old-timers who still make claims to it, but no longer exchangeable for many other resources and rewards in Paradise Valley.[5] These combined processes of resource hoarding and devaluation have contributed to a restructuring of the status hierarchy of Paradise Valley, with newcomers gathering increasing support, power, and efficacy relative to old-timers, whose relevance to and acceptance within the community is diminishing over time.

RESOURCES AND DIVISIONS: SYMBOLIC CAPITAL AND SOCIAL BOUNDARIES

The importance of social capital in high-poverty rural communities has been well documented by rural sociologists who have studied its benefits for families as well as the challenges faced by those families and communities that lack it.[6] As the previous two chapters have illustrated, social capital can substitute for economic capital in multiple ways for individuals and families in Paradise Valley, providing noneconomic benefits that help them survive in the absence of sufficient economic capital and allowing them to mobilize informal networks to fill in the gaps in public infrastructure.

"Pretty Much on Our Own": Social Capital for Some, Social Isolation for Others

My previous research in rural communities uncovered many instances in which social capital was activated, including when well-known families who experienced disasters or illness were helped by the larger community in informal ways, such as throwing community fundraisers to help pay for hospital bills or providing hands-on help with necessary repairs.[7] These practices are certainly not unheard of in urban areas, where churches and other civic and social groups may engage in similar acts of collective, informal charity. But they are particularly common in small rural communities, where formal infrastructure for handling emergencies, disasters, and medical crises may be insufficient or nonexistent, and poor families frequently are uninsured or underinsured. In these cases, social capital compensates for economic capital and aids in survival for socially integrated families who lack significant income or wealth. In rural places without healthy economies, social capital can become extremely important to survival.[8]

The importance of social capital for rural families does not make it universally available to all, however. Families who are not well integrated into their communities will likely lack the social capital they need to get them through difficult times.[9] Lack of integration can occur for multiple reasons, including recent in-migration, prejudices along race or ethnic boundary lines, remote living, or lack of other types of symbolic capital, such as cultural or moral capital.[10] Social capital can provide poor rural families with resources, but its absence can create additional challenges in communities that do not have adequate formal infrastructure to provide for low-income families' needs. As with most resources, in Paradise Valley newcomers tend to have more access to social capital and to better mobilize it to meet their collective needs. This disparity in social capital does not occur randomly or inevitably, but rather is the outcome of systematic processes of exclusion and the hoarding of resources within elite social circles.

Although many old-timers fondly spoke of Paradise Valley's history as a cohesive, supportive community, most felt that social connections, integration, and cohesiveness were fading there. By most accounts, nostalgic as many were, Paradise Valley was at one time a more homogenous and interconnected place, with a smaller population of residents who shared much in common in terms of daily life experiences and struggles and who treated one another with a level of familiarity symbolized for many in a friendly wave and greeting. Although perceptions of the past are often rosier than the lived experience was, Paradise Valley's mythical cohesiveness was an important standard against which residents perceived its current divide. Many old-timers told stories of the ways in which social capital had once existed for them there, often explicitly contrasting with the present-day community, as these comments illustrate:

> When I first came here ... I'd drive down the road and people would smile and wave to me. I didn't know them. They didn't care. They'd smile and wave. But you know what? I've seen a difference since I first got here: The difference is, people are more self-absorbed, basically.
> —Maggie Chambers, seventy-four-year-old single, poor, disabled

> Growin' up here, everybody knew your name. Not quite that way anymore, with all the extra people movin' in. But it used to be that way. You couldn't get away with anything, 'cause by the time you got home, your mom and dad already knew about it.
> —Wes Thompson, forty-five-year-old married, low-income municipal employee

> The community isn't the same as it used to be. Now, it's all the people that moved from Seattle, or Colorado, California. And it is a beautiful area to come and live in, I'll grant them that. But I wish they just would think a time or two about the people that lived here for so many years, kept things going. ... I like people and I usually say "good morning" or "hello" or "how are you" or something, and I have had looks that looked at me, like, Oh, I don't know you.
> —Martha Crawford, eighty-year-old widowed, middle-income retiree

This type of lament was repeated over and over again by old-timers, both native and in-migrant. Their senses of loss and romanticized views of the past spoke to a real sense of decreasing social capital, at least for these residents. As she described the community's social decline, Martha Crawford told me: "I am sure when you are talking to some of these other people that have moved in here recently, they will tell you that's not so, and they have their group of people that they are friendly with." She was correct: as I wrote in chapter 3, newcomers often described a very close-knit community where they felt supported and integrated. Their strong sense of community contrasted starkly with the loss of community described by longer-term and poorer residents, and newcomers commonly talked about how easy it was to make lasting, supportive social ties there. For example:

I feel like we are surrounded by support. I feel really lucky. I feel like the hard part of our job is asking for support. But we have friends—we have a lot of friends that provide support.

—Rachel Wilson, thirty-seven-year-old married, middle-income stay-at-home
  mother

I found it very easy to plug in. I mean, we already were involved with [the outdoor community] fairly intimately for a long period. So we already had [those] connections. . . . Mostly I would say it was the Montessori school that our first went to at two years old, and then our second child went there as well. You know, you are in parenting groups, you are in all of these things. And that pulls you into—you have a group of parents that you are kind of going through that stage with.

—Andrew Bowden, forty-six-year-old married, middle-income carpenter

I have a group of friends, like, with babies and stuff that I have just con-
nected with here. . . . And we meet up once a week and go walking with the kids, or you know, have dinner with the dads included. That kind of thing.

—Sabena Griffin, thirty-three-year-old cohabiting, middle-income nurse

A number of newcomers spoke enthusiastically of the support that they received from their tight communities of close friends and parents of similarly aged children. Many engaged in frequent small group activities such as dinners, celebrations, and outdoor activities within their social circles. Within those friendship groups, resources were shared generously, and help was offered quickly to those in need. For thirty-eight-year-old stay-at-home mother Brooke Gilbert, who had lived just two years in Paradise Valley, her newfound friends through her book club helped her get through a recent separation from her husband. She recounted:

I hadn't had a lot of understanding of what a break-up was like and how devastating that could be. And I had mothers showing up on my door and they would just give me a bag of premade meals and give me a hug and leave, or invite us to dinner. . . . People were fantastic. They were really lovely in a way that was surprising, because I had been here a year, and I didn't feel that particularly close to a lot of them. But they definitely circled the wagons. It was pretty lovely . . . they offered to watch the kids. They're great.

Maria Setzer, a forty-year-old part-time teacher, also experienced the community as very willing to help those in need. She described the type of informal support that is common in many rural areas.[11]

If things were, like, really, really bad, I know that I could call on any of our circle of friends and say, "Gosh, we're in a crisis, we really need help." I know that
my friend, her son went through cancer. Their friends, we all jumped in and
supported them financially even just to keep their mortgage going, getting
paid and stuff like that while he had to get treatment. Fortunately, we haven't
been put in that kind of position, but I do know that if push came to shove and
we were just drowning, we could go, "Help!" and people would help.

For newcomers like these, social capital acquisition often happened
quickly and effortlessly in Paradise Valley, and well-established newcomer
support networks rapidly absorbed in-migrants who shared similar levels of real and symbolic resources. Thus it was that so many newcomers
portrayed the community as generous, open, and quick to come to one
another's aid.

But on the other side of the social spectrum, the community's generosity was less frequently discussed. For old-timers these informal types
of social support were waning, and the well-resourced social networks
neither welcomed them nor offered them aid. Old-timers repeatedly told
stories of lacking social networks to rely on in the long- and short-term.
Beverly Parker, a sixty-seven-year-old poor, retired widow who managed
a small homestead by herself, lacked social capital to aid her through an
extended power outage in the aftermath of a summer storm. She recalled:

> That was the hard part, was being by myself. And people had their own wor-
> ries, so I didn't wanna bother anybody else with, you know, asking for help.
> So I hadta kind of wing it by myself. Uh, how did I cope? I drove the truck
> into the—I backed the truck into the creek over here to get water for the
> pigs, because I had pigs down there. Uh, I just went to bed when it got dark.
> And uh, mostly tried to keep things in the freezer from going bad, which, I
> did OK. I did fine.

For Wendy Harris, the same summer storm acted as the catalyst for
increased social support within her trailer park community—at least temporarily. She explained:

> The [storm] was almost a good thing to just bring the community together.
> The neighbors and I started getting back in touch after two years of [no
> interaction]. They had no contact with me. I didn't have contact with any-
> body. We got together, because [my neighbor], her husband, the neigh-
> bor across the street there, my husband and him went to school together.

They're, like, a year apart. So he would come over and check to make sure we were OK, with the power out and stuff. Then we all got together and people were like, "OK, so I have this in my cupboard. This needs to be cooked because it's goin' bad in the fridge. So let's all get together," and every night we had dinner over there, we cooked on his barbeque, and we all got together and pitched in for that dinner.

When I first met Wendy in late summer, these newly re-formed social ties seemed robust, and she and her neighbor were often seen walking into town and visiting social services together. But over the course of the year that I knew them, their friendship faded, and by the following winter they rarely interacted, although there were no obvious signs of hostility.[12] In their case, limited and transitory social support simply did not turn into a strong or reliable long-term resource.[13] They were unable to overcome the multiple barriers that poverty, the stresses of parenting and long working hours, and the structures of trailer park living posed to the creation and sustenance of community.[14]

For other old-timers, forming even weak social ties was very difficult.[15] Such was the case for Allison Lloyd, whose husband had grown up in the valley. In response to my question regarding social support, she explained:

> We have nothing, which has been really hard on my husband and I just for a long while, actually, but the only support we really had in the past was um, my husband's dad and his wife, and that was only like once every two months, if that. You know, we could have them watch the kids if we needed to, but we're pretty much on our own. You know, and that's really hard to know that um, we don't have anybody to turn to if we need something or if we need help with something, you know.

Beverly and Allison both expressed a sort of reluctance to reach out to people for help, due to combinations of pride and cultural norms, as well as prior bad experiences that led them to be wary. But as illustrated by Wendy's experience, even when old-timers did reach out, they often struggled to form lasting social ties. In addition to failures to maintain ties to other old-timers, several discussed feeling excluded or rejected in their attempts to reach out to newcomers. Maggie Chambers, a seventy-four-year-old retiree who was considering moving away from the valley, blamed what she referred to as "cliques" of newcomers for her decreasing ability to create and maintain social connections there. She said:

I see more cliques, where they don't want to branch out. They don't want to come over and say hi. If somebody looks tired or looks upset, I go to them. I say, "Gee, you have a beautiful smile." What does that cost me, to go over and tell somebody they have a beautiful smile? They usually look shocked but they look pleased. It doesn't cost a thing to be kind. And that's what I'm missing. I have seen it grow more like [California] did. I see people pushing in, that in my opinion don't belong here. [laughs] Because if they did, they would reach out.

Megan Wicker, a twenty-eight-year-old stay-at-home mother, described feeling rejected and marginalized after looking for community in a local church frequented by many newcomers:

When I used to go to church with my first friend [outside of Paradise Valley], I felt very supported, like they wanted to save me, and they wanted to help me, and they would help me any way. And then when I went with my recent friend [here], I don't know if it was just the church or the people that go to the church, but I felt more, like, pushed away, like I wasn't somebody they wanted in their church. . . . I just kind of felt awkward there. Like I wasn't one of them.

Jody Hammond, a forty-five-year-old small business owner, similarly described being snubbed by newcomers with whom she had weak social connections:

I worked up [in Pinedale] washing dishes for eight years. I worked in a restaurant up there. And it was really funny, the other day, the guy who owns the place and I saw each other at the pub and he walked over and basically completely blew me off even though I'm pretty sure he knows who I am. And he is a lawyer and he has his second home in Pinedale. And my neighbor goes, "Isn't that . . . ?" and I said, "Yeah." And she said, "Is he always that way?" And I said, "Well, yeah, he is who he is." You know? And so there is definitely that divide.

For the least advantaged residents of Paradise Valley, these types of minor rebuffs, isolation, and marginalization could grow into bigger problems, exacerbated sometimes by mental health issues, low self-esteem, and fear of further rejection. Poor Paradise Valley residents often told tales of intense social isolation, to the point that it became an impediment to their survival. I recorded the following notes after my volunteering at the food bank, whose clients tended to be both poor and among the most socially isolated in the valley.[16] The first observation occurred around the Christmas holiday, as I was helping to sign up clients for holiday food baskets. The application for the service required a phone number in case the delivery person had trouble finding the residence. I struggled to help sign up a middle-aged man who could not meet this requirement:

> He lives in one of the subsidized housing complexes in Eagle Flat and doesn't have a phone. I asked if he had any friends or neighbors with phones and he said no. I asked if another person there from the same complex was a friend and he said that they were technically neighbors but that they didn't interact. He made it clear that he would rather forgo the food basket than to rely on someone else.[17]

The next passage describes a conversation with an elderly woman who was a regular client, but who had been missing from food distribution the previous week:

> I asked Brenda about how she was doing and why she hadn't come in [last week]. She explained that she just gets pretty depressed sometimes and doesn't feel like going out and seeing people, even though she usually feels better when she does.... She said she shuts herself in sometimes, sick with worry [about her homeless daughters]. I asked her if she goes to the lunches at the Senior Center, in order to get out of the house. She said that she struggles to leave the house alone, but doesn't really have anyone to go out with.[18]

As these quotes illustrate, in Paradise Valley "rural" and "tightly knit" are not synonymous, despite cohesion being an important component of the rural idyll that both newcomers and old-timers referenced among their reasons for being there.[19] A resident's likelihood of experiencing social support versus isolation and abandonment was highly correlated with his or her side on the community's social divide. While well-resourced newcomers generally made strong, supportive ties quickly and easily, and maintained them over years, its less-resourced old-timers usually had the opposite experience. They described isolation and frail social ties that weakened over time, as well as having few people to turn to for help with either daily or emergency needs. They described experiences of rejection and failures to create new ties. Social support was key to surviving Paradise Valley's challenges, and residents' abilities to create and reproduce social capital played vital roles in structuring their basic ease or struggle with daily life there. Without it, old-timers' disadvantages were multiplied.

There were numerous factors that influenced different individuals' and families' abilities to form and sustain social ties in Paradise Valley. Old-timers' stories of isolation and rejection were often peppered with their own fears and insecurities, including distrust of others, desires to avoid judgment, and pride that kept them from reaching out for help. Their own personal problems, including lack of resources and chaotic lifestyles and schedules, but also mental health and substance abuse issues also under-mined their abilities to form and maintain social ties. But even those who had the fewest personal problems struggled to find and maintain durable social networks. Meanwhile, newcomers described much more robust social ties, but it was clear from their discussions that this social capi-tal was reserved for those within their select groups of friends, collected among those who had the most to share and who could be relied on the most to reciprocate.

"Different Ideologies and Ways of Life": Cultural Capital in the Creation of Social Capital

The gulf in social capital in Paradise Valley was reinforced by dividing lines in other areas as well. As has been observed in other rural commu-nities, differences in cultural capital can help create and reinforce social network boundaries.[20] The importance of cultural capital is often dis-cussed in urban settings, where cultural differences can be stark and vis-ible, and culture is easily categorized as high or low.[21] It is less frequently documented in rural settings, where communities are less likely to contain the same level of cultural diversity, and residents typically share cultural norms and understandings with little variation.[22] Where there is greater diversity, however, culture can become another axis upon which social divisions rest and resources are divided and allocated. Particularly in rural communities like Paradise Valley, which have experienced in-migration by newcomers with cultural backgrounds that are distinct from those of longtime residents, cultural differences can come to play important roles in structuring daily life and social and economic opportunities.[23] As with social capital, in these situations cultural capital may help form and maintain social hierarchies, providing resources and access to some families, while simultaneously denying these advantages to others whose cultural norms, beliefs, and expectations mark them as different. Researchers have documented rural community divisions grounded in cultural differences based in ethnicity, religion, politics, and sexuality.[24] In these cases deep cultural rifts allow for judgment and exclusion of one social group by another, resulting in the systematic denial of resources.

Cultural differences do not have to be gaping divides in worldviews and belief systems in order to provide the basis for social boundaries, however. In the case of Paradise Valley, cultural differences were extremely important but not necessarily grounded in deeply held religious or moral beliefs. In this community, cultural capital was not built on variations in ethnic backgrounds or religious belief systems, but rather on significant differences in tastes and preferences for art, music, food and drink, and leisure activities as well as differences in political stances and in aspirations for children's outcomes. The bulk of affluent newcomers to the area shared similar interests in "high culture" forms of art, music, food, and drink, and strongly preferred outdoor sports activities such as hiking and skiing over such leisure pursuits as television, motorized vehicle use, or video games, which were preferred by old-timers.[25]

These kinds of cultural differences can serve to structure social life, including influencing who is in one's social networks. Old-timers and newcomers increasingly chose different venues for eating, shopping, and recreating, effectively segregating themselves in ways that resulted in different levels of exposure to cultural capital for children. Going for coffee at an upscale café versus the grocery store deli impacted whom one interacted with socially, as did drinking Budweiser at a modest bar versus craft beer at an upscale pub. For children, going to dance, ski, and music lessons after school resulted in very different experiences and exposure than did watching television or playing videos games at home. Thus not only was cultural capital tradeable for other forms of real and symbolic capital in this setting, but it also served to maintain and reinforce social divisions.

Yet at the same time, as has been found by other researchers, middle-class residents remained unconscious of social class as a status marker, practicing class blindness even as they deftly drew on cultural differences to police class boundaries.[26] Newcomers had multiple discursive ways of acknowledging the cultural divide while maintaining that it was unrelated to social class.[27] On the occasions that cultural differences were openly acknowledged to be divisive and/or class-related, the speakers tended to be older newcomers without school-aged children, often who were more closely involved in philanthropic organizations around the valley and thus had more interactions with old-timers. Seventy-five-year-old retiree Dennis Wright, who was an active volunteer for multiple organizations under the Angel Food umbrella, described first noticing the valley's cultural divide a decade earlier, when as a new in-migrant he unknowingly patronized an old-timer bar. He recalled:

> We went in there on Super Bowl Sunday. We had just moved here and didn't have a TV, so we went there to watch the game, and it was quite a shock. And the people were really generous and inclusive, in spite of our cultures, which were quite different.... Culturally, the language—very different cultures. The language. Oh, the food. We were invited to share in their food, and there was all of these salads, like macaroni salad and all of the dressing and stuff—very strange. Strange, and not that strange that I didn't recognize it, but I recognized it with aversion.

More often, newcomers were careful not to express explicit negative judgments of old-timer cultural norms and instead tended to focus on a positive preference for their own culture and pursuits in explaining their chosen social activities and networks. Interests and pastimes were key to making social connections for most newcomers in Paradise Valley, and they described multiple ways in which their chosen hobbies and interests helped them to form social ties. For example:

> Of all the various places that I lived, this was the easiest place to make friends.... I think living in town and having the walkability, I met some people that way. But primarily by volunteering... I met a lot of people through [the art gallery]. So I found it very easy to find my niche in this community.
> —Donna Cox, sixty-seven-year-old divorced, middle-income retiree

> We met [our closest friend] last fall during deer-skinning. Kevin went over there and helped her.... Again, it's that exchange of information and skills and heavy labor that has started building a good relationship. And we do have a lot in common.
> —Aspen Reed, twenty-eight-year-old cohabiting, poor subsistence farmer

It's both easy to make friends and connections and that those people, part of the ethic is you look out for each other. Maybe that's in part—well there are certain, there are circles.... The people I've met I met through various activities: a lot outdoors, but you know, uh, common interests.... The first year I did a lot of [volunteer] work, participated in gym classes. That's a very effective way to meet people. So are all the educational opportunities that [a local nonprofit organization] puts on. That's another way to meet people. And then skiing, hiking, biking, uh, so volunteer activities, the educational activities, and outdoor activities.

—Sharon Silver, sixty-four-year-old married, middle-income retiree

For Hannah Lowry, the consultant introduced in chapter 3, her tight community consisted of people who shared her leisure and intellectual interests, in contrast to those with other hobbies. Although she acknowledged that privilege played a role in her chosen interests and social networks, she was careful to neither criticize old-timers' pursuits nor suggest that old-timers were purposely excluded. She said:

On weekends when we're not just trying to buckle down and do work, we're out backpacking with a group of friends or doing a day hike with a bunch of ladies. And then I have a book club once a month. We'd rather spend more time with our friends, but I think we're doin' OK, given the fact that we're all on [nonprofit] boards. I see friends at board meetings, I see friends at work...

I get to go to book club... and not everybody has that luxury. The people I end up spending time with are the people who have that luxury. But there's also a lot of families that go hunting together. I don't want to go hunting, so I'm not friends with those families, because they're going ATV-ing and hunting, and they're having a great time outdoors together with other families who do that. But we're not. We're friends to, like, say hi on the street.

Like many newcomers, Hannah described her chosen social circles in terms of specific interests, not social class.

Nadine Gough had a similar understanding of the boundaries of her social world. The thirty-six-year-old teacher and valley native had left the region for a decade, attending school and meeting her husband in the Bay Area before returning to the valley to raise their children. She described estrangement from her local friends since her return, and she instead surrounded herself with those who shared her adult interests. She said of her childhood friends:

I don't know exactly how they are different, but yeah. Maybe different ideologies and ways of life just in activities—the hobbies that we like and stuff.
I mean, I do really like to be outdoors, and then I don't see them. It is actually a big valley. Some of them I think still party hard, so I wouldn't really
be involved in that. And the others, like I think if we got together and had
a reunion it would be really fun, but I just don't see them in that way after
having kids and a family. My life like gets smaller in the sense of choosing to
be around people that I just really love and that feed me.

It was common for newcomers to acknowledge that their social activities rarely included old-timers, but to contend that there was a mutuality
to the ways in which this occurred, and to steadfastly overlook the role of
social class in structuring cultural interests and competencies in Paradise
Valley. A highly educated, middle-class artist who had recently moved to
the valley with her family explained to me that low-income parents were
absent from certain activities because they were uninterested or unwilling to come out and join things. She insisted that places like art galleries
weren't exclusive, but "those people" simply lacked interest in going to
them.[28] I heard similar statements from other newcomers, who asserted
that old-timers' disinterest in cultural activities explained their absence
from them and questioned why either old-timers or newcomers would
want to spend time with people who didn't share their interests.[29]

This class blindness was often practiced most unwaveringly by newcomers with school-aged children, who had a strong stake in creating
exclusive social networks and portraying this exclusion as value-neutral.[30]
While to some degree it was true that old-timers actively avoided certain
events or activities, such justifications failed to recognize the judgment
that they often felt and the senses of alienation and cultural incompetence
they experienced in these settings—not to mention the often prohibitive
cost of many cultural events and activities in Paradise Valley. Nor did most
newcomers acknowledge the demeaning ways in which low-wage workers were regularly treated by the affluent as they waited on them in service settings around the valley and the degree to which these experiences
reinforced social distance between groups and old-timers' senses of being
unwelcome and unequal.[31]

Thus, while newcomers' descriptions of variations in cultural interests
often made them sound benign, for those on the "low culture" side of the
divide, these differences clearly had a hierarchical and exclusionary qual-

ity. Allison Lloyd described an awareness that her family's leisure interests branded them as outsiders to the valley's elite social networks:

> I think that people think that I'm a—that's why I call myself a redneck. 'Cause, like my brother came up here and he was like, "God, I can't believe that you do that. You go hunting? You let your kids ride a 4-wheeler in your front yard?" You know, I think a lot of people, um, there's a lot of people that have assumptions about me, and that's fine. They can assume all they want, but I think I'm a good person.

Although she asserted repeatedly that she didn't care what people thought of her, Allison made efforts to present her family as middle class and respectable when she could. With regard to her small rented home, she told me:

> My house is usually spotless, because I want them—I don't want them to be one of those kids that have, you know, have their friends come over and the house is dirty and they're embarrassed to have their friends come over. You know?... So, I like—it's important to me to have a clean, safe place for them that they feel comfortable in, and they know, um, that, that stability. I want them to have that stability.

Despite these types of efforts, however, Allison still perceived judgment from the greater community that for her had become a disincentive to partaking in social activities in Paradise Valley. She explained:

> You know, so I—everybody has, in a small town everybody has their own views of you. And that's fine. They can think whatever they want, you know, I'm, as long as I'm happy then I'm fine.... I really don't care what people think of me, but I don't, I guess it does hinder me from doing stuff though too, that I don't wanna... yeah I guess it's easier to just, uh, I can know what they think about me all day long, but having to go deal with it is another thing.

The impacts of Allison's social and cultural discomfort went beyond leisure pursuits, however, and also impeded her ability to take part in leadership activities. She said:

> I tried doing PTA and stuff like that, but that's just a bunch of moms that are not—a bunch of politicians, mom-politicians. I didn't like it. They're not really into doing fun things for the kids. It's more about, "Let's talk about

how we can make it more like a government." Ugh, it was just, I didn't really appreciate it.

Cultural differences and senses of comfort in different settings played important roles in the creation and maintenance of Paradise Valley's social divide. Thus, while newcomers described social lives full of outdoor sports, board meetings, gallery openings, and performances, old-timers like Wendy Harris often described much less vibrant social calendars. She said:

> I'll do stuff that's outdoors. I will not go to the theater thingy. I don't like bein' indoors. The Easter thing every year that they do, I usually go down and hang out for that. Just that kind of thing. It's got to be outdoors, some-thin' I—just somethin' that I can just go and leave whenever I'm comfortable leaving.... They have to be free. They can't cost me money, especially comin' off two years of not havin' any money. It's gotta be somethin' that's—or very minimal cost. We do the farmers' market. Every weekend my aunt and I make a point of going yard sale–ing. I know that's not "community," but you know how many people you see at yard sales? [laughs] We see a lot of people at yard sales, so I get most of my social gathering that way. Almost every other day, now that Ted's working and I can afford a cup of coffee, we go to coffee down at [the grocery store].

Newcomers' cultural pursuits put them into regular contact with many of Paradise Valley's elite residents, but many old-timers' activities ensured that they only interacted with other low-income families who also lacked cultural capital and had few other resources to share.[32] Families like Wendy's and Allison's did not join book clubs, nor send their children to private schools, nor were they active in the valley's elite outdoor-ath-lete community. Instead, they felt a sense of alienation from the better-resourced community. Without sufficient exposure to newcomers and their robust social networks, old-timers had few opportunities to build cultural capital. Their resulting lack of it helped to create and reinforce their low social capital as well, trapping them in cycles of marginalization and isolation. Although she acknowledged that social capital existed for some, for Allison it seemed perpetually out of reach. As she put it:

> I know people have friends aside from having kids, but we have—you know, Chad works all the time, and then comes home, and he tries to spend time

with the kids, and I'm trying to get the kids to bed, and we're trying to give them a stable life. And we really have no life outside of our family and um, you know.... But yeah, we've been—if we need something, we figure it out. If we have somewhere to go, we take the kids with us. If we have—we really have always been on our own, and it's really, it's a rough place to be. But we make it work.

In Paradise Valley, social and cultural capital were mutually reinforcing. Families with interests in high-culture activities took advantage of (and often helped create and sustain) the community's opportunities to enjoy art, theater, music, dance, and outdoor recreation, and were exposed to others with similar interests and similar resources through these pursuits. Through these exclusive social networks they shared multiple resources— from goods and services to power positions within the community. This contrasted starkly with the experiences of old-timers with more traditionally rural backgrounds, who experienced economic and social exclusion from both cultural activities and the social networks that formed around them. Instead of interacting, sharing, and learning about each other's interests, old-timers and newcomers effectively separated themselves into distinct groups with increasingly fortified boundaries. Even the educational system, in which children of old-timers and newcomers mingled daily, failed to facilitate significant mixing across this ever-deepening and self-reinforcing divide.

"Turning Their Backs on Kids": Human Capital and the Social Divide

Like social and cultural capital, human capital in the form of education and skills can play an important role in creating and exacerbating social divisions as well as reproducing them in the next generation.[33] In Paradise Valley, education and the local schools served not only to prepare children for their adult futures but also to provide social and cultural opportunities to some, while systematically withholding them from others. By most old-timers' accounts, social class had long mattered in Paradise Valley's schools, which had historically disenfranchised the community's most disadvantaged residents through both the structures of school programs and the ways in which children were treated by teachers and administrators.[34] Parents, school children, and local alumni described experiences with the local schools that reinforced dividing lines and prepared some children for brighter futures than others. As is the case in many communities both urban and rural, in Paradise Valley the local schools acted to sort and divide children more than to even the playing field.[35] The results of these multiple structural barriers and social processes included very different experiences with schooling—and very different levels of adult human capital acquisition—for newcomers versus old-timers.

Parents' own levels of education and experiences in school frequently influenced their goals and attitudes toward education for their children. As with many rural communities, in Paradise Valley education was both a vehicle for upward mobility and a mechanism that perpetuated "brain drain," the process whereby young adults, often the community's most advantaged and promising, selectively out-migrate to pursue educational and work opportunities elsewhere.[36] Many newcomers were extremely clear regarding the importance of children leaving Paradise Valley for higher education, while old-timers were often more ambivalent with regard to out-migration. Out-migration was an explicit parenting goal for 35 percent of newcomers, but only 11 percent of old-timers with children.[37] Nonetheless, both old-timers and newcomers discussed the importance of education, although to differing degrees and often with different goals. A higher proportion of newcomers who were parents, 55 percent versus 40 percent of old-timer parents, listed education as a top parenting goal.[38] The differing reasons for education as a goal reflected both divergent cultural norms and parents' own levels of human capital. While newcomers often described education as an important end in and of itself, old-timers more often stressed it as a means to securing local work and achieving upward mobility.[39]

This was the case for Chad Lloyd, the sawmill worker who had four children with his wife, Allison, quoted at length earlier in this chapter. Chad had not finished high school and instead later pursued his GED. For him, education was a tool that would allow his children to increase their employment options. He explained:

> I want 'em to go to college. I want 'em to get a good job where they don't have to work so many hours that they don't get to see their kids. My biggest thing is, "You're goin' to college. I'm not goin' through all this so you can do what

I did!" [laughs] Yeah. All I want is them to be happy and do better than I did. I think that's every parent's wish. "Do better than me, dang it!" [laughs]

Tilda Conner, a care worker who had only a high school education, expressed a similar sentiment for her teenaged daughter: "I hope that she goes to college. She's got so many great ideas. And I want her to be—every parent wants their kid to be better than they were, and I do."

For newcomers, educational goals were often more ambitious and less focused specifically on employment outcomes. Newcomers tended to have much clearer understandings of what was needed to achieve educational goals. They spoke specifically about the costs of different types of colleges, the potential for different types of scholarships, and the importance of grades and extracurricular activities to securing admission into more competitive and prestigious colleges and universities. For example:

> My hope is that I can at least ensure my kids' ability to go to a state school and, um, you know, I guess I view that as a minimalist goal as far as creating an opportunity for them. Um, beyond that, we'll see. I mean, I don't know, I don't know how they could afford to go to [a private college].
>
> —Shawn Murphy, forty-three-year-old divorced, low-income carpenter

> I think in this family there is an expectation that they go to college. I think we are in a little bit of denial. I am not sure exactly how we are going to make that work financially, but we just kind of hope things work out.... So I have been reminding him, you know, every Ivy League school has a soccer team. He could do worse.
>
> —William Turner, sixty-two-year-old married, middle-income retiree

> We certainly hope that they are bright, and we hope that they push it, and we hope that they—you know, partly one of the incentives is if they do well, there will be help with college. If they don't do well, we are paying for all their college and money isn't going to be that easy.... I am hoping that they push it—you know, [their mom] went to Berkeley. Well, right away our son wants to go Berkeley. OK, well, then you need to do the bonus work. You know? That's a pretty good school.
>
> —Andrew Bowden, forty-six-year-old married, middle-income carpenter

Although both groups described sincere desires for their children to go to college, their abilities to guide their children were influenced by their different orientations and understandings of how to navigate the process, starting with K–12 education. Different levels of parental cultural and human capital often translated into much more proactive involvement and direction for educational experiences of newcomers' children. Newcomers were much more likely to send their children to private schools prior to high school and to actively manage their children's participation in different courses and extracurricular activities. They were also more likely to feel like they had efficacy within the school system in ensuring their children's needs were met, also commonly associated with higher social class and education.[40] Old-timers, in contrast, were much more likely to complain of problems in the local schools—their own as well as their children's. Many described multigenerational feelings of abandonment and bias in the school system that ultimately undermined their support for their children's education and their abilities to advocate for them.

For old-timers the sense of being treated unfairly in the local schools was pervasive, and both parents and alumni told stories of unfair treatment in school. It was common for old-timers, including many with low educational attainment themselves, to homeschool their children after repeated frustrations with local schools.[41] Their complaints ranged from children not receiving enough help with special needs; to feeling that children were unjustly targeted by teachers and school officials; to the extra costs for participation in certain activities, including sports. Asa Hobson, who had lived most of his thirty-eight years in the valley, had experienced problems with the local schools himself, although he went on to eventually get an AA degree. He described feeling abandoned at Paradise Valley High School, where he received no guidance about how to pursue college:

> It just was like this mentality back then that they could get away with because it was a small town, that there were good kids and bad kids. And I was a bad kid. And that was it. It was just as simple as that. If you weren't from a Christian household, if you just misbehaved, or if your family didn't have money—you know, if you weren't in school sports—all of those things. And I was none of those things. And I graduated with, like, a D average from high school, and graduated college with a 3.8. So it is like, you know, where was the problem? You know? I just—yeah. Still to this day I haven't gotten to a point where I have gotten old enough to say, yeah, I was the problem. I mean, yeah, I was a tough kid to deal with, but they just had a way of turning their back on kids.

Although he strongly hoped that his children would have better experiences and greatly valued education, Asa voiced multiple complaints and frustrations focused on his daughter's needs not being met in the public schools. "Some of those limitations are still there," he said. "And I think you get them with small towns and communities."

Old-timers repeatedly complained of unfair treatment as well as social and economic barriers to their children's success in Paradise Valley's schools. Tilda Conner's complaints had to do with a combination of poor communication with school officials and the feeling that they treated her daughter unfairly. She recounted:

> The principal and I, we didn't get along . . . we did not like each other, almost to the point where I was gonna pull her out of public school. . . . She was getting bullied by a boy who is at least 100 pounds bigger than her. . . . And he would pick her up out of her seats and throw her. And when I would call and complain, [the principal] would go, "She shouldn't instigate. She shouldn't say things to him." I was like, "No, because verbal things are way more different than physical, and if it happens again, I'll call the police." And when I threatened that, he put [the bully] on a different bus, but [the principal] was out to get her.

Like Asa Hobson, Wendy Harris had struggled in Paradise Valley's schools. She felt that she was targeted for being from a troubled family:

> Well, I was a straight-A student up until high school, and then from there, that's when—I don't know, things changed. I don't know why. . . . And I would get in trouble for the stupidest things at times. It got to the point where—and this was because my cousins were ahead of me. And I'm the spittin' image of my cousin. So [the principal] figured I'd be just as much trouble. So the slightest thing I did, I got in trouble. And that's when I gave up. I gave up trying to pull the straight-A's and stuff like that. I gave up. If I'm gonna be in trouble for stupid things, you know, forget it.

Wendy had hoped that her son might succeed where she had failed, but she found that her family's financial constraints held him back from full participation, particularly the "pay-to-play" fees attached to after-school sports:

> The pay-to-play is ridiculous, I think that's what's stopping him [from playing sports]. It'll cost $150 just for one sport right now. I'm sorry. I think

that's ridiculous. We didn't have to pay when I was in school. I don't understand why it'd be $150 just for one sport. . . . I'm like, "Are you kidding me?
It would cost me almost $150 [for him] to play a stupid sport. You people
are rippin' me off. " He's not gonna do a sport. I'll go out and play with him
instead. [laughs]

Problems like those encountered by Asa and Wendy often left old-timers
with lower levels of human capital as well as disadvantages that ranged
from lacking information about how to pursue higher education to lacking money for school fees. Their lack of confidence and sense of frustration further impeded many in their interactions with school officials, low-
ering their abilities to negotiate to get their children's needs met.[42] These
barriers helped to ensure that their children faced numerous struggles in
their educational trajectories in Paradise Valley and beyond.

In contrast, newcomers tended to have few complaints about the local
schools, and when they did express frustration, it tended to be focused on
the lack of opportunities for their children to excel, such as competitive
sports teams and advanced curricula.[43] More frequently they discussed
satisfaction and a sense of gratitude for the high quality of local schools.
Shawn Murphy, whose children were in grade school, commented: "Our
school is an incredible school that has provided a great opportunity for
support as a parent." William Turner, whose children were in high school,
also expressed contentment with local offerings. He explained:

Paradise Valley High actually shows up on the—within the top ten or fifteen
of state high schools, so I think—because there is enough people here—people who have moved here from—you know, there is a few other Microsoft
retiree types, and people who come over here from the west side generally came from strong academic backgrounds. So I think there is reason-
able expectations at school. And our kids get mostly A's and are active in
things. . . . So I think they are going to have reasonably good opportunities.

Although fewer newcomers had attended Paradise Valley schools, those
who had often described positive experiences as well, further suggesting that social class had long helped shape school trajectories. The adult
children of earlier generations of better-resourced in-migrants tended to
speak of special treatment they had received in school there, particularly
when their parents were well known or well connected to the schools.
Nadine Gough, whose mother was a teacher herself, recalled:

I definitely got accused of being the teacher's pet a little bit. But my parents never did that. Like my mom was harder on me than the other kids, probably. Again, I sort of teetered between, I knew how to get good grades and check all the boxes academically to stay relatively on top. But also was partying and skipping—you know, shucking and jiving—but I didn't really get in trouble because I was one of the good kids. You know?

The same was true for Toby Cook, a thirty-two-year-old Paradise Valley native. When asked if his parents teaching in the school system made a difference for him, he replied:

> Yeah, plenty. I think it made um, a big difference in how teachers thought of me.... It got me a lot of tickets to act bad and still have a good reputation.... I had a lot of freedoms that other kids didn't because I, uh, I could get away with stuff that other kids couldn't.

In general, newcomers expressed fewer problems of their own in Paradise Valley's schools and fewer problems for their children. Instead of concerning themselves with individual issues, they were more likely to focus on improving the overall educational or extracurricular offerings in Paradise Valley's schools, to ensure that their children were not missing out on opportunities by growing up there versus a larger city. These educational agendas, which were often strongly resisted by old-timers, generally prevailed.[44]

These different orientations and experiences with local schools helped to shape children's attainment as well as their social circles and levels of inclusion or exclusion within the valley more generally. College-bound high school senior Jason Hill, and his mother, Emily, explained how the social world of Paradise Valley High worked for him:

> JASON: I think there is a little bit of a separation between beliefs and stuff, um, like all my friends are mostly like liberal families and uh—
>
> EMILY: Have their masters or PhDs, the parents—
>
> JASON: Yeah, the parents. Um, but we get along fine with everybody else and I think we just hang out with each other more than the others. I guess.

These processes had predictable results. On the one hand, newcomers' children tended to excel in school and generally went on to pursue college education outside of the valley, gaining access to more human and cultural capital. A handful returned as adults who were often absorbed into the next generation of more privileged newcomers. Old-timers' children, on the other hand, generally did not perform as highly in school; did not participate in as many extracurricular activities; and were less likely to either pursue or earn college degrees, particularly from more prestigious colleges or universities. They were more likely to remain in or return to Paradise Valley as adults but also more likely to struggle to find meaningful and lucrative work there. Adults across the social class spectrum, but especially newcomers, expressed concern and judgment about the fortunes of young adults who did not leave the valley to pursue higher education, often suggesting that those who remained were both intellectually and morally flawed. For example:

> It seems to me that the ones who are born and raised here and stayed here and never left are pretty ignorant—not in an academic way necessarily—but they just don't have that broader perspective of humanity and what's out there.
>
> —Claire Woods, forty-two-year-old married, middle-income nonprofit consultant

> Most of the kids that stay around here, that's the ones that end up using [drugs] and falling, you know? You can only go so far in this town.... I just know that if you stay here, you are either going to be flipping burgers for the rest of your life or waiting tables.
>
> —Megan Wicker, twenty-eight-year-old married, poor stay-at-home mother

> Nothing good happens to kids who stay here without going somewhere else. It's a very small community there are a lot of small—"small-minded" is too harsh—conservative values. There's nothing a kid can do here work-wise after high school that's at all challenging or rewarding....
>
> You know, there are people here who were born and raised here and didn't ever leave, and I don't want my kids to become that.
>
> —Hannah Lowry, forty-five-year-old married, middle-income consultant

In Paradise Valley, human capital was yet another resource that was unevenly distributed between newcomers and old-timers. Given the importance of parents' educational attainment to children's adult attainment, it is unsurprising that children of more-educated newcomers would have multiple advantages in the attainment of human capital.[45] These advantages took multiple forms, including the important roles of parental aspirations, cultural orientations, and knowledge about how to achieve educational goals.[46] But in Paradise Valley, as in many other rural school settings, other social class factors and community divides also played important roles in encouraging or limiting student achievement.[47] Like many rural school districts, Paradise Valley struggled to fund the cost of education and passed some of these costs onto students themselves. Thus low-income and poor families faced multiple economic challenges to their children's full participation in Paradise Valley's schools.[48]

As with other forms of symbolic capital, human capital advantage and disadvantage reproduced themselves, putting newcomers' children on track to high educational attainment and likely out-migration for college and beyond, while old-timers' children were more likely to struggle in school, have lower aspirations for college, and to end up as adults with lower human capital—as well as fewer job opportunities both within and outside of the valley. For those who failed to pursue out-migration and higher education, stigma resulted, branding them as ignorant at best, deadbeats and drug users at worst. Thus education in Paradise Valley not only served to help the advantaged in their replication of human capital, but further hindered the disadvantaged in building this resource as well as in maintaining claims to moral capital.

"We Don't Ask for Help": Moral Capital and Social Stigma

I first wrote about moral capital as I uncovered it in an isolated rural field site, where outwardly exhibiting one's moral worth resulted in opportunities that were denied to those who appeared to lack it.[49] I found that in rural settings morality worked to create boundaries between people and could be traded for other resources such as job opportunities, encouragement in school, and social capital. Research suggests that for people living on the margins of US society, struggling with both poverty and job loss, conceptions of morality can help create new understandings of what it means to be successful.[50] In homogenous rural communities notions of proper work ethics and morally acceptable activities often help create those definitions of success. Moral understandings also influence the choices people make about how to best survive unemployment and poverty, dictating proper behaviors and coping strategies.[51]

In rural US communities, iconic American qualities such as independence and hard work often form the basis of moral capital, tradeable for both economic benefits and social status.[52] In many such communities people's activities are visible and known. For those who manifest their work ethic and moral values through culturally acceptable work activities like paid jobs, subsistence work, and even through the receipt of "earned" government aid like Unemployment Insurance, there can be payoffs in terms of both social support and economic opportunities. For those who fail to properly illustrate their morality, either through the receipt of means-tested government aid or through involvement in illicit activities like drug dealing, both labor market opportunities and informal charity are frequently limited.[53] Thus morality is both a positive force, helping people to access social and economic capital, and a negative control that helps discourage behaviors that are seen as damaging to the community, whether or not they might aid individuals in survival.

Old-timers' words and actions were often infused with positive references to morality in the forms of work ethics and self-sufficiency, which newcomers were far less likely to discuss this way. Old-timers frequently discussed these moral issues as important to their own senses of self, and they made behavioral choices based upon moral values, including refusing to ask for or seek out help and other outward displays of morality. Many old-timers asserted that this sort of moral fortitude was a distinctly rural quality, which was currently in decline in Paradise Valley. Greg Rossi, a fifty-seven-year-old retired Forest Service employee, described old-timers' understandings of the rural values that were being lost. He said:

> They talk about back when they were kids, [manual labor] was mandatory. You've gotta help. You didn't even whine, because your mind philosophy is that you've gotta do this...the whole mentality was, you had to help out. There was no crying or whining.

The importance of teaching a stoic work ethic to children was expressed by many old-timers, who often took great pride in the degree to which they had imparted these values. This was the case for Audrey Patterson, a fifty-nine-year-old SSI-reliant mother of four grown children, who proudly described her family's value system as it related to teaching children the importance of work. She recalled:

> You know, growing up, yeah, my kids had chores. They hadta go feed and water the dog. Uh, when they had their own animals, they hadta go out and take care of 'em. We've had horses, we've had goats, we've had chickens, we've had rabbits. [laughs] You know, so they, and you know, they were taught when they were little.... When it was bedtime, my kids' toys got picked up and put in their room. I mean, that's just the way it was.

The moral universe of Paradise Valley's old-timers generally required this type of unwavering work ethic as well as a refusal to ask for help. While newcomers repeatedly lauded the support they received from friends and family, old-timers tended to extol the virtues of self-sufficiency and described the shame they felt in asking for help and lengths that they would go to in order to avoid it. The shame around asking for help was particularly difficult for men, who often saw need as antithetical to rural masculinity. For example:

> I wish I didn't have to do it [ask my brother and aunt for help with money].... I know they don't really care. If they can help, they will. But it's more like a kick to my manhood, metaphorically speaking.
> —Caleb Daniels, twenty-six-year-old single, poor, unemployed

> I think [my wife] got WIC, which I wasn't really for, but I don't think she gets it anymore. She got it for a few months. We qualified, but I was like, "I'll go grow a garden. I don't need [it]."
> —Donald Barnett, fifty-four-year-old married, low-income carpenter

> You just try to do well and do right by your people and live as honest a life as you can, and you know, try not to be a burden. And that's the other part. We don't ask for help, you know. That's what this community doesn't do . . .
> Q: And what keeps you from asking for help, do you think?
> Proud. Pride. Yeah. And ability. You don't want to give it up. You want to be able to do as much as you can, you know?
> —Pam Rhodes, fifty-seven-year-old cohabiting, low-income service worker

For old-timers, discourses and displays of work ethics and family values helped to create positive sources of meaning amid the difficulties and privations that they endured.

As these and numerous other declarations and performances attested, Paradise Valley's old-timers clung tightly to the values of hard work and self-sufficiency, taking as many opportunities as they could to demonstrate their claims to these distinctly rural American moral values.[54] But these assertions generally went ignored by Paradise Valley's new power brokers, who often dismissed old-timers' claims to these types of morality and valued other qualities more. As chapter 4 illustrated, youthful mistakes often became permanent stains on individuals' characters, undermining their abilities to compete for jobs and housing long after the specific incident or behavior occurred. Old-timers' receipt of formal aid was also stigmatized, often taken as further evidence of their laziness, lack of morality, and lack of work ethic. Newcomers tended to deny the existence of structural inequalities in the labor market and to practice class blindness to hold old-timers individually and personally responsible for their disadvantages. Their impressions of old-timers often included explicit or implicit moral judgments, and the conflation of poverty and employment struggles with a lack of work ethic and morality. Thus, whereas old-timers saw themselves as continually enacting and demonstrating dignity and morality in their struggles to survive, newcomers often saw only stigma and moral turpitude amid self-imposed poverty. For example:

> I also think there's a reason for some people to live in rural communities, and we talked about the good side to that. There's also a bad side to that, that it's—it's—communities can cut slack to some people that—it allows them to be more dysfunctional. . . . And then there is a fringe economy, and I'll just say this. You can drive around and you can see it, small old travel trailers packed behind houses. And what they—those are rental units. People are renting those out to people and a lot of those people are doing things in exchange for their rent that are not good . . . criminal activities of various sorts, whether it's drugs or whatever, prostitution.
>
> —Jim Kelly, fifty-six-year-old married, middle-income business owner

> We talk about these kids that don't really eat enough and whose parents aren't there, or they're in jail, or they're on meth. We have—not a very big population like them, but it's there. And I wish we could get that taken care of . . . 'Cause you see those kids that are always absent and never have their homework in, and always losing every library book. Well, that's because your mom's high all the time.
>
> —Emily Hill, forty-seven-year-old married, middle-income teacher

[There are] mothers, young obese mothers, with their babies that are, are livin' on food stamps, good chance their father isn't there anymore, there's domestic violence, unwed mothers, teen pregnancies—that stuff is gonna happen to them, and then to their kids. And it's gonna stay here in Eagle Flat. They're never gonna go anywhere.

—Peter Williams, sixty-eight-year-old married, middle-income retiree

Newcomers used old-timers' real and imagined addictions and illegal behaviors to rationalize their exclusion from labor markets and social networks, allowing themselves to feel justified in fortifying the boundaries between the two groups. On the rare occasions when newcomers did acknowledge old-timers' work ethics and self-sufficiency, they often stopped short of seeing these qualities as morally virtuous. Hannah Lowry ended her interview by commenting, "I think so many people [here] have the pioneer mentality. Like, the locusts came and they lost all this year's seed potatoes, but somehow we're gonna eat the furniture and get through the winter or something, you know? [laughs]." Nonetheless, as previous comments from her suggest, she did not value this sort of mentality highly and believed old-timers to be overly conservative in their values and lacking future prospects.

Thus it was that the one type of symbolic capital that old-timers fought to create—moral capital in the form of work ethic, family values, and self-sufficiency—was of little exchange value to them in Paradise Valley. Despite the multiple ways in which they demonstrated their morality, from teaching their children the value of hard work to refusing necessary aid, they were repeatedly viewed by newcomers as lacking moral virtue. Judging them often on the basis of their lack of economic, human, cultural, and social capital, and the widespread (and largely unsubstantiated) belief that they engaged in stigmatized coping strategies, newcomers generally assumed that old-timers also lacked moral virtue. They repeatedly suggested that old-timers didn't want legitimate jobs or weren't willing to do hard work and that they focused their energies instead on drug use and illegal activities. Newcomers often assumed that adults who struggled with poverty had chosen dependence on aid over work, rather than that they were unable to find decent work or to support their families comfortably through low-wage jobs. When their children struggled in school, they were assumed to have drug-addicted parents, rather than parents who had been themselves marginalized in the valley's schools and labor market. And when they failed to out-migrate as adults, they were assumed to be drug addicts continuing a generational cycle of poor work ethics and immorality. Given the social divide and the limited interactions between old-timers and newcomers, there were few opportunities for old-timers to demonstrate their morality directly to newcomers to counter these assumptions.

This gulf in perceptions of old-timers' work ethics and moral values had significant impacts on their abilities to compete for jobs and other resources in Paradise Valley. It was common for employers, many of whom were newcomers themselves, to explicitly criticize old-timers as employees and to express hiring preferences for newcomers. I was told multiple times by newcomers that the community's local adults were poor workers and that local kids weren't being raised to work hard. Most poignantly, during a public Chamber of Commerce forum multiple business owners complained repeatedly about the lack of skilled and trained workers locally who knew how to do specialized tasks required by their businesses. They discussed at length strategies for attracting individuals with these skills from outside the valley.

Eventually I spoke up and asked if bringing in outsiders was truly necessary and was told vehemently that it was. I went on to suggest that training local teenagers through summer jobs and internships could be another avenue for creating a workforce with the specific skillsets that their jobs required and might provide a viable path to adult success for those who prefer not to leave the valley or who lack the resources to leave for training and education elsewhere. Although at least one business owner in the meeting admitted to having had a similar training trajectory himself, he and multiple others got quite agitated by my comments and went on to protest that local young adults lack skills, work ethics, education, and the willingness to take financial risks. One pursued me after the meeting to continue the heated conversation and further defend his stance. He told me that there are some people who shouldn't stay in the valley and who don't want to work or contribute anything to the place.[55]

Thus for old-timers, moral capital mostly existed as a negative force, as their assumed lack of it worked against them in multiple social institutions, causing them to be excluded from jobs, housing, and social and educational opportunities. Beyond newcomers' failure to recognize their moral capital, however, old-timers also were faced with the declining value of this type of resource in the community. Despite their contentions that the unemployed were responsible for their labor market failures due to their lack of work ethics, newcomers rarely actually traded in moral capital as an important resource. It was unusual for them to invoke moral attitudes and stances of this sort as positive values that they looked for in others, particularly as friends and acquaintances. And though they sometimes discussed work ethics in the negative while complaining about their difficulties in finding trustworthy employees in the valley or justifying old-timers' exclusion from housing, educational, or social opportunities, generally the valley's best options went first to those with social connections, cultural capital, education, and job experience. A reputation as a hard worker might benefit local adults in their job searches but was seldom the main or primary factor that aided them in finding work locally and was generally of the most benefit to those who already possessed multiple other real and symbolic resources. Social connections, education, and job skills generally paid off much more in the job search than did local reputations and known work ethic. Even those old-timers with the strongest work histories often struggled to find jobs that could comfortably support them and their families.

The values that old-timers espoused and around which they structured their lives, including idealized visions of rural morality, were thus devalued by newcomers, for whom social status rested within cultural capital, education, and social exclusion, versus moral capital and social cohesion. The new social world of Paradise Valley was an easy place for those with economic, social, human, and cultural capital to live, work, and recreate, but an increasingly difficult place for those without abundant amounts of these real and symbolic resources to survive, let alone to thrive. However, moral capital, which tends to flourish in homogenous, cohesive, isolated communities, steadily diminished in importance there, as newcomers devalued it relative to other forms of real and symbolic capital, and questioned old-timers' claims to it.[56] This shifting in the meanings and values of this form of symbolic capital is one of the most significant micro-level processes that disadvantages old-timers relative to newcomers in Paradise Valley.

SYMBOLIC CAPITAL AND THE REPRODUCTION
OF INEQUALITY

For newcomers with high amounts of wealth, human, and/or cultural capital, it was relatively easy to build and maintain social capital, which was vital for filling in the gaps in Paradise Valley's infrastructure, services, and labor market. Newcomers were absorbed quickly into well-resourced social circles whose members offered numerous forms of support that helped them to navigate the challenges of rural living. Those without these forms of real and symbolic capital, however, increasingly found themselves on the wrong side of symbolic boundary lines that effectively excluded them from many of the community's other resources, exacerbating both financial strain and social isolation. They lacked sources of support through daily challenges as well as emergencies and disasters, and increasingly felt alone and abandoned in Paradise Valley.

For many who had lived in the valley longer, the exclusion was experienced as a loss of community. For Paradise Valley's old-timers the decline in social cohesion was noticeable, a stark contrast with the tight-knit community that they once took for granted and that many associated with the rural ideal. Although Paradise Valley may not have ever been the social utopia that old-timers wistfully described, their perceptions of loss reflected real struggles to survive in a rapidly changing rural landscape in which new skills and preferences were necessary to reap the bulk of social and economic rewards. Alongside the growing economic divide described in earlier chapters was this insidious and deepening social divide, in which the old-timers perceived their social status melting away.

The loss of social capital was both reinforced and exacerbated by differences in other types of symbolic capital that newcomers possessed and produced in greater amounts than old-timers. No longer a homogenous, working-class community with distinctly rural customs and traditions, the new Paradise Valley was divided by significant differences in cultural norms, interests, and values. Newcomers generally used neutral language and practiced class blindness when describing these differences but nonetheless engineered social lives built around specific cultural norms, values, and activities, while explicitly excluding those with more traditionally rural-focused interests and unfamiliarity with more elite forms of recreation and leisure. Constructing social connections and friendships around their specific interests and activities allowed newcomers to effectively trade cultural capital for social capital. Old-timers' lack of high-cultural interests and discomfort in elite cultural settings, along with their lack of time and money required to participate in many such events and activities, exacerbated the gulf in social connectivity and social capital, further segregating old-timers into circles that lacked access to multiples types of resources.

Paradise Valley's schools, both private and public, also played into these dynamics by reproducing and exaggerating, rather than leveling, differences in human capital. Children of newcomers were prepared from early ages by parents and schools for academic excellence and aspirations to out-migration and college attendance. Within Paradise Valley's private and public schools they were sorted by teachers and administrators, as well as by academic, cultural, and extracurricular interests, into social circles that included mostly the children of other advantaged and well-resourced newcomers. Old-timers' children, in contrast, often began their academic careers with disadvantages that included less-educated parents, lowered access to information about how to succeed in school and beyond, and financial constraints that put both private primary schools and full participation in the public schools out of reach. They encountered more problems in the public schools, received less encouragement from teachers and counselors about college attendance, and faced cost barriers to educational and extracurricular activities. They thus tended to end up with lower human capital and less access to both cultural capital and the social connections it engendered in Paradise Valley. They were less likely to out-migrate for higher education, and more likely to remain in Paradise Valley, where their job prospects were constricted and their morality was questioned.

Many old-timers clung to moral capital as their one abundant resource, showcasing through word and action their work ethics and family values. These performances and declarations mostly went unnoticed by newcomers, however, who rarely interacted closely with old-timers and who assumed from their disadvantaged and stigmatized circumstances that most were lazy, unmotivated, and struggling with drug and alcohol addictions. Thus moral capital went unrecognized and brought few rewards, more often working against them as a negative force. Beyond newcomers' dismissal of old-timers' morality was the reality that the community's new power brokers seldom traded in this resource, which they systematically devalued relative to the forms of symbolic capital that they owned and traded in abundance. Thus moral capital was of little exchange value in modern-day Paradise Valley, where newcomers did not need to rely upon or trade in it, and old-timers were seen as lacking it regardless of their own claims to it. It failed to act as a significant tradeable capital and instead became one more boundary between old-timers and newcomers, which ironically served mostly to further justify newcomers' withholding resources and opportunities from old-timers.

The gulf in symbolic capital between old-timers and newcomers was somewhat organic in its origins, given the vastly different social, economic, and educational backgrounds of the mostly rural old-timers and more urban-based newcomers. But the growth and reproduction of this gulf was not inevitable or necessary. Earlier in Paradise Valley's history, urban in-migrants tended to be more seamlessly absorbed into the larger community, resulting in a mixing of rural and urban, middle- and working-class customs, culture, and values. As many of the valley's old-timers explained, in the late twentieth century it was common even for in-migrants with higher levels of education and more liberal political stances to slowly acclimatize to the rural lifestyle and culture, and to be integrated into the social fabric of the community's longer-term inhabitants. This mixing of groups resulted in a community that came closer to approximating the cohesive, supportive, and homogenous rural community that both old-timers and newcomers idealized. However, as the pace and degree of in-migration grew, integration decreased. Instead of sharing resources, values, and day-to-day experiences, the newer generations of in-migrants effectively closed themselves off from the community's less-privileged residents, creating a separate and unequal society that amassed the bulk of the community's resources among themselves. At the same time, those who lacked these resources were both excluded and vilified, judged as immoral and unworthy of either inclusion or opportunities to achieve the American Dream.[57]

Over time, as differences in real and symbolic resources within Paradise Valley, and between rural and urban America have grown, the result for old-timers has been growing exclusion from multiple forms of real and symbolic exchange as well as marginalization from economic, social, and civic life in their home community. Their disenfranchisement echoes that of a growing sector of the United States, including large numbers of the ever-shrinking working class. As the nation itself grows more unequal and divided, we grow further from understanding and relating to each other's experiences and from concerning ourselves with the problems of other groups.[58]

6 Paradise Lost

MAKING SENSE OF COMMUNITY CHANGE
AND THE ELUSIVE AMERICAN DREAM

Early on in my time in Eagle Flat, I took note of an interesting juxtaposi-
tion. At the grocery store parking lot, I noticed two cars that were parked
side by side. My field notes described:

> A green jeep that looks like either a past or current US Forest Service vehicle
> with two bumper stickers: one says "Back off city boy," and the other says
> "Welcome to Eagle Flat, now go away." Next to it is parked a fancy sedan
> with a bumper sticker that says "Ski Paradise Valley."[1]

For me these two vehicles were a perfect visual representation of two very
different worldviews and experiences that collided daily in Paradise Valley.
On the one hand, there were the rural working-class roots symbolized in
the Forest Service jeep, with its strong sentiment of protectionism from an
invading urban force. On the other hand, embodied in a high-end sedan
were the middle-class privilege, leisure, and resources, beckoning others
to join in the expensive and exclusive outdoor recreation activities that a
rural setting offers. Inside one of the valley's two full-size grocery stores,
these incompatible understandings and populations circulated with minimal interaction, maintaining an uncomfortable peace across lines of difference and a divide that at times seemed impassable.

Modern-day Paradise Valley is simultaneously a rural utopia of community and social support for some and an increasingly divided community
where disenfranchisement, misunderstanding, and judgment dominate
the social landscape for others. The deepening divide influences residents'
outlooks and worldviews as well as their understandings of what community is and how community is done. As rural and urban communities are
increasingly dependent and interdependent upon each other, these clash-
ing understandings of community, civic responsibility, and morality structure and reinforce social divides and conflicting experiences in rural places
like Paradise Valley and across the larger nation.[2] The impacts of the divide
in Paradise Valley include feelings of dissatisfaction for some members of
the community as well as an increasing sense of marginalization from and
conflict with a hostile outside world. For many old-timers this feeling contributes to the type of sentiment exemplified in the bumper stickers, the
desire to close off and protect oneself from outside threats and invasions.

This sense of protectionism and closure has long been associated with
small rural communities, including what researchers Michelle Kondo,
Rebecca Rivera, and Stan Rullman have referred to as the "last settler
syndrome"—the desire to preserve a rural community exactly the way you
found it.[3] This sentiment was commonly expressed by old-timers like
Ruth Cooper, a seventy-year-old retiree who had moved to the valley thirty
years earlier: "I was one of those that wanted to shut the gates behind me
when I moved here, and I don't want anything to change. But logically,
we know it's going to change." Change was hard for old-timers not only
because they liked the valley the way that they had originally found it, but
because many of the recent changes resulted in their feeling disenfranchised and struggling to survive as they chased an increasingly elusive and
diminished version of the American Dream. This desire to close the valley
off contrasted with many newcomers' visions of the valley as improving
through growth and the importation of others like themselves. As newcomer Anya Wilburn put it: "There's more people keep moving here, but
at least they're all usually really cool people."

Newcomers and old-timers found different ways to live with and make
sense of the community's divide, coexisting mostly through limited interaction. Their separation entailed living unconnected lives but also seeing
the world and their community through very different lenses that reflected
their distinct cultural norms, personal experiences, and senses of self. For

newcomers this process included class blindness, often with a focus on their positive contributions and sincere desires to help the larger community. For old-timers it often took other forms, such as blaming either newcomers or other disadvantaged residents for the community's problems and thus distancing themselves from these concerns. Old-timers also frequently engaged in discourses that focused their alienation and frustration in other directions, including toward larger and impersonal groups like urbanites more generally or social structures like the government. They drew on larger societal messages, including those provided to them by right-wing media outlets, to help them make sense of how the American Dream had been stolen from them and whom to blame for the theft.

During the final years of the Obama administration, twenty-four-hour news networks and right-wing media outlets broadcasted relentless messages of anger and rage that spoke to various experiences of loss across America. In Paradise Valley experiences of exclusion and marginalization fueled personalized interpretations of this anger discourse for old-timers and allowed them to blame distant and faceless institutions for their losses, instead of their more proximate new neighbors.[4] Newcomers, however, mostly saw themselves as positive forces for good and felt proud of their contributions to the community and the larger society, while turning a blind eye to the ways in which their advantages negatively impacted others in their adopted home. These differing orientations contributed to particular social and political understandings as well as a social landscape of division and exclusion rather than empathy and cohesion. Paradise Valley's experience provides a window into processes that are occurring across the nation, as Americans become increasingly divided in their daily lives, interactions, politics, and worldviews. It illuminates the forces driving the national-level divisions between those who have extra to give and those who are losing access to the American Dream.

"WE TRY TO GIVE BACK": CLASS BLINDNESS AND HELPING WITHOUT INTERACTING

The stance of class blindness described in previous chapters did not mean that newcomers were unaware of social problems, the community's divide, or the growth of inequality. Class blindness allows the middle class to benefit from the valley's inequality without acknowledging their own relative advantages or taking responsibility for perpetuating class inequality through their behaviors, choices, and privileged access to opportunities.[5] Nonetheless, newcomers (many of whom saw themselves as the community's benefactors) frequently showcased genuine concern for social issues and made concerted efforts to address them in the abstract and at the community level, while simultaneously failing to take responsibility for perpetuating them at the individual level.

Newcomers frequently described liberal political outlooks, which often included a number of social justice orientations and interests. When asked to describe the specific concerns and interests that were important to them, they spoke of a number of social, political, economic, and environmental issues, including poverty and inequality, health care, food system concerns, LGBTQ rights, and environmental protection. The following are a sample of newcomer responses to my questions regarding issues that were important to them:

> Well, you know, saving the earth, conservation and reaching out to the poor, and the—you know, gay rights, and that kind of thing.
> —Roy Watson, seventy-four-year-old married, middle-income retired teacher

> Environmental issues. Social issues. Um, financial issues. You know, I pay a lot of attention to national politics. Um, and the organization of our country and the way things are run. Gay rights. Um, so yeah, social justice.
> —Walter Perry, fifty-nine-year-old married, middle-income US Forest Service employee

> The corporatization of everything and everything that goes along with that—the buying of politics, the genetic modification of everything, the increasing gap between wealthy and poor, the concerted effort to polarize people.
> —Claire Woods, forty-two-year-old married, middle-income nonprofit consultant

> Corporations, Monsanto, blah, blah, blah—it's like, the environment should be first.... I don't want to poison my children, and no GMOs kind of thing, because I just don't know. Save the environment and la, la, la—all of that.
> —Sabena Griffin, thirty-three-year-old cohabiting, middle-income nurse

These concerns drew heavily upon concepts and rhetoric associated with liberal and Democratic stances, which reflected interests in improving lives across society, protecting themselves as well as others from a host of social and environmental harms. The sources of information for this group were mostly forms of print media, including the *New York Times*, the *Washington Post*, and *BBC News* as well as the local (left-leaning) newspaper, *National Public Radio*, and political humor programs like *The Daily Show*. Thus they tended to have very consistently liberal understandings of political issues and concerns, and as chapter 2 described, they mostly voted in line with these beliefs. Most newcomers were politically active, and 88 percent said that they voted regularly.[6] A number expressed skepticism of the democratic process but voted nonetheless:

> I'm pretty cynical when it comes to politics in general, and, uh, so, yeah, certainly socially liberal, economically kind of a little more conservative, and I also don't feel like either of the political parties really represents—it's just such a flawed process and all that I have a hard time—like, I vote, but I'm not like, "Yay!" It's just like, OK, lesser of evils kind of deal.
> —Shawn Murphy, forty-three-year-old divorced, low-income carpenter

> The difference between the two parties is now very marginal, since we're a corporatocracy. We've lost most of the features of democracy. The corporations own most of the—virtually all the senators and congressmen. So there's not a whole lot of difference between the two parties. . . . So yeah, such as they are, I always pick the Democrats.
> —Howard Jenkins, seventy-five-year-old married, middle-income retired teacher

Despite reservations like these, many newcomers expressed a sense of mastery through political knowledge, as was the case with fifty-six-year-old bartender Jim Kelly, who explained, "I regularly vote. I advocate. I study. I research." Maya Ferrer, a thirty-four-year-old massage therapist, expressed a similar confidence in her political efficacy, which she tied directly to living in Paradise Valley: "I actually felt like living in a rural place I had more of a say than like, so, but yeah, and now I do my civic duty. I read the voter's pamphlet and think about it and ask people about their informed decisions, and I vote."

Political and social concerns were not simply abstract interests but the basis of tangible action for newcomers, many of whom were interested in contributing to the community in positive ways and passionate about working to address social problems. Previous researchers have found that in-migrants to amenity-rich rural communities often have a lowered sense of attachment, civic responsibility, and/or desire to contribute to the community than longer-term residents.[7] Far from being the case in Paradise Valley, as discussed in chapter 3, both place attachment and a deep sense of civic responsibility contributed to newcomers' volunteerism and desires to improve the community in perceptible ways. As chapter 3 explored, newcomers described a vast array of altruistic activities that helped those within their social circles but also many that focused on tangibly improving and giving back to the larger community. For example:

> LOUISE: We try to give back to the community as much as we can. And we have cleaned out part of the stuff out of our closet every year—things that we haven't used for a while and take them down to the community center, they can use to sell down there.
>
> ROGER: And we give food to Angel Food, which feeds people in the community.
>
> —Louise and Roger Clark, sixty-eight- and seventy-year-old married, middle income retirees

> I'm involved a lot with the Paradise Gallery. . . . I've done some volunteer stuff with the theater. We had a benefit garage sale for one of the families that lost their home here just last weekend.
>
> —Maria Setzer, forty-year-old married, low-income substitute teacher

> Over the years I have done a lot of organization-participation stuff. I was very much involved in the partnership for sustainable Paradise. . . . I volunteer to help at a lot of things for Home Front and for Eagle's Nest, and blah, blah, blah.
>
> —Lea Fern, fifty-nine-year-old divorced, poor artist

> We donate a lot to the foodbank. We get a lot of surplus out of the garden.
>
> —Claire Woods, forty-two-year-old married, middle-income nonprofit consultant

Volunteer and charitable work with local organizations allowed many newcomers to put their strongly held beliefs around political and social issues into action. As they discussed the multitude of ways in which they donated time, money, and resources around the valley, these newcomers evoked social, political, and occasionally religious stances as justifications for their high levels of civic engagement and concern. Although, as these quotes illustrate, much of their action focused on donating surplus goods or resources that they no longer needed, these efforts were vital to sustaining the community's many nonprofit organizations.

However, as these quotes also illustrate, newcomers' political views often were somewhat rote and lacking substance. When it came to crafting solutions to the issues they raised, they were often vague. Ideas ranged from more libertarian to more socialist approaches, but the bulk of newcomers expressed liberal ideologies in the abstract, but few concrete political or practical solutions to the problems they discussed. Within this sample, there was little support for federal social programs like welfare. Instead, many newcomers favored loosely neoliberal approaches including private charities and market-based solutions. What was more consistent among this group was that many of those who expressed earnest concerns regarding issues like social inequality and poverty did not extend their concern to specific *individuals* in need.

Although newcomers repeatedly espoused the importance of social justice concerns on a theoretical or ideological level, when it came to making sense of the individuals experiencing these problems within the valley, they often had very different understandings. Newcomers gave money and time to a plethora of nonprofit organizations, donated old clothes and excess garden produce, and attended festive events that celebrated the work being done around the valley to help sustain its physical environment, arts, and social services. Nonetheless, most newcomers did not directly rub elbows with the people their efforts helped to sustain, and thus true connections and bonds were rarely formed across the social divide. As a volunteer with Angel Food and Home Front, I worked alongside a number of newcomers who defied this pattern in important ways, but the majority of newcomers engaged in charitable activities across the valley did not make direct or personal connections with old-timers in need.

Judgments of the valley's less-fortunate residents as lacking work ethics, morality, and future prospects were not limited to newcomers who were unconcerned about social issues or who failed to recognize inequality in their community. Many of those who worked earnestly on social inequality and poverty issues, and who showed a clear understanding of the valley's social divide, nonetheless expressed similar judgements of the valley's poorest individuals as ignorant, drug-addicted, lazy, and immoral. Peter Williams, a sixty-eight-year-old retiree who had lived in the valley for eight years, was deeply involved in its charity sector and conveyed a serious concern for issues of poverty and inequality in the community. I met him at his stunning, recently built home, with high vaulted ceilings and exposed wooden beams, and expansive views of the valley below. As snow clouds gathered across the horizon, Peter spoke at length about the importance of local charity efforts to address social problems, to which he contributed by making sizable monetary donations. He explained:

> In some ways this is a real microcosm of the haves and the have-nots around here. So I, you know, I can't respond to a lot of the issues that other people you've talked to probably have to grapple with, you know. But I know about 'em. And we do what we can to help them, you know. . . . We have narrowed it down to two pretty big donations a year to two local groups. One is Home Front, which is a vital organization as you well know. And the other is the Paradise Valley Citizen's Council. To try to, uh, protect the valley itself. And thereby the people in the valley, you know. But this, this other business about the, the poverty here, the rural poverty, people's inability to move around, mobility, transportation, some of those needs are beginning to be addressed, a lot of it through the efforts of Home Front and other groups too.

Peter took pride in being educated about social concerns in Paradise Valley, yet he also spoke from a stance of self-conscious removal from individuals in need, demonstrating judgment and class blindness regarding the choices and outcomes of the group he referred to as the "poor, uneducated, or uh, undereducated, underprivileged, underaware." He told me:

> You know, it's a tough place to live. And I, I understand that. And I sit up here on the hill and watch it all, you know . . . It's a, it's a tough place to live. . . . I really do understand that there are people in this valley who need to go to Home Front to get a coat. Or a carrot. Or they go to Angel Food. It's tough. They drop out of school. They can't get a job. [The grocery store] is a career move.

A similar set of sentiments were expressed by Lea Fern, an artist who had been in the valley for fifteen years. She articulated heartfelt concerns about social justice issues that she translated into direct work with several local nonprofit groups. She spoke of the importance of this kind of civic engagement: "There are issues everywhere you look. Find one, pick one, and work on it. You know, whether it is a local issue, national issue, or something around the globe. Do something, because we all need to." However, she also described the valley's poor in terms that focused on their moral failures and individual behaviors. She said:

> There is some really—I don't want to judge them, but for lack of a better term, sort of down-and-out people here. You are really aware of that. OK. I mean, heroin is bigtime on the rise, and there is meth. . . . That's part of the spectrum.

Walter Perry, a Forest Service employee who described himself as "born with that social justice gene," nonetheless worried openly about the possibility that growth in local poverty might impact him personally. He explained his fear regarding the following:

> Things that I value, that feels like it's kind of trickling away. So the ability to enjoy a place where you don't have to worry about robberies or rapes or shootings, or things like that, you know, not knowing where the key to the front door is, and you don't care. . . . I mean, if the [economic] collapse continues, then when people start coming to try to find food and they can't find food here at [the grocery store], instead they find food in my garden or my back door.

Despite understanding many of the social forces at play, socially aware and active newcomers like these often spoke of the poor as personally flawed, threatening, and morally contaminated on the individual level. For a number of its most philanthropically minded newcomers, involvement in the community's charity sector and concern about its social problems did not overcome class blindness and did not translate into either close relationships with many old-timers or real empathy for their individual plights.

On the contrary, the nature of the charitable and nonprofit sector was such that more often than not, those who gave the most resources were the least intimately involved with local populations. Rachel Wilson, a nonprofit board member who had lived in the valley for seventeen years, had this to say about the forces that sustained many such organizations:

> In some ways there is this idea that the valley takes care of itself, and at the same time there is this amazing outside—it is almost like we have a wealthy uncle or something like that. And I mean really, the number of nonprofits that host events on the west side is incredible. . . . I think that is great.

We should tap in on some of those resources. But sitting in on some of the meetings and realizing that I have no idea who the players are—the people that are giving the big money around here, and that are being courted by the local nonprofit sector to give big money I think has changed. Whereas it used to be let's have a contra dance and raise $1,500 so we can put new carpeting in at the art gallery or whatever.

For newcomers, understandings of how to give back to a community resembled the rural idyll in the focus on concern for local issues but also drew heavily from urban-based, middle-class philanthropy practices that tend to be less personal and interactive.[8] Thus, like their urban counterparts, they showed concern by filtering their efforts through local organizations, donating time, interest, and money to institutions that would help populations in need, rather than interacting directly with individuals in the community.

This sense that newcomers were socially removed from the valley's less fortunate populations was shared by old-timers as well, although filtered through very different lenses. In the wake of summer fires and floods, newcomers came together in the community theater to collectively process the experience through performances, including poetry, songs, essays, and dance. One prominent local philanthropist and volunteer read an essay describing how after the disasters she drove around the valley observing the devastation, and how deeply moving she found this experience.[9] Asa Hobson, a field scientist who had grown up in the valley, experienced such behaviors very differently. He described the following experience, from the same floods, as an example of what he saw as newcomers' hands-off mentality when it came to directly helping others:

> When [our friend's] house was washed out, we had people in a red Audi Quattro wagon, I remember it perfectly to this point, and they were stopped and they're taking pictures of us. Well, we were tryin' to emergency get his stuff outta the house, as quick as we could. And they're blocking the trucks that we had lined up to get the stuff outta there. And I started yelling at them, "There's two types of people in this situation: people that are helping and people that are getting out the fuck out of the way! So get the fuck outta the way!" And just, it's just a real disconnect, even when people, they're like right there, they feel like they're watchin' it on TV somehow. You know? It's not, instead of taking a picture—like that was the thing that made me so mad—like instead of taking a picture, get out of your car and help!

For Asa, such behaviors were an example of a larger trend among new-comers, which was out of step with Paradise Valley's previous norms: "If you are not willing to help somebody else around here or have your door open to people, or if you are goin' to put up a gate, like a gated community style, then you shouldn't be here, because that's not what the place has ever been." Many old-timers similarly found newcomers' behaviors to be incompatible with rural norms of directly helping individuals in the community and were unimpressed with their hands-off style of philanthropy through financial contributions.

The more urban-influenced structure of charity and nonprofit work in Paradise Valley both grew out of and perpetuated the class blindness of many middle-class residents. It allowed them to care about people in the abstract versus in person, to be concerned with issues rather than individuals, and to give to those in need without actually bridging the social divide between the haves and the have-nots. Thus, despite the sincere social justice interests of so many newcomers, such concern was rarely translated directly to individuals in the community, and instead judgment, social boundaries, and exclusion flourished even among those who both recognized social inequality and expressed a desire to change it.

Many newcomers viewed charitable giving as an important part of what it meant to contribute to a rural community. But for old-timers it represented a sea change in the way community is done and what it meant to be part of a rural community. Philanthropic giving allowed newcomers to acknowledge the social divide while feeling that they were taking concrete action to address it, but for old-timers the changes in the ways community was enacted on the ground left them feeling angry, abandoned, and betrayed. As Penny Carpenter, a forty-year-old hair-stylist, told me:

> I feel like a lot of people move here and they are like, I want to be a part of the community, but then when they move here they want to change it to more like a city community. Or—that's how I feel . . . It is just a lot of focusing on not so much on the community as individuals and families and what not, it is more focusing on basically everything revolving around tourism and recreation. Instead of actually like a hometown feel.

Even a number of middle-class residents with longer histories in Paradise Valley had noticed the changes in how "community" was performed there.

Kristine Girard, a sixty-five-year-old ski instructor who had lived in the valley for thirty-five years, attributed these changes to growth in the valley's population and the increasing urban influence. She explained:

> [People] used to be much closer-knit. Now everybody, we're still pretty close, help each other, but they look after number one first, kind of, um, there's not as much helping.... I'd say it's just kind of [due to] population density. I mean, when you can no longer go to every event in the valley, when you can no longer recognize everybody, you still have a circle of friends, but there's a whole bunch of people you don't know. So the traditional wave when you pass people you know on the street or in their car doesn't happen most of the time, because people, in fact when you're walking on the street, look the other way, city-style.

By and large, however, most newcomers were unaware of the ways in which their conceptions of community and philanthropy differed from those of the more traditional rural populations among whom they now lived. They created an urban-rural hybrid model of community that focused on caring about local community and social justice in the abstract, while also blaming struggling individuals for their situations and distancing themselves from neighbors in need. Class blindness facilitated this understanding of themselves as charitable, liberal, and community-focused, while simultaneously allowing for social exclusion and resource hoarding that deepened the social divide. Although they generally felt very satisfied with their community, for old-timers making sense of the growing divide was often a much bigger challenge that resulted in more negative outlooks and outcomes.

THE BAD SIDE OF COUNTRY: MANAGING MARGINALIZATION THROUGH SOCIAL BOUNDARIES

> I would've liked all these innocent, more country, less dynamic people, you know, to inhabit the valley, but you know, there's a bad side to them too. The trailer trash, stuff like that.
>
> —Ryan Boyle, thirty-nine-year-old cohabiting, poor stay-at-home father

The struggles that old-timers faced in Paradise Valley were often difficult for them to accept and comprehend, particularly while so many others with shorter tenures and fewer ties to the area appeared to flourish
there. Although most old-timers spoke of their multiple labor market and
related challenges as facts of life, they were seldom unaware of how their
social status colored their experiences. Many old-timers consciously recognized that their struggles were intertwined with newcomers' successes.
Unlike newcomers, however, old-timers seldom saw themselves as having
agency in addressing the divide or contributing to solving Paradise Valley's social problems.

Instead, like Irene Nelson, a fifty-four-year-old artist, many expressed
feeling judged, excluded, and disempowered. Irene told me:

> You are ending up with this social clash.... Unfortunately, I really do see
> a different—like a class war starting to really develop. Before, nobody had
> a huge amount, but it was still within this broad band. Now you are see-
> ing some folks up here, and they are very disdainful to everybody else.
> Personally, I don't give a shit. They can have whatever. But they still need to
> have respect for basic human issues.

The frustrations of not garnering respect and being treated differently
permeated many old-timers' narratives, which were sometimes peppered with statements that attempted to counter disrespect and assert
self-worth. Their anger at feeling judged often caused old-timers to lack
empathy for newcomers, and many responded to the sense of marginalization by judging the newcomers in turn, further contributing to the social
divide. They also asserted dignity through more subtle means, including
making claims to work ethics and family values. In addition to assertions
and performances that old-timers used to externally exhibit their moral
worth, many old-timers often described other old-timers in disparaging
ways that allowed them to separate themselves from those whom they saw
as lacking such claims to morality.[10]

Work status is often a focus of such discursive boundary work for
low-income and poor populations, allowing individuals to construct
collective identities in opposition to "undeserving" others deemed to be
flawed.[11] Thus old-timers' recognitions of class differences and economic
struggles were frequently combined with statements that evoked claims
to moral capital, often overtly or subtly contrasting their own work ethics

or values with those of morally inferior others, including both newcomers perceived as entitled *and* old-timers perceived as lazy.[12] In creating
and reinforcing these social boundaries, old-timers were able to counter
newcomers' narratives of their laziness and moral contamination. Yet at
the same time, their own sense of solidarity and community was further
eroded and undermined through these individualistic assertions and
understandings.

Fifty-seven-year-old Pam Rhodes pointed her comments directly at
newcomers while describing her work history. The low-income service
worker had come to the area thirty-two years earlier and had held many
different jobs there. She described her long work history with both pride
and bitterness, which she directed at those whose "people" helped them
survive: "Welcome to Paradise Valley . . . You want to make—you want to
live here, and if you don't have the buy-in from your people, work. You
work." For Pam, the struggles to find sufficient income highlighted what
she perceived as a contrast between hard work and privilege, which she
identified as a gulf between old-timers and newcomers. She depicted her
own family and fellow old-timers as moral in their work ethics and dedi-
cation, compared to newcomers who didn't have to work hard in order to
succeed. She explained:

> It is a struggle to make ends meet as a mom and wife and family member. . . .
> We didn't really want a handout in any which way, but it made it hard. And
> I still see that now in the folks that have stayed here—it is pretty hand-to-
> mouth for some segments of the community. And then other folks come
> in—and you know, bless their hearts—but they have mommies' and daddies'
> blessings and then they get things bought for them like homes, and tractors,
> and cars, and it's just a really different place than it used to be. . . . People
> who have lived here a really long time who have built community, who have
> made it a really safe, friendly, accessible place are getting taxed out, you
> know? And it is just like, well, wait a second. It doesn't seem fair.

Lillian Mitchell, a fifty-five-year-old store owner, suggested that not only
were newcomers themselves lacking traditional rural work ethics but
that they were passing their flawed values and entitlement onto their
children. Unlike the participants quoted in chapters 3 and 5, Lillian
argued that it was newcomers, not old-timers, who refused to work hard
in local jobs:

You see the ranch small farmer go to a yuppie hobby farmer. That is probably one of the bigger [changes] I have seen. I have seen that generation
that doesn't want to see their children work hard. So we lack for kids that are
raised now to do any kind of work ethic, know how to work.

Such assertions of work ethics were one common way for old-timers to
push back against the increasing sense of marginalization, while also
asserting their own claims to dignity.

Overt comparisons with newcomers were not the only way that old-
timers made claims to morality, however. Even more common than comments that questioned newcomers' work ethics were comparisons with
other, often more disadvantaged low-income and poor community members who served as examples of moral degradation.[13] In Paradise Valley
this process was a common reaction to perceived judgment and exclusion, and in their attempts to make sense of marginalization and protect
themselves from shame, old-timers often lashed out against even more
challenged old-timers, in discursive attempts to create social distinctions
between themselves and these stigmatized others.

Owen Roberts, the struggling maintenance worker, railed against other
poor residents as frequently as he complained about newcomers. For him
there was a clear distinction between the ability of old-timers and newcomers to survive in Paradise Valley. "You can make a good living here, but
you are never going to be rich," he said. "Never. No. The people that are
rich didn't live here. They moved here. They did not live here to start with."
Yet despite his acknowledgment of newcomers' advantages in the labor
market, Owen complained at length about the valley's disadvantaged residents lacking work ethics, contrasting them with himself. As he put it:

People that are working are paying for people that don't want to work. And
a lot of people around here are on food stamps that shouldn't be. Because
there is work out there if you want to work. But [they don't] because it is
easier to be on food stamps. . . . Like the food bank. They serve about a hundred families a week. They shouldn't have to do that because there is people
there that could work, but they don't want to, because it is easier not to. I
love to work. I have always loved to work.

Owen returned to this theme throughout his interview, often dismiss-
ing aid seekers as not only lazy but also drug-addicted and/or criminal—

the same stereotypes that newcomers often applied to old-timers. He explained further:

> A lot of [aid recipients] have been in jail. A lot of them are on probation. And they don't have to be there. Go find a job. They don't want to. They can do things without worrying about it. They got Angel Food to help them out.... If they tried, I would be 100 percent for them. But they don't try.... They can work in a restaurant or something. But people that have been in jail, they are not to be trusted very far—no. But there is jobs out there—they can rake leaves for somebody. Clean somebody's yard up for them. They don't want to do that. They don't want to get their hands dirty.

Like those whom he judged as undeserving, Owen also sometimes received aid. In response to a question about his receipt of Unemployment Insurance during seasonal layoffs, he responded fervently, again distancing himself from people who misused and abused aid, asserting his own work ethic:

> I hate [Unemployment]. I hate it with a passion, but you have got to have money coming in somewhere. I have been on it for probably fifteen to twenty years. When I worked for the government I was a summer employee, so I was on it from about, oh, say from 1980 to '89 I was on it from about September through April, and I hate it with a passion because there is so much stuff. And there is so many people that misuse it, just like everything else. People misuse it. Food stamps, income. They misuse it. Some people living better than I do. It bugs me, but I'm not going to do that. I want to work, and if I can, I'm going to do it.

For old-timers like Owen, such strong assertions of work ethics were an important buffer against internalizing shame, which allowed them to create distinctions between themselves and others in similarly stigmatized positions.

Asserting morality through contrasting themselves with substance abusers was another common technique for old-timers, mirroring many of the ways in which newcomers described the low-income community. Drinking, methamphetamine use, and increasingly opioids were all acknowledged to be problems in Paradise Valley, particularly for its poorest residents.[14] Old-timers sometimes portrayed substance users as both morally compromised and bad parents, discursively separating themselves from them and blaming them for a number of the community's current problems, including their decreasing sense of community. For example:

> You see, back in those days, people helped one another. They don't now, because they can't afford to help anybody. Alcohol, dope, marijuana—this is terrible things that has happened in our lifetime. And a lot of times you think people would wake up and see what's going on with their kids, but too busy.
>
> —Fred Foster, eighty-two-year-old married, poor farmer

> We have some people who are challenged now with the whole drug, methamphetamine stuff. And that's a huge burden on our community. Huge. And I just want those folks to go straight. That's all. I mean, they are missing out so bad, and they are going to be so compromised. And their children are compromised.
>
> —Pam Rhodes, fifty-seven-year-old cohabiting, low-income service worker

> I think there's a difference [from when I was growing up here]. We drank. Now they do all sorts of other stuff. All we ever thought, I mean, all we ever did was go out and drink beer. I mean, we didn't do the meth and crap like they do now, you know, just didn't do it.
>
> —Audrey Patterson, fifty-nine-year-old married, poor, SSI-reliant

As with work ethics, assertions of morality through judgment of substance users were often the most vehement among those who had faced these problems themselves, who wanted to distance themselves from the negative stereotypes. Several of the above-quoted participants had adult children who struggled with drug and alcohol addiction. Megan Wicker, a twenty-eight-year-old stay-at-home mother, strongly judged local young adults as she attempted to separate herself from her own troubled past. Megan was struggling to stay clean after kicking a methamphetamine addiction. She described being introduced to the drug in high school and continuing to use off and on for years, even after temporarily losing custody of her children. Megan connected her drug problems directly to her own struggles to find work. She told me that "boredom is the hardest part for an addict," and explained: "In the wintertime there is a lot—there is nothing to do, and people are out of work, and you get bored, and boredom is not good for addiction." Despite her understanding of the ways in which the local labor market impacted her own drug use, Megan asserted that other young adults who used drugs were "just horrible children. . . . That whole generation, apparently, they are all into heroin and it is horrible." She elaborated further, linking drug use to bad parenting:

> They are just—I don't know. They were younger parents to begin with and they just—they figured since they were doing [drugs], their kids could do it, kind of thing, and they didn't take very well care of their kids. It's horrible. Like the Tucker family, like I don't know, they just got into heroin and using needles and they think it is socially acceptable and it is not. It drives me crazy.

While newcomers usually discussed these problems from a stance of removal, old-timers frequently experienced them as more proximate threats. These types of statements, which denigrated the morality of others, were often made most passionately by those who had the greatest fear of being judged for similar behaviors.[15] They commonly applied these negative statements to specific subsections of the old-timer population, such as drug users or aid recipients, versus the entire old-timer community more generally. Nonetheless, these discourses of morality versus deficiency helped to shape old-timers' understandings and social interactions, in ways similar to those I found in my previous rural research.[16]

Although the creation of symbolic boundaries allowed many old-timers to assert dignity, it also resulted in old-timers turning their frustrations upon each other, thus diminishing their capacities to maintain social capital and create strong social networks. It also meant that they often failed to see themselves as a cohesive group in Paradise Valley, further undermining both their capacity for building community among themselves and their collective efficacy in terms of promoting their own needs and interests in the larger community. Thus unlike newcomers, old-timers often failed to see themselves as part of a cohesive and protective social group to whom they could turn for help. They also felt that they could not turn to the community's better-off newcomers, or outside institutions for significant aid or protection. The disdain that many felt for both newcomers *and* other old-timers constrained their abilities to create and take part in any type of community in Paradise Valley.

"NOT THERE TO HELP YOU": PROTECTIONISM, VULNERABILITY, AND ANGER DISCOURSE

Social boundaries between old-timers themselves allowed many to make sense of their diminished dreams, which still might compare favorably against those of even less fortunate individuals and families. However, along with the sense of being judged and excluded by newcomers, boundaries of this nature contributed to the sense of being socially isolated or abandoned, a common theme for many old-timers.[17] These feelings of exclusion combined with the sense of being invaded or attacked by an outside force, and many old-timers expressed feeling vulnerable within their home community and beyond. Powerlessness and vulnerability helped to shape their worldviews, including the sense of distrust and self-protection that many described as well as pessimistic understandings of the larger social and political climates in Paradise Valley and throughout the state and nation. It was common for old-timers to tell me that they didn't trust the democratic process and that their concerns weren't addressed by local or national leaders and institutions, although the majority (72 percent) had voted at some recent time.[18]

In response to the question of whether they voted regularly in any types of elections, old-timers had the following answers:

Very seldom, because I don't think they do any good, and I don't like the political machine...

Q: Do you follow any political issues?

Nope. Unless it's farm issues, and then I'll follow farm issues, but that's about it.

—Beverly Parker, sixty-seven-year-old widowed, poor, Social Security–reliant

I haven't voted yet. I, uh, I have weird political views [laughs]. Um, I don't know if it actually does anything to vote, really, you know? I don't know.... I know my husband doesn't vote. I've thought about it. And every year I'm like, I should go vote. Oh, but I don't have time.

—Allison Lloyd, twenty-eight-year-old married, low-income stay-at-home mother

I don't—I think—I don't think my vote matters.... I think that the whole voting process is a show. I think that they already have it figured out and that they're gonna do whatever they want to do.

—Chad Lloyd, twenty-eight-year-old married, low-income sawmill worker

Only thing I can tell you about politics, I don't trust 'em. Absolutely not.

—Greg Rossi, fifty-seven-year-old divorced, middle-income retired US Forest
Service employee

I don't think any of our voices are heard anymore. I just think it is just a
political football game. I think we are paying into the big game—all of us.
At our expense. I am tired. Really tired.

—Pam Rhodes, fifty-seven-year-old cohabiting, low-income service worker

"My Vote Doesn't Count for Much": Distrust in the Political System

Old-timers' political understandings drew from their own experiences
of abandonment but also reflected the national discourses of the time,
including the widespread antigovernment rhetoric. They described senses
of being both invaded and abandoned but did not talk of either moral
outrage or minorities having cut the line, as previous researchers have
found.[19] Instead, much of the frustration that old-timers expressed had
to do with the experience of being unimportant or unheard, whether at
the local, state, or national level—often reflecting macro versions of the
dismissal and marginalization they experienced within Paradise Valley.
Many old-timers expressed more conservative political views, and they
often felt that their concerns were drowned out by louder and more liberal voices, particularly from the more urban west side of the state.[20]
Municipal employee Wes Thompson, who voted regularly, explained his
understanding that rural Washington was ignored in favor of more urban
concerns and needs:

> You see a lot of the stuff, it's like, "Let's raise the taxes to fix the roads." Hmm.
> We don't get much road repair over here. Seattle's always got roads bein'
> repaired, but you drive up and down these valleys, their idea of repairing a
> road here is throwing some chip seal on it. Over there, they're tearin' whole
> lanes out and rebuilding the roads. They just throw some gravel on our
> roads. It's like, we pay our taxes too.

Wes's wife, Adeline, expressed a similar concern:

> I feel for the most part that that—um, [pause] my vote doesn't count for much.
> 'Cause it ends up happening a lot here especially. Even though we're a large
> county, there's more people stuffed into a smaller space, and they're more
> liberal on the coast than we are over here.

Care worker Tilda Conner articulated a related sentiment, but for her the abandonment translated into a reason not to vote. She said:

> I felt like, had I—well, you know, here's the problem. We're so little over here, it doesn't matter what we vote, 'cause Seattle's denser, they'll get the vote anyway, and often they vote exactly what I don't want to do.

Although not everyone was this concerned about state-level politics, the theme of being ignored and under attack by a political machine that favored other interests was powerful throughout old-timers' interviews. Allison Lloyd didn't vote, but she did feel strongly about political issues, expressing a preference for the Tea Party. Her political beliefs focused on self-protection from outside forces. She explained:

> I mean, honestly I feel like, um, the government's going to shit and that they're trying to take away a lot of our civil liberties. And I'll be damned if they take that from me. They're gonna have to pry my guns out of my hands, you know, that kind of a thing. And I know that sounds—that's where my redneckedness comes in, is that I fully think that I'm gonna do what it takes to protect me and mine.

Allison's husband, Chad, expressed similar views, focusing on independence and self-protection:

> My kind of view is, stay to yourself. I don't know. I guess I don't—the whole gun rights and stuff, and stuff like that, it's—[pause] don't tread on me [laughs]. I'm more of a—I stay to myself, don't bother me kind of—I wouldn't say reclusive, but yeah.

As described in earlier chapters, Allison and Chad felt very isolated and lacking support in Paradise Valley. Allison connected her political conservatism directly to her family's sense of abandonment by others within the community as well as by larger social structures. As she put it:

> We don't really have anybody we can ask [for help] because everybody we know is in the same boat as us. And I don't think we would really ask if, uh, you know. It's just we wanna try to do it as much as we can on our own. I mean, I have applied for like, food stamps before when we were really broke. We never qualified for it. Um, we never could get any help from the government, so we uh, that probably has influenced me a little bit in my political beliefs. You know, that everybody else seems to be able to get help but we can't.

This sense of lacking support from larger social institutions was echoed by old-timers across the political spectrum. Fifty-two-year-old Kim Henderson lived in subsidized housing but still struggled to survive. She didn't have a strong political preference but expressed the concern that people in need were being abandoned in the United States. She explained:

> Internally we really aren't taking care of our own. When we are giving money to feed people in a foreign land—which I agree with—and we have children going hungry here, I feel that that is a two-faced statement. You must take care of your own before you try to take care of someone else. And that bothers me. That has richly bothered me for a long time.

Asa Hobson, who consistently voted liberal, gave a more succinct version of this sentiment: "I have never liked government. And people have always said, you know, they are there to take from you and they are not there to help you." For many old-timers the sense that no one supported them—including community, society, and social institutions—fueled a deep distrust of the political system and fear of attack from powerful interests. Regardless of their political stances and voting outcomes, old-timers repeatedly made connections between their direct experiences of loss, powerlessness, and inability to get help, and their distrust and fear of the government and its potential to cause them harm. For most, these concerns emerged organically in their interviews long before I asked them specific questions about their political interests and voting behaviors. As the next section illustrates, old-timers focused their concerns on the most immediate threats to their livelihoods, including land use policies and government regulations.[21]

"Less Rule Is Good": Antigovernment Discourse

The combined sense of being under assault and being abandoned by the larger society was felt at both the local and the national level for many old-timers, frequently linked to antigovernment sentiments. This antigovernment anger discourse did not necessarily arise organically from the rural experience, although it rang true for them. Most old-timers adopted this discourse after being exposed to some version of it through national media outlets. During the time period of this field work, right-wing news sources both centrist and extreme focused on the theme of government as enemy force and combatant—a notion that resonated intensely with old-timers around the valley. In many of their homes, cable news played on continual loop in the background, with commentators repeatedly stressing this theme. I knew numerous locals who rarely turned off *Fox News*, and I conducted multiple interviews in which it remained on screen, playing muted as we spoke. When I asked these old-timers to describe the sources of their political understandings, it was not local sources but national outlets like this that they named. They discussed turning to *Fox News*, *The Drudge Report*, *Breitbart News*, and Rush Limbaugh, as well as more centrist sources like *CNN*, *Yahoo News*, and the *Associated Press*.

Many old-timers' understandings of "the government" were ambiguous, encompassing multiple federal and state agencies and different types of laws, regulations, and legislation. Often their grasps of the complexities of particular legislative agendas and agency mandates were also vague. Nonetheless, the antigovernment rhetoric resonated for many. In addition to aligning with their sense of abandonment, it echoed their personal trials, including individual experiences with seemingly capricious agencies, institutions, and agendas that had negatively impacted their lives and livelihoods. Theirs was not a false consciousness, nor a "deep story" that a researcher needed to explicate for them, but raw frustration with specific agencies and interventions that impacted their daily existence and way of life.[22] These concerns were often at the top of their consciousness, arising unsolicited throughout their interviews and casual interactions.

Antigovernment themes were particularly salient for those with long histories in logging, farming, or ranching, occupations that had been directly affected by changes in federal, state, or local resource management policies.[23] The antigovernment discourse, steeped as it was in anger and fear, gave many old-timers a concrete, albeit behemoth and unstoppable, enemy upon which to focus their resentment and blame for the different struggles and losses they had endured. In the rural-wildland interface, government agencies including the US Forest Service, the Bureau of Land Management, and the Department of Ecology play important roles, structuring many people's work lives and daily practices. Thus many old-timers connected antigovernment sentiments to concrete experiences of vulnerability or abuse at the hands of these larger entities. Often this sense

of powerlessness was exacerbated by the feeling that those same agencies gave back little to the community, abandoning local populations while
continually imposing new obstacles.

Fifty-seven-year-old Greg Rossi had worked for the Forest Service for
decades, which informed his sense of the government as bloated and serving the interests of outsiders rather than the local population. "Logging
created a monster," he told me, which remained in place even after the
industry collapsed in the region: "It's like monsters. They have total control of the money, of everything, and they're gonna keep it that way, protecting their jobs and their lifestyle and the way they do it, where they're
destroying it." He explained that despite this control, the Forest Service
provided little local employment or other benefits:

> Now the government, the Forest Service, is an upside-down pyramid. Very
> few people are on the ground, and they're all up on top, and they're all the
> high-paid, GS9, 10, 12.[24] They're suckin' a lot of money and doin' very little.
> A lot of 'em have jobs that just—the jobs shouldn't be there. You don't need
> that many people, and they do things to justify their own job.

Greg's feeling of having been betrayed by an agency that once was necessary, but had become oppressive in the wake of logging's collapse, influenced his understanding of the government more generally as failing the
people of Paradise Valley.

> I'm just a big advocate, I'm huge on freedom. Everyone can live their dreams.
> And when I see the government, just less rule is good. You need government.
> You need rules. I like the environment and stuff like that. And so I'm just
> worried about the government dictating. Like, here, we don't do anything
> for the public. I've got friends that I'm more right, they're more left, hard
> left, but we all agree that we do nothing. I think the Forest Service needs to
> do a lot for the local communities, at least try. And no one's doing anything
> for the local economy.

Fifty-four-year-old construction worker Donald Barnett, whose favorite news sources included *Fox News*, Rush Limbaugh, and the *Drudge
Report*, felt similarly about the potential dangers the government posed.
Donald connected his belief that the government served mainly outside
interests directly to his time in the agricultural industry. His experiences
in the 1980s with government buyouts for small farmers had convinced

him that the government served only large corporate interests.[25] He told me that politicians were "all a bunch of criminals," and explained that these early experiences informed this view: "I had over 350 clients that I was servicing, and in a year [after the buyout] I lost a third of my clients. And I just—that kinda pissed me off. I just added it to my antigovernment sentiments." Donald translated this anger at the government into political beliefs focusing on individual freedom and self-protection.[26] He said:

> I think my basic philosophy is that people should be able to do whatever they want so long as they're not hurtin' somebody else, unless that person is a sadomasochist and they're into that kind of thing. I think the government has too much control. Politically my belief is that the power structure starts with the individual and goes to the county to the state to the federal level. It's not now. It's top-down...
>
> Gun control, the right to keep and bear arms, I don't see where it's that nuclear because of the potential that we have to protect ourselves against the tyranny of government. That's a touchy issue for some of my more liberal friends. "As long as the police have guns." Yeah, if you could trust the government, that would be great, in an ideal world, but I don't, and I'll keep my guns, thanks.

Many old-timers similarly found federal rules and regulations capricious, serving large and outside interests while oppressing and impoverishing small-scale operations. Fred and Doris Foster, a Social Security–dependent couple in their eighties, had struggled for years to make a living farming and ranching on their marginal plot of land. I met them at their home, a 1960s-era ranch house with its exterior a mixture of peeling and missing siding, including a large section that was just exposed plywood and tarpaper flapping in the wind. Despite having lived there for more than forty years, Fred told me that the house "still isn't completely finished." The couple, who said that *Fox News* was "about the only thing we watch," blamed the government for most of their difficulties. Fred told me: "You can't do anything without having an inspection or somebody telling you what you can do and what you can't do." Doris explained that over the years government regulations and interventions had repeatedly challenged their livelihood:

We had to get out of the orchard industry because [of] regulations that we couldn't keep up with the changing of what the government wanted to do, because the insurance company made stipulations that the people that were doing the agriculture work, made it almost impossible for a person that's trying to make a living and keep up with what they wanted, like wearing glasses to go up a tree or a ladder. It was something that—it was ridiculous, but it was the law.

While changing labor regulations made it difficult for the Fosters to continue orcharding, they also struggled with changing rules regarding irrigation. Fred explained:

The Department of Ecology wanted us out of the river because the water that we were using, they felt that there wasn't enough water left in there for the fish. . . . And that's the reason why we are now out of a well, because we agreed to go out of the river, and they would drill us a well and put us in a pivot system, and now the pivot system costs too much money to operate.[27] PUD [Public Utilities District]. So you are getting to see why we are so bitter.

Fred and Doris, like a number of other farmers and ranchers in the area, experienced the government as an outside force whose whims were unpredictable and seldom responsive to their needs. The installation of a well and pivot irrigation system, while an expensive upgrade to their farm, was useless to the Fosters because they couldn't afford to operate it.[28] Thus, rather than viewing its installation as the subsidized investment that it was, the Fosters experienced it as an invasive intervention that destroyed the profitability of their farm.[29] In addition to their struggles in navigating regulations and keeping their farm afloat, the Fosters, like Allison and Chad Lloyd, felt that they were overlooked when in need of help. With regard to their Social Security checks, they explained that because of the low income they had made throughout their lives, the amount they received now was insufficient: "When you retire on a small amount of money, the amount you paid into after so many years, it doesn't keep up with the expense. But the people that probably get, oh, retirement and Social Security, they probably get about $2,000 to $3,000 a month. But not us . . . Maybe $700." Beyond this meager amount, they received little additional help from a government that they saw as mostly hostile to their needs:

DORIS: We can't get food stamps.

FRED: We don't qualify.... Because we own our own place.

Q: *Too much value in the property here?*

FRED: There you go. Government.

Fred returned to the theme of government as enemy throughout his interview. "See," he told me, "I am a bitter guy." In their failures to adequately address or respond to the pressures faced by small-scale farmers and ranchers, government agencies like the Department of Labor and the Department of Ecology became the enemy of old-timers like the Fosters. Unable to navigate increasingly complex bureaucracies, agricultural practices, and regulations, the Fosters found themselves fighting and consistently losing symbolic battles against poorly defined and faceless foes.

Ranchers and farmers often faced overwhelming challenges related to changing regulations. In addition to labor laws and water regulations, grazing permits were a major source of frustration for a number of old-timers in the cattle industry, many of whom complained at length about the decrease in public land available to them.[30] Barbara Phillips, a seventy-year-old rancher, had struggled for years with permit issues. "Here in this valley," she said, "there's a lot of—not a lot, there are a few, small, family-farm ranches. And they have a real hard go in my opinion." Her complaints were numerous, from restrictive regulations to being harassed by government agencies. She described fighting with the Fish and Wildlife Agency over grazing rights to public lands, explaining that it failed to recognize that grazing was only detrimental to ecosystems when cows were fenced in too tightly.

> And I think that they don't really—in these plans, they have attorneys writing these things up, and attorneys answering why you shouldn't graze, but they don't address animal health or biosecurity or things that are important.... They kind of harassed us and it's unbelievable. Really, I wouldn't have believed it, what they did.... We had to sell a lot of cows because we just had our private land to graze them on.

Keeping a cattle farm afloat in an era of shrinking public grazing lands was a difficult endeavor for the Phillips family, despite having a large amount of quality land. Barbara described a constant struggle and sense that something had been stolen from them:

Well, you could be more financially—it would be better if they didn't take away a grazing permit and you didn't get paid for your labor. Which really isn't legal . . . If you are always defending yourself, and they are taking away, literally the fruits of your labor and saying you go out and do this and do that—and that is a big problem with those, in my opinion with these leases. You could have a state—some DNR [Department of Natural Resources] lease—and the lease would be twenty-eight pages long. It would be full of orders. You do this, and you do that. And it is ridiculous. That's not right. That's just ridiculous. It does not—it is not economically possible, to work and not have benefitted from your labor in terms of having it conscripted by agencies. To me, that is terrible.

Antigovernment rhetoric spoke to some of the most serious struggles that old-timers had faced in the changing social and economic landscape, where federal interventions and agency changes contributed substantially to the diminishing of their opportunities. As Paradise Valley became more densely settled, new pressures and needs for land and water required changes to existing regulations and uses in order to ensure conservation of increasingly scarce resources. But for those who had long seen these resources as infinite and shared openly by community members, such changes contributed to their experiences of loss and betrayal. As local priorities shifted from a resource extraction model to one of conservation and recreational use, older generations of Paradise Valley residents felt the squeeze. The sense of abandonment that accompanied their economic struggles and social marginalization within their home community was easily directed toward the government, which did little to respond to their concerns or address their most pressing needs.

This anger discourse appeared to be the modern corollary of the morally focused political discourses that I studied in the rural West ten years earlier.[31] Rather than focusing on issues like family values and morality as their main concerns, marginalized old-timers adopted the language of anger and fear, of attack by behemoth entities against which they were powerless. While the political outcomes were similar—in both time periods and settings the population voted mostly conservatively—I found the anger discourse to be significantly more pernicious. Rather than focusing on sources of pride and simple accomplishments as proof of your own or another's value, this newer discourse focused on powerlessness and victimhood, without providing any clear blueprint or hope for improvement.

It turned away from positive and achievable goals, letting go of chasing the American Dream, and focusing instead on how it had been stolen. In so doing, it provided structure and narrative to an extended experience of economic challenge, downward mobility, and status loss. This message was broadcast across national media and was carefully constructed to resonate with a generalized sense of loss, which has been the experience in many US communities including rural places like Paradise Valley. Longtime valley residents focused on the aspects of the discourse that were most meaningful to them, particularly those that provided explanations for the diminishing fortunes of western ranchers, loggers, and farmers.

Although in 2014–15 the anger discourse was focused mostly on "the government" as the enemy, this simmering rage could easily be turned against Americans themselves, particularly among those who felt marginalized in their home communities and saw themselves as victims.[32] At the time, concerns with issues like immigration were not the main issue in Paradise Valley, but the stage was already set. Donald Barnett voiced a preview of the racialized anger that would soon help carry the Trump administration into power, which combined with the antigovernment discourse and continued disdain for the "undeserving poor." As he explained:

> When I hear there's thirty thousand to forty thousand illegal aliens comin' across the Arizona border every month, I think of a football team and the quarterback keeps gettin' sacked. You've gotta protect the quarterback. If we're under such a terrorist threat, which, I think we probably will be here soon, why would you let that many people come across your border? That just doesn't make sense to me. I have nothing against the immigrants themselves, they're comin' over here tryin' to make their lives better, and most of—a lot of the people who are here don't want to work, really. They're on the government dole and they don't want to work. So they're comin' over here and they're fillin' in these jobs, and these people around here are complainin', "I don't want to work. I've gotta have 20 bucks an hour." So you're an unskilled laborer and you want $20 an hour. And ultimately they don't really want to work.

For old-timers this combination of understandings helped them to make sense of their current situations, the diminishing of their American Dreams while so many others seemed to flourish in the place they considered to be their home. Although they expressed frustration with newcomers and the changes they brought, many old-timers also directed their dissatisfaction at other old-timers who struggled more and at large and powerful enemies against which they were defenseless. The messages they received from mainstream and national media built upon American cultural concepts including freedom, independence, and white entitlement to the American Dream. They portrayed the Obama administration and Democratic Party as the agents of Big Government and adversarial to these principles. The anger discourse combined reification of American values with understandings of the government itself as threatening them, allowing Paradise Valley residents to connect their unique experiences of economic loss, status threat, structural change, and government intervention to specific political beliefs and voting outcomes.

The result for many old-timers was an internalized sense of anger and powerlessness with no concrete plan for addressing their concerns and no hope for help from either within or outside of their community. Their resentment seldom translated into concrete action items that helped them regain some sense of efficacy within their community, larger state, or nation. Instead, many old-timers continued to feel abandoned within their own community, having lost both their sense of being cared for by others and their hopes for a better future. They were left instead with bitterness about the ways in which the American Dream had been stolen by more powerful individuals and interests.[33]

UNDERSTANDING COMMUNITY AND INEQUALITY IN THE NEW RURAL AMERICA

In Paradise Valley, understandings of community both informed and were informed by political understandings and individuals' senses of efficacy. Newcomers generally framed their roles in the community as positive forces for social change, as good citizens who both cared about and took concrete—and frequently monetary—action to improve the community. Their actions often matched their larger beliefs in ways that corresponded to their understandings of what it means to be community-oriented. Their understandings of how "community" is done were heavily influenced by their experiences in urban settings, in which social and community concerns are often addressed at a distance and through the intervention of the nonprofit and social services sector. Newcomers contributed substantially to the development of this sector in Paradise Valley, which similarly facilitated their abilities to address the community's needs in tangible and positive ways.

What this form of community intervention seldom did, however, was provide direct and humanizing interaction across social boundaries. With the exception of programs that matched individuals in need directly with volunteers who helped them, most opportunities provided by the nonprofit sector enabled donors to have minimal to no interaction with the recipients of services. Thus charitable giving rarely translated into the creation of meaningful social interactions or relationships across the social divide. To the contrary, in many ways it contributed to the flourishing of class blindness that allowed even those newcomers who expressed serious concern about poverty and inequality to see themselves as part of the solution versus the problem and to blame poor, unemployed, and addicted individuals for their misfortunes. Newcomers' class blindness when it came to their own contributions toward old-timers' struggles, along with their judgment of these individuals as morally flawed "others," contributed to the community's deepening divide.

For old-timers the palpable sense that newcomers didn't care about them as individuals or families was often the outcome of this new form of community, in which socially minded people expressed concern through financial contributions or performance art, but nonetheless failed to get out of the car and help a neighbor in need. They described a sense that newcomers excluded them and judged them, and contrasted this with their own understandings of rural community, in which all members look out for each other, care about each other's concerns, and treat each other with casual friendliness and respect. In their frustration with the modern social landscape, they frequently overlooked the reality that even more homogenous and traditional rural communities tend to have their own social divides and outcasts, and they often spoke wistfully of a time before the tourism industry, when everyone supposedly took responsibility for one another and interacted regularly as friendly neighbors.[34]

At the same time, old-timers often failed at doing and being the kind of community that they idealized. Although many told stories of the ways in which they had come together in the wake of natural disasters like fires and floods, they frequently failed to create and sustain community cohesion on a daily basis. As much as they denounced judgment by newcomers, many engaged in similar processes of judgment themselves, either implicitly or explicitly separating themselves from those who were less fortunate, less hardworking, or less successful at avoiding self-destructive behaviors. Their judgments often mirrored those of newcomers as well as the common stereotypes of the poor that have long been perpetuated by politicians and pundits intent on dismantling the social safety net and deflecting blame for social problems.[35] They spoke in ways that made clear the boundaries between themselves and these supposedly immoral others and in so doing reinforced separations that played out in their daily lives, contributing to the isolation and vulnerability that further undermined their chances of achieving even a diminished version of the American Dream.

For old-timers the resulting experience of being unsupported and under attack helped to shape a worldview of fear, anger, and victimhood. They spoke of needing to protect themselves from outsiders and powerful interests, and of the frustration of not getting help when they needed it. Fueled by political rhetoric and the media, they lived in fear of each other as well as of "the government," in the form of institutions, agencies, and programs that had disappointed or caused them harm over the years. Without a sense of how to fight or influence these institutions, they were overwhelmed by powerlessness. They expressed anger at the government but also distrust of the democratic process and political machine. Their anger had few outlets and provided little sense of accomplishment, instead leading them into negative spirals with no resolution or hope for the future. Despite actions and declarations that exhibited and proclaimed their moral values and work ethics, they remained powerless to help each other or help themselves fight the external forces that waged war on their community, their economy, and their basic survival.

Paradise Valley's divide represents differences not just in social and economic resources but also in understandings of what community is and how community is done. Although itself a unique community experiencing a particular set of conditions and pressures, in other ways Paradise Valley is not very different from other rural communities or the United States as a whole. It is in many ways a microcosm of the nation, emblematic of larger divides. Across communities and across the country, polarization and inequality have facilitated class blindness that allows the more privileged to care about poverty and inequality in the abstract, without actually interacting with or including the poor in their social worlds, or exposing themselves directly to the types of concerns or pressures they face. Class blindness and the failure to connect structural concerns with individual outcomes allows the middle class to feel positively about their concern for the less fortunate, while simultaneously benefiting from the current power structure and separating themselves from struggling individuals, whom they blame for their own flaws and misfortunes.

For people who live in the nation's forgotten rural and exurban spaces and places, this abandonment and dismissal is profound and easily harnessed by leaders looking to rule by division and fear. Neither newcomers nor old-timers were bad people. Both groups were made up primarily of well-intentioned, hardworking individuals and families who desired to provide the best for their loved ones and feel supported by their communities. Both cared about others in their ways, and both wanted to feel cared for in return. But the gulfs between their lived experiences, struggles, perceptions, and abilities to survive and get ahead grew larger over time, despite sharing the space of a small, isolated valley. Their divisions and inabilities to find ways across them mirror those occurring across the United States as a whole, as we as a nation grow increasingly unequal. Throughout the United States, as in Paradise Valley, the past fifty years have been dominated by rising inequality and increasing divergence and polarization in worldviews, interests, experiences, and life chances.[36] These types of differences reinforce themselves over time, contributing to an ever-deepening divide and decreasing abilities to see one another as equally deserving of societal investment and achievement of the ever-more-elusive American Dream.

7 Crossing the Divide
and Reclaiming the Dream

> I think there is a perception—as far as the valley chang-
> ing—there is this perception that all of Paradise Valley is
> being brought up economically. And I think we are just see-
> ing more and more disparity. We are just getting further
> ends of the spectrum. There is no more middle.
>
> —Rachel Wilson, thirty-seven-year-old married, middle-
>   income stay-at-home mother

This book has explored the growth and persistence of social and economic inequality in a rural community, including its origins and the processes by which it is reproduced. Long-standing land-based industries gave way to amenity tourism and in-migration as the community's main economic drivers, producing both economic growth and new struggles. This progression is similar to trends occurring across the nation, as manufacturing and production are replaced with service-sector employment, which tends to be low-paid, insecure, and less than full-time. As has been found by previous scholars of rural tourism development, this type of amenity-led growth had many positive impacts but also a number of unintended results, including the division of the community into more-resourced newcomers and increasingly disadvantaged old-timers.[1] Differences in resources including income, wealth, human capital, social capital, and cultural capital reproduced themselves within a setting of limited opportunities, resulting in increasing inequality within what was once a more homogenous and working-class community.

As has occurred in other rural communities experiencing this type of development and growth, in Paradise Valley in-migration did not lead to mixing of new and old residents, and the boundaries between them instead grew hard and fast.[2] Rather than improving all prospects, the resources and rewards that newcomers brought failed to reach old-timers and instead contributed to the growth of inequality there. Multiple factors created and sustained inequality in Paradise Valley, with impacts across the social spectrum. On the one hand, newcomers pooled their resources in order to combat the community's lack of support, labor market options, and infrastructure, allowing them to make comfortable and satisfying lives there despite the many urban advantages they gave up. On the other hand, old-timers experienced a number of economic and survival struggles, and their dearth of real and symbolic resources meant they were much less able to navigate these same conditions. Their losses were often directly connected to in-migrants' gains, as both groups struggled to make a living in a situation of limited opportunities. Old-timers were systematically hindered in their attempts to get ahead by a combination of structural, cultural, and social factors that resulted in a thin and diminishing set of relationships and resources as well as decreasing access to jobs, housing, and civic opportunities.

This divide reproduced itself through multiple means, including the uneven distribution of social, cultural, and human capital between the two groups. Social structures and institutions played into this dynamic, including the lack of infrastructure for childcare and work-family balance as well as the unequal access to support and opportunities in the public schools. Newcomers used their real and symbolic resources to ensure that their own children were well prepared to get ahead in life, steadily providing them with human, cultural, and social capital that was not shared with old-timers' children. Like other middle-class parents combatting the menacing possibility of their children's failures to get ahead in an increasingly insecure world, newcomers provided their children with as many resources as possible, thereby subtly and overtly policing the boundaries of children's social and cultural worlds.[3]

While these processes contributed to unequal access to human, social, and cultural capital in Paradise Valley, moral capital was devalued in the valley, with diminishing returns for old-timers who made claims to it. Their attempts to build and manifest their morality through self-denial of aid and other performances of values and work ethics brought little payoff and little access to other benefits in the community. Through the continuing unequal access to real and symbolic forms of capital, the community's divide grew, as the two groups shared little in common. They lived separate lives with divergent goals and struggles, not knowing each other well enough to even understand one another's worldviews and motivations. Newcomers and old-timers came to conceive of each other in negative ways, including old-timers' frustration and resentment toward newcomers whom they believed were changing the valley and taking jobs, homes, and status away from its longtime residents. Meanwhile, newcomers often described old-timers as lazy, ignorant, drug- and alcohol-addicted, and responsible for their own economic misfortunes and disenfranchisement in the community.

There were a number of social impacts of the growing divide in this community, including the loss of cohesion and civility, a growth of social isolation for some, a failure to relate to and understand those on the opposite side of the divide, and growing blame and hostility against those who suffer the most. These types of moral judgements created boundaries for old-timers among themselves, permitting them to point to their own virtues in contrast to someone else's vices. These moral and social judgments are based in stereotypes of the rural working class as well as of the poor more generally in a nation that has for decades focused on blaming and punishing the poor for their poverty.[4] These judgments are also based in deep-seated class prejudices that are unconsciously held by many Americans, including those whose class blindness keeps them from seeing others' misfortunes as being directly tied to their own privilege.[5] Class blindness works through multiple mechanisms, including the failure to recognize the advantages that social class status provides and perpetuates; the assumption that the same chances are available to all; and the tendency to ascribes both one's own successes and others' failures to individual rather than structural or societal causes. This stance allows the privileged to avoid taking personal responsibility for the perpetuation of class inequality, while blaming disadvantaged groups for their own fates.

Although class blindness works in these ways in Paradise Valley, many newcomers did nonetheless recognize that a divide existed within the community and had real concerns regarding its damaging effects. A number connected this divide to larger national trends, including the growth of inequality on a national and even global scale. For many it was difficult to pinpoint how to address this issue, however, and despite recognizing it as a problem, they often did not fully grasp how they could become part of its solution. Newcomers and old-timers envisioned and enacted community differently from each other. Unlike the more rural old-timers, more urban-based newcomers generally expected that social problems could be solved through the intervening and impersonal structures of the nonprofit network and social safety net and felt that by giving money to charitable organizations they had done their part.

Yet despite Paradise Valley's extensive social service offerings, inequality festered and social problems persisted. Furthermore, both old-timers and newcomers described a divided social landscape in which neither group fully understood the motivations and intentions of the other, but with minimal interaction were able to assume the worst. Class blindness created the space for social boundaries between the two groups that allowed the advantaged to avoid putting a human face to the inequality that they knew was there. Avoiding its immediate manifestations allowed many to ignore, justify, and rationalize their privilege. Caring in the abstract and giving money to charitable middlemen allowed them to wash their hands of responsibility to make real changes to their local or national social and economic structures.

The impacts of these dynamics went beyond just a deepening divide, resulting in deeply embedded anger and frustration for old-timers, who saw their chances for achieving the American Dream slipping away but often could not pinpoint the exact cause or cure for their losses. They described a sense of being under attack and powerless against large and abstract forces. Their feelings of powerlessness and vulnerability helped to undermine social trust and cohesion at the local level and beyond, filtering up to their understandings of larger societal and political realms as well. These experiences of abandonment and assault by outside forces were easily harnessed by the growing anger discourse propagated by political and media interests to sustain the current structures of inequality, thus helping to perpetuate the cycle of incivility, division, and powerlessness. As subsequent events would evidence, this same anger discourse would help to propel into political power administrations that further focused on division, blame, and demonization of the nation's most vulnerable groups. Paradise Valley's experiences were in many ways a small-scale version of social, economic, and political trends occurring across the nation, in communities of all sizes, makeups, and locations.

INEQUALITY COME HOME

The dynamics I describe in Paradise Valley are not isolated to this isolated place; rather, they represent a small-scale version of the class divide, class blindness, loss, and anger that are currently afflicting the nation. The inequality described in this book is not unique to Paradise Valley, and it is not unique to rural America: it is an expansion of the growth of inequality throughout the United States, visible in large cities, small cities, and increasingly even its small towns and isolated places.[6] Inequality has grown significantly in the past half-century in the country, including growing disparities in income, wealth, opportunities, and outcomes.[7] Along with the unequal distribution of wealth and income, increasing numbers of Americans are losing access to upward mobility, a key component of the fading American Dream.[8] Although these trends have impacted a broad spectrum of Americans, they have affected those without college educations—those who once belonged to the working class—most severely.[9] Paradise Valley residents recognized the universality of their community's problems:

> I think we are a microcosm of that gap between the rich and poor that is happening all over the country.
> —Claire Woods, forty-two-year-old married, middle-income nonprofit consultant

> What I think is we really need to address the issues of the class divide and income inequality. I think it is a nationwide and worldwide problem. It is interesting to see it come home to this little rural community.
> —Lea Fern, fifty-nine-year-old divorced, poor artist

The US population is a nation of divides now, between white and minority, immigrant and native-born, college-educated and not, rural and urban, wealthy and poor, powerful and disenfranchised. Until recently, however, rural communities were seen as insulated from this trend to a degree, as they are often more homogenous and thus exhibit less diversity along many axes, including income and wealth.[10] The physical isolation of rural places does not fully insulate them from the larger problems of the nation, however, and rural communities throughout the United States are increasingly impacted by the growth in national inequality, including the importation of urban wealth and income into small towns with limited resources.[11] Rural and urban are not as distinct and removed from each other as they once were, sharing cultural references, media and information, and, increasingly, social problems across space and distance. The loss that Paradise Valley's old-timers expressed can be seen as a microcosm of that experienced by rural, working-class, and low-income populations across the United States.

Scholars have raised multiple concerns about the potential consequences of the growth of inequality in the United States. Sociologists Kathryn M. Neckerman and Florencia Torche have discussed the intergenerational reproduction of inequality through decreasing mobility opportunities and caution that this process can occur through social institutions including health care, schools, and the political process. They further warn of the potential "loss of social cohesion as the social worlds of rich and poor diverge."[12] Citing studies mostly focused on urban areas, Neckerman and Torche discuss issues such as the preference for associating with those most like ourselves, increasing residential segregation by economic status, and reductions in social capital.[13] They argue that these outcomes "are associated with rising income inequality and that levels of trust and civic participation are lower in areas with greater income inequality."[14] In Paradise Valley one can view these very processes as they unfold, undermining this small town's social institutions and relationships.

For this reason Paradise Valley is an important case study, illustrating not only the processes by which rural and working-class Americans are disenfranchised but more generally the processes by which inequality negatively impacts everyone. This is not simply a story of one rural population's division and loss; it should instead be read as a detailed exploration of how inequality is produced and reproduced and at what costs to our communities, our society, and our democracy. As two groups within one small town become more and more separated, divided, and polarized, they become increasingly unable to truly respond to one another's concerns. This divided community mirrors communities and regions across the nation, in which social class differences reproduce themselves through geographic, social, and cultural segregation, separating and insulating us from the daily routines and experiences as well as the larger goals, struggles, and joys of groups on the other side of the divide.

Although this book focuses on a rural community, it is not a story or a set of concerns that is limited to rural America. On the contrary, it is important to see Paradise Valley for what it is: a small-scale version of larger processes of inequality, resource hoarding, and disenfranchisement that are occurring across the nation. It is important to focus not on why rural Americans are angry, frustrated, or delusional, but rather on the processes by which inequality is maintained through mechanisms that create frustration, judgment, anger, and self-blame but not civic unrest or large-scale social change. The political realm has coopted these negative emotions to turn all of us against one another in ways that ultimately disempower and further disenfranchise the most vulnerable among us. It is important to see this book not as simply a story of rural America, because focusing just on what is wrong, misguided, or irrational about rural Americans misses the larger picture of a nation internally divided. Blaming rural and working-class Americans for their misfortunes and cultural understandings further contributes to class blindness, through erasing their dignity and humanity as well as ignoring middle-class and urban responsibility for creating, sustaining, and reinforcing social divisions and social segregation.

Neither is this book meant as an indictment of the middle class or the poor, either urban or rural. It is instead a call to both sides to recognize the toxic impacts of deepening inequality and the damage it does to our communities and our nation. As long as we see others as different from, less deserving than, and threatening to ourselves, we will continue to foster anger, judgment, and lack of empathy or concern.[15] We will be ever more vulnerable to the poisonous effects of inequality and disenfranchisement as well as to the politics of anger and blame.[16] Ultimately, everyone will be unable to access a fuller version of the American Dream, in which all citizens have the chance to live in comfort and prosperity and pursue their own goals and accomplishments through their own efforts and talents.

Given how inequality and social division lead to these negative outcomes, with both the privileged and the disadvantaged contributing to an increasingly divided society, how does a rural community—or the nation at large—divided on itself begin to heal its wounds? How do we build upon our best instincts, those for concern and help and sharing with others, in order to create a more equal society? Can it be done in a place in which disparity means that one group of people has so few resources and so little power while another group has so much of both and thus so much to lose? What might it look like to heal Paradise Valley's divide, and how would such efforts impact both its haves and its have-nots? Paradise Valley has long attempted to answer these questions for itself, and energetic locals across the class spectrum continue to put their talents, interests, and resources toward supporting the community as a whole as well as its most disadvantaged residents specifically. There nonetheless remains a need for more action and substantive changes in perspectives, behaviors, and the structure of our communities and larger economy to overcome class blindness, apathy, and anger, and (re)create communities and a nation in which we are united in our shared desires to flourish together and pursue our dreams.

MAKING A DIFFERENCE: EXEMPLARY EFFORTS FROM PARADISE VALLEY

> I'm not cynical on the ability of people to make a difference
> on the scale of this community. And that's the beauty of it.
> You don't need to, like, you know, change our foreign policy.
> But you can choose to live your life in a way that represents
> those things.
> —Shawn Murphy, forty-three-year-old divorced, low-income
>   carpenter

Although Paradise Valley evidenced some of the more destructive impacts of inequality, class blindness, and social boundaries and judgment, it also had a number of strengths that enabled it to effectively combat these dynamics and build a supportive community. Given its impressive array of both human and economic resources, Paradise Valley is well positioned to address many of its own social problems, including finding innovative ways to reestablish connection between social groups. Despite the social divide and difficulties in accessing each other's experiences across it, Paradise Valley's residents both old and new were often very generous and making real efforts to address the community's needs.

It is important to acknowledge some of the community's best efforts to both support its most vulnerable residents *and* to build community connections across its social divide. In their 2003 book *Better Together*, coauthors Robert D. Putnam and Lewis Feldstein argued that building social capital within communities "takes time and effort. For the most part it develops through extensive and time-consuming face-to-face conversation."[17] Help without connection can only go so far in improving lives and efficacy. Ultimately, Paradise Valley's disadvantaged residents need to be reintegrated into their home community in multiple ways that will allow them not just access to the very basic survival requirements—food, shelter, heat, and electricity—but also access to symbolic resources including social, cultural, and human capital that will empower them and provide access to a larger set of social and economic resources in turn. A number of local organizations and individuals make significant efforts to address ongoing needs in education, family support, and poverty alleviation, which are actively addressing not just economic strain but also social integration and the community's divide.

"Equity and Excellence for All":
Reducing Gaps in Education and Childcare

The Paradise Valley school system plays an important role in the reproduction and maintenance of inequality within the valley. Although public schools have the potential to be instruments of meritocracy, more often they are sorting mechanisms by which societal hierarchies are reproduced.[18] As chapter 5 illustrated, Paradise Valley has a long way to go in terms of addressing educational inequality. And while some of the school board's choices have been extremely controversial, it has also made important strides toward narrowing gaps and increasing inclusivity in some areas, including the "pay-to-play" fees that made sports, extracurricular activities, and even certain classes prohibitively expensive. In 2014 the superintendent of schools explained to me that he was aware of this issue and working to remedy the problem:

The concern it raised for me is we might have students that have a strong passion or a high interest in certain coursework that elect not to sign up for that coursework because they can't afford the course fees. And yet are too embarrassed to tell anybody that. So with that, one of our six strategic areas of focus is equity and excellence for all. So we have eliminated all course fees at Paradise Valley Junior High. And we had families that were hugging us at the start of the year as they came up prepared to write a check for something they really couldn't afford, but their child wanted to take ceramics or photography, or whatever it may be. We also eliminated all supply fees in grades K–6. Next year we expand that to eliminate all supply fees across the district. And then we start covering some of the enrichment fees.

The school district has continued to work on these issues, and prior to the start of the 2018 school year, it announced the following fees had been eliminated: all school supply and course fees, some testing fees, and many enrichment fees. In addition, the district had made significant reductions to pay-to-play fees. By the fall of 2019, pay-to-play fees were eliminated as well. While these fees are only one of the multiple ways in which inequality is reproduced through the schools, their reduction and elimination undoubtedly is a major help to many schoolchildren across the valley. Nonetheless, there is still work to be done on making all aspects of the educational experience equally accessible.

The school district has recognized the need for more access to prekindergarten education as well. It has supported a partnership between a local private school and several other nonprofit organizations in the valley to create year-round childcare and education opportunities for infants and toddlers. The families of children served by this collaboration are offered wrap-around services through Home Front, including parenting resources, health resources, and nutrition services and education, while the private school partner offers access to financial aid for parents who struggle to afford the fees, which begin at approximately $9 per hour. Importantly, the service is focused on including parents from a diverse range of economic and social statuses, including young and low-income parents who through it are exposed to new social networks for themselves and their children. Although this partnership serves only a small number of families, it provides a model for inclusivity in service provision that reaches out to parents across the social class divide.

Supporting All Families: Home Front's Ongoing Efforts

Home Front was one of several local organizations where I volunteered regularly during my time in Paradise Valley, allowing me to witness first-hand the delivery of their impressive array of services. The organization had a dedicated and hardworking staff made up mostly of newcomers with shorter tenures in the valley. The interactions I witnessed between staff and clients were generally focused on service provision and managing client expectations, but real connections between staff and clients were rarely forged. Leadership at the time expressed a desire to improve interaction between social groups and build community, and to make affordable access to cultural activities more available and less stigmatized. We discussed ideas such as providing free passes for their clients to attend fundraising events around the valley, where many of the area's most advantaged newcomers hobnobbed but whose entrance fees were mostly excessively expensive for the low-income community.

Since my time in Paradise Valley, Home Front has redoubled efforts to bridge the community divide and provide necessary services. This includes focusing more energy on exposing clients to social, educational, and cultural activities across the valley through multiple initiatives, including those just described. These efforts to bridge the social divide are small in comparison to the considerable number of services the organization provides, which include emergency funding for housing and heating; food and cooking classes; parent support groups; and an extensive array of family planning, health, mental health, and domestic abuse services. Nonetheless, these efforts represent an important recognition that connections between individuals of differing social strata can have vital impacts on improving community life across the divide. As researchers of social capital have found, such local interactions and personal contacts are necessary for creating trust relationships that are vital to building resilient and cohesive communities.[19] The lack of such connections results in exacerbation of suffering across multiple axes of social, civic, and economic life.

Distribution with Dignity: Angel Food's Efforts
toward Poverty Alleviation

Over my career I have done fieldwork at multiple food banks, both urban and rural, but I had never worked at one like Angel Food. The service operated out of a small storefront in Eagle Flat's main thoroughfare, and its cramped and chaotic space created a surprisingly comfortable atmosphere. Angel Food's umbrella organization was a nondenominational faith-based group whose stated mission included "honoring and respecting one another at difficult times in our lives." The food bank's promotional materials explained that the service focused on "getting to know your neighbor, [providing] a coffee shop atmosphere, tables and chairs and a free lunch." This sense of respect, community, and an open environment where interaction was encouraged were key to creating its unique climate. Angel Food was set up to minimize social distance between clients and staff, and maximize interaction. The staff consisted mainly of retired adults, both newcomers and old-timers, who understood that their mission went beyond providing food and included forging connections with clients.

The service had several unique aspects that worked toward this goal, including providing lunch to clients before food distribution began. Many regular clients—particularly those who were elderly, had extra time on their hands, or who needed special help—came in early to eat and "visit" with each other and with staff before receiving groceries for the week. No identification or proof of financial need was requested prior to being served lunch or receiving food; clients were only asked for their names. During food distribution they were individually brought into a private area, where they sat down one-on-one with a volunteer interviewer who asked them about themselves, their situations, and their food needs, and ultimately created an individualized shopping list of items that were available that day. If the interview uncovered other unmet needs, clients were referred to additional services. According to the food bank's director, the interview was a vital step toward "treating each client like a human being and taking time getting to know them, rather than being impersonal like other food banks."[20] It was crucial in giving the clients choice over their food decisions, simultaneously humanizing the encounter and empowering the individuals.

Distribution was similarly individualized and focused on humanizing clients, who were introduced by name to each volunteer who helped provide them with food. When finished, clients were offered help with carrying groceries to their cars or to their homes. The system was volunteer-heavy, capitalizing on the availability of civic-minded adults in Paradise

Valley, whose backgrounds spanned the social spectrum. It was one of the few charitable venues in which old-timers and newcomers appeared to be equally comfortable volunteering and in which old-timers regularly took on leadership roles and responsibilities. Angel Food's unique setup encouraged interaction and sharing while minimizing social distance between workers and clients. Its "café-like" atmosphere encouraged clients to interact with each other, and they frequently talked, laughed, hugged, and offered help to one another.[21]

The interviewer model increased social interaction and created personal investment in the client on the part of the staff, who came to understand the challenges individuals faced and got to know them and their needs. I noted numerous examples of volunteers praising the positive attributes of troubled clients, as well as going above and beyond necessary duties to help those in need. Staff regularly delivered food to drug-addicted and disabled clients who lacked transportation; called regular clients at home to check on them if they missed a week; and provided clients with extra food when they knew that they were in particularly difficult situations or had very large families. Volunteers were often consciously aware of social class issues and actively worked to avoid judging clients, at times explaining problems like drug addiction and substance abuse as reactions to earlier trauma and struggle.[22] Clients in turn repeatedly praised the service and staff for being nonjudgmental, describing them as caring, friendly, and like "family." For example:

> Oh, I love going there! . . . Yeah, I mean, it's like my secondary family almost.
> —Carl Young, seventy-two-year-old single, poor, Social Security–reliant

> I don't feel as if they're lookin' down, 'cause there's so many people there. Even if they don't need it, they usually go in there just for social. . . . It makes it seem—it doesn't make it seem like you're gettin' handouts.
> —Wendy Harris, thirty-seven-year-old married, low-income stay-at-home mother

Beyond simply the friendliness of the staff, clients were often consciously aware of the steps they took to minimize social boundaries and the degree to which they succeeded, as explained by regular client Kim Henderson:

> It's always been great from the first time I went in and I knew no one. They have always been kind. . . . I never feel shamed or less than. I have always

felt like part of. And it is funny, sometimes I will be sitting there waiting my turn, and people will go, don't you work here? No, I don't. I just came to get food today. Which is a compliment to those people who are working there that you can't really tell the line between who is helping and who is not—who is there to get the help, and who is giving the help. It's pretty cool.

The other organizations under Angel Food's umbrella operated with similar mandates and included home visits for the elderly and people with disabilities as well as food and gift services for the holiday season.[23] Although no single organization can provide everything a community needs, this one did more to address both poverty and the social divide than any other with which I worked. It provided an inspirational model for helping while building mutual respect and social connection. It alone could not heal the rift in this rapidly changing community, but Angel Food provided an important foundation as well as vital services.

These three examples exist alongside numerous others in Paradise Valley that aim to expand access in areas including housing, health care, transportation, and elder care. As all of these efforts illustrate, despite the deepening divide, Paradise Valley has many chances to craft creative solutions to its own problems. Endeavors like these demonstrate the importance of providing aid and forging connection while preserving dignity as well as building bridges across the social divide in different ways. Although differences in resources can result in unequal access to life chances, those same abundant resources can be harnessed in multiple ways to help improve prospects and outcomes in this and other communities experiencing similar challenges. The in-migration of well-resourced outsiders can have numerous potential benefits for communities beyond their financial contributions to local economies. They often bring new skill sets and ideas as well as openness to diverse viewpoints and populations that can mitigate the potential for rural communities to become closed societies.[24] These best practices illustrate the different ways in which communities can foster the connections that create space for understanding and empathy to flourish and for concern to become tied to real individuals, rather than just abstract ideals.

However, on their own such efforts will not succeed at healing Paradise Valley's or any other community's divide. Focused as nonprofits' efforts often are on providing direct services to those facing the greatest needs, they necessarily miss many members of a community who struggle in some ways but do not actively seek help due to cultural norms, individual pride, and/or failures of services to provide for those with less intense or immediate need. Nonprofits also exist in limited and bounded time and space, and too often the connections forged in service environments do not translate into ongoing relationships across other places, spaces, and situations. Despite all of these sincere efforts to help the less fortunate and to create social interaction in Paradise Valley, it was rare for volunteers and clients to socialize outside of the service spaces, and thus only limited social capital was built through these exchanges. While increasing both the interaction and comfort of newcomers and old-timers with one another is an important goal, alone it is insufficient to change what has become a long-term pattern of resource hoarding and social exclusion. Efforts like these do little to address broader structural issues, including larger-scale economic, social, and political trends. While each of these players and programs have contributed to improving lives in Paradise Valley to some degree, truly addressing social problems in this community or anywhere requires both grassroots efforts like these and macro-level changes to the US cultural, economic, and political systems.

BUILDING A FUTURE IN A DIVIDED COMMUNITY AND NATION

The United States is beset by multiple types and sources of division, with manifold origins. This book has focused on just one of those axes of inequality: social class. Investigating this issue in a setting of minimal other sources of division allowed me to highlight the deleterious impacts of social class divisions on access to resources and social and economic opportunities. This focus is not meant to minimize the impacts of other types of divisions, nor to suggest that class inequality is more important than inequality by race, ethnicity, gender, age, or sexual identity. Each one of these axes of division can have similarly destructive impacts on affected populations and communities, similarly enabling some groups' privilege and others' deprivation. Each of these is worthy of its own in-depth treatment, concern, and continuing efforts to combat it.

That said, from this book we can learn much about social class itself, the often ignored form of division in a nation in which most residents imagine themselves fitting somewhere in the middle of the distribution, rather than at its extremes.[25] Like other forms of division, when ignored and unchecked it can lead to numerous negative outcomes, including exclusion, dehumanization, frustration, and anger. Being born on the wrong side of the class divide results in systematic marginalization within multiple social institutions, and this book has explored this outcome with regard to only a few. Unequal access to housing, labor market opportunities, education, childcare, and the political realm are more than sufficient to produce unequal outcomes, and in so doing to reproduce the divide that created them. Addressing these divisions must occur through multiple means, including public policies that support all families and adults as well as through small-scale actions like the ones described in this chapter.

Although the book does not offer large-scale solutions to the problems facing the nation, its findings suggest that the future success of rural communities like Paradise Valley, as well as of the United States, must be addressed at the macro scale, along with action at the community level. Without economic policies that provide more equitably distributed access to income and wealth across the social class and occupational spectrum, we cannot hope to include all Americans in the dream of prosperity, security, and mobility.[26] If we continue to focus only on corporate profits and GDP over the lives and opportunities of individuals, we will continue to foster competitive economic environments in which desperation, anxiety, and fear divide us into groups too afraid of losing what little we have to share with those who have even less.[27] To change the current trajectory, it is necessary for all Americans to feel secure in their abilities to survive and thrive in their own versions of the dream, in which hard work provides its own material rewards, along with symbolic ones.

At the same time, for individuals there is still much room to improve our abilities to understand, care about, and interact with others whose life experiences, chances, and outcomes are different. Many who espouse ideologies of social justice and concern still need to come to deeper and more respectful understandings of those individuals who have been less fortunate in finding ways to navigate the current economic and social conditions. When working-class and rural populations fail to be won over by vague and patronizing sentiments of concern, and continue to reject lib-eral ideologies and politicians in favor of those promoting self-protection and "freedom," judging them as ignorant, unaware of their best interests, or simply delusional in their anger will only contribute to the nation's divide.[28] In order to address and heal it, those with power and resources must learn to respect and understand them and include them in the coun-try's prosperity. As long as middle-class, wealthy, urban, and educated liberals view working-class, low-income, rural, and less-educated popula-tions as expendable in the fight over scarce resources, the nation's increas-ingly disenfranchised groups will continue to see their political, cultural, and economic agendas as hostile and threatening.

It is in environments of disconnection and division that stereotypes, judgments, and selfishness flourish, and in moments of interaction, com-munication, and real connection that empathy and understanding grow. This is not to argue that the political and policy realms do not matter or do not shape our underlying realities. Inequality must also be addressed through national policies that support education, living wages, affordable housing, work/family balance, health, and income support for those who cannot work. But a better understanding of one another will allow for better-informed policies in multiple arenas, from the local to the national.

As this book has illustrated, despite good intentions and even sincere concern for social issues, individuals are often unaware of the unintended impacts of their personal choices, beliefs, and actions on others in their communities. Often those impacts can only be seen on the aggregate level and are not discernable to the individuals who help construct the pat-terns. Yet when multiple individuals with privilege and resources act in similar ways, they can in fact have negative repercussions for those who lack access to these same advantages. Knowing and understanding more resource-challenged individuals can help those with resources to better understand the effects of their behaviors and decisions on others in their own communities. It can also enable all of us to create more effective poli-cies, including antipoverty policies that focus not on punishing the poor for struggles to find work, housing, or work/family balance, but instead on addressing real needs for training, living wages and salaries, market interventions, and additional supports.

In addition, for individuals in poverty to know more people of privilege can help expose them to cultural experiences and institutional knowledge as well as help make them feel heard, understood, and empowered in ways that might make discourses of anger and frustration less appealing or intuitive. It is not enough to look across the divide and blame one another for our separate roles in creating it, or to focus on one another's shortcomings, whether they be perceived laziness, apathy, irrationality, or greed. The story of Paradise Valley is one that challenges all of us to get to know the neighbors that are least like us, to hear their stories and come to understand their challenges, pains, goals, and victories. It challenges us to recognize that our own gains may contribute to others' losses, and to work together toward a more inclusive society on both local and national scales. For in those moments of crossing the social divide and abandoning our class blindness, the hope for increased access to the American Dream still endures.

Epilogue

Amid the coronavirus pandemic, Paradise Valley faces new challenges, and the types of inequality described in this book are escalating. Although remote rural areas like Paradise Valley have been mostly spared the worst of the pandemic thus far, there nonetheless remains the potential for disastrous impacts should the virus begin to spread there, particularly given the lack of medical infrastructure and the high concentration of older adults who move to the region for retirement.[1] Beyond these concerns, early reports suggest that other social dynamics set in motion by the outbreak may further exacerbate the current trends in rural inequality. In the wake of the global pandemic, which in the United States began in earnest just a few hours west of Paradise Valley in Seattle, the pull of the rural idyll has grown even stronger. It will likely have results that permanently alter the nature and future trajectory of Paradise Valley and many places like it.

In the valley the pandemic unfolded in many of the same ways as it did elsewhere, beginning with shutdowns, job loss, and increased need. It meant instant unemployment across the valley, as small businesses— the only kind there ever were there—were heavily impacted. Angel Food reported a 40 percent increase in patrons immediately following Washington State's initial stay-at-home orders. Along with this increase in demand, the outbreak required changes to their delivery model including outdoor-only distribution and limits to congregation in groups, effectively putting the café-like atmosphere and interviewer model on hiatus. The ability to create community was undermined as social isolation intensified for all. Food insecurity rose for children as well, and the food bank went from supplying approximately 130 weekend food backpacks each week to more than 400, which now went out on busses for distribution to children across the valley. While in previous years, the program paused during the summer, in 2020 it continued all year.

By early May, with the summer tourist season rapidly approaching, small towns were unprepared for influxes of visitors, and across the West there was concern about tourism bringing the virus to rural communities that lacked the medical infrastructure to handle it.[2] Facebook pages representing Paradise Valley interests asked people to stay away. By early summer, however, the valley was still a relative safe haven from the coronavirus and was allowed to proceed into the state's reopening phases. Within a few weeks the local messages shifted to promoting safe recreation and mask-wearing, and the valley slowly, tentatively began to reopen. Restaurants and hotels commenced summer business, albeit at diminished capacity and with fewer employees. Visitors returned and the valley hummed back to life. While business was slower than usual in most areas of the local economy, one particular sector bucked the trend: real estate. Local realtors experienced an onslaught of prospective buyers and an intense shortage of available real estate to sell. Both finished homes and land without structures were selling faster than new listings became available. Homes and land were commonly selling for above the listed price and selling quickly. Prices were rising rapidly. The rush for rural real estate had begun.

Regardless of whom I asked about the housing trends, I received the same explanation for the inflamed real estate market: the coronavirus pandemic and COVID-19 fear inspired people to flee cities in search of safer places to live, or at least to retreat to. One local realtor explained her impressions of the situation:

> It looks to me like all of the people living in increasingly crowded coastal cities who have ever thought of having a second home in the valley, moving here, retiring here, etc. all of a sudden want to get the hell out of the city right now. It's like there is a frenzy to get away from the chaos toward a more

peaceful slower pace of life in a community where there is tons of open space but also coffee shops and decent restaurants and fun shopping.

I heard versions of this narrative from everyone I asked. I experienced it in my own rural hometown as well and heard about it from friends and family on the opposite coast. In the pandemic's aftermath rural housing markets across the nation heated up, as working from home became acceptable and commonplace, and people increasingly feared the crowded cities that had been the early epicenters.[3] The rural idyll called even more loudly as the pandemic clarified for many the virtues of rural peace, solitude, and safety.

It's unclear at this moment whether the rural real estate rush will be a long-term trend or a momentary blip in the otherwise long history of rural exodus. But at least in the short term, its impacts on Paradise Valley have worsened or may worsen many of the issues highlighted in this book. With slow business in local retail and service establishments, wages remain low and unemployment is high. The valley's service-sector workforce struggles even more than before the pandemic to afford local rents, which for many are now nearly equal to monthly incomes. Despite efforts to increase affordable housing in the valley, subsidized rentals are still scarce and have long waiting lists. Local service providers report an increase in doubling up and couch-surfing as poor and low-income individuals struggle to find shelter, and express concern about what the winter will bring.

Even those who are stably employed are struggling, as both rental and real estate sale inventories have shrunk to shocking lows while prices have skyrocketed. By midsummer the local electronic bulletin board was filled with posts from increasingly desperate residents looking for homes to rent as well as to buy. The housing insecure included a stably employed parent of three who pleaded: "I just really need to find something before winter hits and I know I'm not the only person looking, but I am once again reaching out in hopes that you or somebody might know of a place." It included a couple who were "born and raised" in the valley and hoping to buy a house before it was formally listed. They explained: "We all know just how competitive the housing market is around here, and we would love to find something before it hits the market and we have to compete with those looking for a second home here." Post after post offered prospective landlords assurances of jobs, good references, connections in the valley, and cautiousness with regard to the coronavirus. One post that ran repeatedly over multiple weeks even offered to improve a rundown rental:

> I am still looking for a cabin or small house to rent. Even if it needs repair and is a fixer-upper and you've never considered renting it before; I am a finish carpenter and can repair, refurbish and restore your place toward renting. It will provide you with an income property and a revenue gainer. And you will be providing housing in a still existing emergency housing shortage.... There has to be a place out there that is not being occupied; so if you have something to offer; or even a lead, please call me.

There are, of course, winners in the housing game—particularly those who can afford homes priced at more than $500,000, mostly coming from outside the valley. By most accounts the new waves of in-migrants are similar to those described in this book: wealthy, well-educated, professionals with liberal leanings and good intentions, who bring art, education, and charitable giving to the valley. The local newcomer population continues to care about the community and its vulnerable populations as well. At Angel Food they received donations of more than a thousand dollars in gift cards to local restaurants and businesses to share with their clients to combat food insecurity. However, when asked if the food bank clients were likely to patronize upscale restaurants to use the vouchers, staff expressed concern that they might feel uncomfortable and worry about things like what to wear and what to order. It is thus unclear whether these gift cards will really help feed the hungry versus help keep the local businesses afloat, although both goals are important and worthwhile.

The pandemic has provided many opportunities for the nation to pause and become more aware of the divides that plague us, particularly those based in race and ethnicity. It has stimulated a dialogue in which terms like "racial bias" and "white fragility" have become commonplace even in mostly white Paradise Valley. Although it has not yet become the catalyst for a similar reckoning with class blindness, I hope that it may still. In the meantime, however, in the valley and throughout the nation the pandemic exacerbates inequalities in income and wealth as well as unequal access to the most basic of human needs: food, health, shelter, and safety. As these problems grow, I fear that the qualities that have drawn generations of Americans to beautiful and remote rural places will be undermined, or perhaps worse, reserved only for the enjoyment of the most privileged.

Methods, Sample, and Local
Demographic Information

DATA COLLECTION AND ANALYSIS

Interviews were focused around several thematic areas, including history in and perceptions of the community and its changes; family history; work history; leisure; marriage, relationships, and family; religion and faith; political interests and voting behaviors; and demographics and background information. There was also completely unstructured time at the end of the interview for participants to discuss issues that were important to them. Interviews were digitally recorded (with participants' consent) and transcribed verbatim. Each interview transcript included detailed field notes and memos written generally within twenty-four hours of the interview to provide additional insight and observation. The final sample was 43 percent male and 57 percent female (n = 36 and 48, respectively). About 56 percent of participants (n = 47) were under the age of fifty, and 44 percent of participants (n = 37) had dependent children at home. The average number of years spent in the region was twenty-three. Based on self-reported income and the federal poverty guidelines, about 24 percent (n = 20) of the sample is classified as poor; 30 percent is low income (above the poverty line but less than 200 percent of it; n = 25); and

46 percent (n = 39) are classified as middle income (above 200 percent of the poverty line).

Interview transcripts and field notes were analyzed and coded for both anticipated and new themes that arose repeatedly throughout the interviews, using an Extended Case Method orientation, a reflexive methodology that positions the researcher in dialogue with existing theory and the perspectives and understandings of actors on the ground, "in order to extract the general from the unique, to move from the micro to the macro."[4] According to the sociologist Michael Burawoy, "Reflexive science sets out from a dialogue between us and them, between social scientists and the people we study.... It starts out from a stock of academic theory on the one side and existent folk theory or indigenous narratives on the other."[5] Thus, to practice this method, I allowed participants' own perspectives, interpretations, and boundaries to help guide my understanding, adjusting my own interpretations as I went and throughout the analysis process, while also testing my growing insight against existing theoretical understandings. The transcripts and field notes were coded and analyzed using NVivo software, which allows for the creation of multiple levels of coding and thus identification of themes in the data as well as variations within those themes. As I analyzed the data through these multiple stages of coding, I continued to check my understandings against those of participants and locals in the field, both through comparison against their interview narratives and through discussion with clients, coworkers, acquaintances, and friends across the income and class spectrum.

PARADISE VALLEY DEMOGRAPHICS AND ECONOMICS

As shown in Table A.1, despite some variation (due in part to the small population size and in part to development-based speculation that occurred in the late 1980s), employment in natural resource–based industries, construction, manufacturing, and retail have remained relatively steady or fallen between 1980 and 2010 in Paradise Valley's two most populous towns. Employment in the arts, entertainment, recreation, and accommodation and food services sector, however, has grown steadily during the time period, falling from 9.5 percent in 1980 to a low of 1.4

Table A.1   Employment by selected industry for Paradise Valley's two largest
               incorporated towns (%)

Industry	1980	1990	2000	2010–14
Agriculture, forest, fisheries, and mining	10.9	6.4	7.2	6.4
Construction	6.5	11.6	7.4	7.5
Manufacturing	20.7	10.3	2.7	6.4
Retail	17.2	25.3	13.0	10.5
Entertainment and recreation	9.5	1.4	24.7	30.8
Unemployment rate (all working age)	24.2	11.9	8.8	13.1

SOURCE: US Census Data for 1980, 1990, 2000 (Minnesota Population Center 2016); American Community Survey source for 2010–2014 (US Census Bureau 2016).

percent of employment in 1990, and then rising to nearly 25 percent in 2000 and close to 31 percent by 2010.[6] In 2010 this tourism-focused sector employed as many workers as did the other four categories combined. At the same time, between 2000 and 2010 Paradise Valley's unemployment rate rose considerably after falling in the previous decades, reflecting both the impact of the Great Recession and the instability inherent in heavy reliance on this sector for local employment.[7]

Due to these employment factors, as well as other demographic and labor market shifts as explained in chapters 2, 3, and 4, Paradise Valley was disadvantaged compared to Washington State as a whole. As shown in Table A.2, Paradise Valley's median income was close to $20,000 lower than the state's, with lower labor force participation, resulting in significantly higher poverty rates for both children and all individuals. Meanwhile, as is common in rural communities, despite higher poverty, Paradise Valley residents were less likely to receive aid in the forms of SSI, public assistance income (GA and TANF), and food stamps (SNAP) than in Washington as a whole. The one form of aid that was more common in Paradise Valley than in Washington State was public health insurance, resulting in a smaller percentage of Paradise Valley residents going without coverage.

Despite the economic and demographic shifts, Paradise Valley has

Table A.2   Poverty and aid in Paradise Valley's two largest towns and Washington State, 2015

Indicator	Paradise Valley	Washington State
Median household income	$41,884	$61,062
Not in labor force	43.8%	35.6%
Poverty, all people	18.3%	13.3%
Poverty, under 18 years	30.1%	17.5%
Supplemental Security Income (SSI)	3.6%	4.8%
Cash public assistance income	2.9%	3.9%
Food stamp/SNAP benefits in the past 12 months	13.0%	14.3%
Public health insurance coverage	43.9%	30.9%
No health insurance coverage	10.6%	11.4%

SOURCE: US Census Bureau 2015.

Table A.3   Racial breakdown for Paradise Valley's two largest incorporated towns (%)

Race	2000	2010	2015
White	96.7	95.4	94.1
Black	0.1	0.3	1.5
American Indian/Alaska Native	0.7	0.8	2.5
Asian	0.5	0.5	0.7
Native Hawaiian	0.0	0.2	0.2
Biracial	1.5	2.2	2.6
Hispanic	2.8	3.6	8.6

SOURCE: US Census Bureau 2012, 2016.
Note: Numbers do not sum to 100 percent because of the ways in which the US Census counts race, which allow for multiple racial identifications as well as defining "Hispanic" as a separate category.

remained racially and ethnically quite homogenous. As shown in Table A.3, although racial diversity is growing, the area is still close to 95 percent white, a figure that has changed little since 2000. Native American populations were the main residents of the region throughout the nineteenth century but were almost entirely relocated to reservation lands further east between this time period and the first half of the twentieth century, when gold and silver miners first began staking claims to the region. Currently the area's largest communities do include a small Hispanic population, which nonetheless still makes up less than 10 percent of the local population. This remains in stark contrast to nearby nonmountain communities in Eastern Washington's prime orchard and fruit packing regions, which are heavily Hispanic.[8] The combination of Paradise Valley's high housing costs and its lack of agricultural employment have contributed to its isolation from these larger state trends.

The Newcomer/Old-Timer
Distinction

Table B.1 categorizes the in-depth interview participants in this research (by pseudonym) according to the newcomer/old-timer typology, illustrating the multiple facets of these terms in order to clarify the degree to which each individual exemplifies the newcomer or old-timer position within the community.

Table B.1   Newcomer/Old-Timer Classification

Pseudonym	Years in Paradise Valley: *N < 20; O >= 20	Income: N = middle-income; O <= low-income	Education: N >= BA; O < BA	Politics: N = liberal; O = conservative	Culture: N = high; O = low	Category
Allen, Bobby	N	O	O	**	O	old-timer
Baker, Carrie	N	O	O	O	N	old-timer
Banks, Lisa	N	N	O	N	N	newcomer
Barnett, Donald	O	O	O	O	O	old-timer
Bowden, Andrew	N	N	N	N	N	newcomer
Boyle, Ryan	O	O	O	**	O	old-timer
Brooks, Frank	N	N	N	N	N	newcomer
Brunet, Max	N	N	N	**	N	newcomer
Carpenter, Penny	O	O	O	N	N	old-timer
Carter, Janice	N	O	N	**	O	old-timer
Chambers, Maggie	O	O	O	O	O	old-timer
Clark, Louise	N	N	O	O	N	newcomer
Clark, Roger	N	O	N	O	N	newcomer
Conner, Tilda	O	O	O	**	O	old-timer
Cook, Toby	O	N	N	N	N	newcomer
Cooper, Ruth	O	O	N	**	O	old-timer
Cox, Donna	N	N	N	N	N	newcomer
Crawford, Martha	O	N	O	N	O	old-timer
Daniels, Caleb	O	O	O	**	O	old-timer
Douglas, Tracy	N	N	N	N	N	newcomer

Edwards, Marilyn	O	O	**	O	old-timer
Engle, Moira	N	O	**	O	old-timer
Farley, Amy	O	O	**	O	old-timer
Farley, Emmet	O	O	N	O	old-timer
Fern, Lea	N	N	N	N	newcomer
Ferrer, Maya	N	O	N	N	newcomer
Foster, Doris	O	O	O	O	old-timer
Foster, Fred	O	O	O	O	old-timer
Gilbert, Brooke	N	N	N	N	newcomer
Girard, Kristine	O	N	N	N	newcomer
Gough, Nadine	O	N	N	N	newcomer
Graham, Katrina	N	N	O	N	newcomer
Graham, Matt	N	N	O	N	newcomer
Griffin, Sabena	O	O	N	N	newcomer
Hammond, Jody	N	O	O	O	old-timer
Harris, Wendy	O	O	**	O	old-timer
Henderson, Kim	N	O	**	O	old-timer
Hill, Emily	O	N	N	N	newcomer
Hill, Jason	O	N	**	N	newcomer***
Hobson, Asa	O	O	N	O	old-timer
Jenkins, Howard	O	N	N	N	newcomer
Kelly, Jim	N	N	N	N	newcomer
Larson, Edna	O	O	O	O	old-timer
Lloyd, Allison	N	O	O	O	old-timer
Lloyd, Chad	N	O	O	O	old-timer
Long, Julie	O	N	N	O	old-timer

(continued)

Table B.1   Newcomer/Old-Timer Classification (continued)

Pseudonym	Years in Paradise Valley: *N < 20; O >= 20	Income: N = middle-income; O <= low-income	Education: N >= BA; O < BA	Politics: N = liberal; O = conservative	Culture: N = high; O = low	Category
Lowry, Hannah	N	N	N	N	N	newcomer
Martin, Kevin	N	O	O	N	N	newcomer
Mendez, Hope	N	O	N	N	N	newcomer
Miller, Beth	N	O	N	N	N	newcomer
Mitchell, Lillian	O	N	O	O	O	old-timer
Morris, Joyce	O	O	O	**	O	old-timer
Murphy, Shawn	N	N	N	N	N	newcomer
Nelson, Irene	O	N	O	N	O	old-timer
Parker, Beverly	N	O	O	**	O	old-timer
Patterson, Audrey	O	O	O	**	O	old-timer
Perry, Walter	O	N	N	N	N	newcomer
Phillips, Barbara	O	O	O	O	O	old-timer
Pinter, Adam	N	O	O	N	N	newcomer
Poole, Kate	N	N	N	N	N	newcomer
Reed, Aspen	N	O	N	**	N	newcomer
Rhodes, Pam	O	O	O	N	O	old-timer
Roberts, Owen	O	O	O	O	O	old-timer
Ross, Scott	O	O	N	**	N	old-newcomer
Rossi, Greg	O	N	O	O	O	old-timer
Setzer, Maria	N	O	N	N	N	newcomer

Silver, Sharon	N	N	N	N	newcomer
Stevens, Phillip	O	N	N	N	newcomer
Stewart, Molly	N	N	N	N	newcomer
Stewart, Todd	O	N	N	N	newcomer
Tate, Marc	N	N	O	O	old-timer
Thompson, Adeline	O	O	**	O	old-timer
Thompson, Wes	O	O	**	O	old-timer
Turner, William	N	N	N	N	newcomer
Watson, Roy	O	O	N	N	newcomer
Wheeler, Jessica	O	O	O	O	old-timer
Wicker, Megan	N	O	**	O	old-timer
Wilburn, Anya	N	N	N	N	newcomer
Williams, Peter	N	N	N	N	newcomer
Wilson, Rachel	N	N	N	N	newcomer
Wolfe, Gary	O	N	N	N	newcomer
Woods, Claire	N	N	N	N	newcomer
Wright, Dennis	N	N	N	N	newcomer
Young, Carl	N	O	N	O	newcomer

SOURCE: Author's calculations.

Notes: * = years in Paradise Valley counted from time as full-time resident, minus time spent living permanently elsewhere. ** = no political preference expressed. *** = this college-bound eighteen-year-old was categorized as O under time in Paradise Valley, despite having lived there for fewer than twenty years, as he had spent his entire life there to date. He was also categorized as having higher educational attainment, although he had not yet earned his college degree. He had already been accepted into an elite private college and was very directed toward specific educational goals.

Notes

PROLOGUE

1. See, for example, Crowe 2006; Deller 2010; Hamilton et al. 2008; Krannich and Petrzelka 2003; McGranahan 1999; and Reeder and Brown 2005.

CHAPTER 1. RURAL DEINDUSTRIALIZATION,
DECLINE, AND REBIRTH

1. All names in this book, including those of people, places, organizations, and institutions, are pseudonyms to protect the anonymity of participants and the field site. Only the state name remains unchanged. In some cases, identifying details have been changed to further protect participants' privacy, including names of people and places in quotes as well as details of participants' families and employment.

2. Halfacree 1995; Howarth 1995; Shucksmith 2018; Wuthnow 2015; Yarwood 2005.

3. Shucksmith 2018:163.

4. Howarth 1995; Shucksmith 2018.

5. Case and Deaton 2017; McCoy 2017; Monnat and Brown 2017; Porter 2018; Silva 2019; Wuthnow 2018.

6. Hacker, Rehm, and Schlesinger 2010; Piketty and Saez 2014.

7. Freudenburg 1992; Lorah and Southwick 2003.

8. Jensen and Jensen 2011; Lichter and Graefe 2011; Sherman 2014.

9. Freudenburg, Wilson, and O'Leary 1998; Hamilton et al. 2008; Sherman 2009b, 2014; Smith and Tickamyer 2011.

10. Brown and Schafft 2019; Hamilton et al. 2008; Lichter and Graefe 2011; Thiede and Slack 2017.

11. Biddle and Mette 2017; Carr and Kefalas 2009; Koricich, Chen, and Hughes 2018; Sherman and Sage 2011.

12. The term "feminized" refers to work and occupations that tend to be dominated by women and often stigmatized as "women's work" that is inappropriate and/or emasculating for men. Brown and Schafft 2019; Nelson and Smith 1999; Sherman 2014; Smith and Tickamyer 2011.

13. Mattingly, Smith, and Bean 2011; Sherman 2009b, 2014; Smith 2011, 2017.

14. Grusky, Western, and Wimer 2011a; Hout, Levanon, and Cumberworth 2011; Parker, Kusmin, and Marre 2010.

15. Hamilton et al. 2008; Wuthnow 2018.

16. Jensen and Ely 2017; Kusmin 2014; Lichter and Schafft 2016; Thiede and Slack 2017.

17. Schafft et al. 2018; Thiede and Slack 2017.

18. Judt 2011.

19. Autor 2019; Telford 2019; U.S. Census Bureau 2019.

20. Jensen and Jensen 2011; Lichter and Graefe 2011; Sherman 2014.

21. Jensen and Ely 2017; Wuthnow 2018.

22. Ashwood 2018; Cramer 2016; Hochschild 2016; Wuthnow 2018.

23. Krannich and Petrzelka 2003.

24. Carr and Kefalas 2009; Crowe 2006; Deller 2010; Hamilton et al. 2008; Hunter, Boardman, and Onge 2005; McGranahan 1999; Reeder and Brown 2005; Ulrich-Schad, Henly, and Safford 2013.

25. Armstrong and Stedman 2013; Brehm, Eisenhauer, and Krannich 2004; Hunter, Boardman, and Onge 2005; Jennings and Krannich 2013; Jones et al. 2003; Krannich and Petrzelka 2003; Lichter and Brown 2011; Reeder and Brown 2005; Sherman 2018; Smith and Krannich 2000; Stedman 2006; Ulrich-Schad and Qin 2018.

26. The term "working class" has many meanings to many people. It is often associated with specific occupations, including a number of manual labor and factory jobs. However, as the nature of the labor market has shifted and such jobs are increasingly scarce, the common understanding of "working class" focuses more on power within the workplace and degree of education required. Zweig (2007:11) characterizes working-class jobs thusly: "Most jobs share a basic powerlessness in relation to the authority of the owner and the owner's representatives who are there to supervise and control the workforce." In the case of Paradise Valley, the

term "working class" refers to a group of people with generally less than college education, whose employment history includes manual labor and/or service-sector jobs.

27. On gentrification, see Ghose 2004; Hines 2010; Nelson, Oberg, and Nelson 2010; Pilgeram 2019; Thompson, Johnson, and Hanes 2016. On social and cultural clash, see Armstrong and Stedman 2013; Fortmann and Kusel 1990; Lichter and Brown 2011; Smith and Krannich 2000; Ulrich-Schad and Qin 2018. On better resourced in-migrants, see Lichter and Brown 2011; Ulrich-Schad 2018.

28. Conley 1999; Oliver and Shapiro 2006; Spilerman 2000.

29. Collins 2008.

30. Bourdieu 1984; Lamont and Fournier 1992; Lamont and Molnar 2002.

31. Lamont et al. 2016.

32. Bourdieu 1984; Lamont 2000; Lamont and Fournier 1992; Schwalbe et al. 2000.

33. McDermott and Samson 2005; Shirley 2010; Wray 2006.

34. Lamont 2000; Prasad, Hoffman, and Bezila 2016; Sherman 2009b.

35. Bonilla-Silva 2009; McDermott and Samson 2005; Schwalbe et al. 2000; Shirley 2010; Williams 2017.

36. Lamont et al. 2016; Williams 2010, 2012.

37. Bourdieu 1986.

38. Bourdieu 1986; Lareau 2003; Putnam 2001.

39. Duncan 1999; Flora and Flora 2013; Whitley 2013.

40. Bourdieu 1977; Lamont 1992; Schwalbe et al. 2000.

41. Smith 2010; Woodward 2013.

42. Schwalbe et al. 2000.

43. Becker 2009; Coleman 1988.

44. Carr and Kefalas 2009; Corbett 2007; Petrin, Schafft, and Meece 2014; Sherman and Sage 2011.

45. Regarding the notion that morality may not always become a tradeable form of symbolic capital, see Lamont 1992, 2000. Sherman 2009b:6.

46. Sherman 2006, 2009b; Sherman and Sage 2011; Whitley 2013.

47. Curran 2016; Gilbert 2014; Lichter and Ziliak 2017; Morris and Western 1999; Piketty and Saez 2014.

48. Bonilla-Silva 2009; Gallagher 2003; Hartmann et al. 2017.

49. Using an Extended Case Method approach, see Burawoy 1998.

50. Field Notes, October 13, 2014; November 30, 2014; December 17, 2014; January 16, 2015.

51. Field Notes, June 25, 2015.

52. Burawoy 1998.

CHAPTER 2. CHANGING TIMES IN PARADISE

1. Grusky, Western, and Wimer 2011b.

2. Hamilton et al. 2008; Tickamyer, Sherman, and Warlick 2017; Wuthnow 2015.

3. Dolsak and Prakash 2018.

4. Clark 2017; Yardley 2011.

5. See Appendix A for more detail on local employment trends.

6. Freudenburg, Wilson, and O'Leary 1998.

7. Recent estimates find that more than 50 percent of all homes in the valley are not primary residences and are occupied only part-time.

8. See Appendix A for more information on the racial makeup of Paradise Valley.

9. Field Notes, September 9, 2014.

10. Field Notes, September 10, 2014.

11. The numbers are as follows: sports and recreation (n = 15); community building and support (n = 14); education (n = 10); conservation and the environment (n = 10); the arts (n = 8); safety and rescue (n = 6); poverty and social services (n = 6); and politics (n = 2).

12. On cultural capital, see Bourdieu 1977; Lamont 1992.

13. This categorization includes anyone with household income more than 200 percent of the poverty line, thus including a number of very high-income individuals. Based on self-reported income and the federal poverty guidelines, about 24 percent (n = 20) of the sample is classified as poor; 30 percent is low-income (above the poverty line but less than 200 percent of it; n = 25); and 46 percent (n = 39) are classified as middle-income (above 200 percent of the poverty line).

14. In Washington State, 32.9 percent of residents have a bachelor's degree or higher (US Census Bureau 2015).

15. Five of those old-timers (13 percent) had issues with methamphetamine use in particular; no newcomer discussed current or past methamphetamine usage. However, though rarely discussed openly in interviews, use of marijuana was known to be relatively common among both groups. By 2014 marijuana was legal in Washington State for recreational use.

16. Most of these respondents were not enrolled members of federally recognized tribes.

17. See Sherman (2009b) for an in-depth discussion of these issues.

18. Equal numbers, just three old-timers and three newcomers, brought up racial justice concerns as among their political interests.

19. Field Notes, December 4, 2014.

20. Bonilla-Silva 2009: 3–4. He goes on to describe "color-blind racism" as aiding "in the maintenance of white privilege without fanfare, without naming those who it subjects and those who it rewards."

21. Several white newcomers had adopted children of either mixed or minority race.

22. SSI is a federal program for low-income people with disabilities.

23. Field Notes, April 26, 2015.

24. Field Notes, October 30, 2014.

25. Field Notes, August 26, 2014.

26. Field Notes, October 1, 2014.

27. Leif Jensen, Ann Tickamyer, and Tim Slack (2019: 283) have found that subsistence activities of this sort are more prevalent in rural than urban areas, and that "rural households appear more likely to say informal work is critical for economic survival." They argue that this type of work is inherently social in nature.

28. Hamilton et al. 2008; Jensen, McLaughlin, and Slack 2003; Sherman 2014; Tickamyer, Sherman, and Warlick 2017.

29. For more on the issue of "openness," see Golding 2014a.

30. Carr and Kefalas 2009; Corbett 2007; Sherman and Sage 2011.

31. Christofides, Neelakantan, and Behr 2006; Golding 2014b; Lichter and Ziliak 2017.

CHAPTER 3. LIVING THE DREAM

1. Cloke and Little 1990; Hines 2010; Nelson and Nelson 2011; Phillips 2004; Salamon 2003b.

2. Sociologists argue that wealth is in many ways more important than income in determining life chances, because of its stability, inheritability, and self-reproduction (Conley 1999; Gilbert 2014; Oliver and Shapiro 2006). For more on human capital, see Becker 2009; with regard to cultural capital, see Bourdieu 1977, 1984.

3. For more on discursive strategies by which whites abdicate admitting racism, see Bonilla-Silva 2009; Ferber 2012; Gallagher 2003. For discussions of rural idyll as implicitly escaping racial concerns, see Sherman 2009b.

4. Regarding "pull of the rural idyll," see Howarth 1995 and Wuthnow 2015; regarding "communities as slower-paced, safer, and more family-friendly," see Halfacree 1995; Salamon 2003a; Sherman 2009b.

5. N = 30. Of the 11 newcomer renters in the sample, 7 had little to no income and lived below the poverty line. Several were engaged in subsistence activities and practiced forms of primitive survivalism, a popular subculture in the valley; 80 percent (n = 32) of newcomers lived in houses, 19 of which were newer homes. The remaining 20 percent (n = 8) lived in yurts, primitive cabins, and double-wide trailers.

6. Over time, as housing prices have risen in the valley, an increasing amount of wealth and income is required to make housing in the valley "affordable," even for many urban out-migrants.

7. Jobes 2000; McGranahan 1999; Smith and Krannich 2000; Thompson 2006; Winkler et al. 2007.

8. Field Notes, September 22, 2014.

9. Just three out of forty-one newcomers (7 percent) moved to the valley specifically for job opportunities, and in all of these cases the location was a major factor in the decision to apply for the job.

10. Field Notes, September 4, 2014.

11. In addition, anecdotal evidence does support the contention that some business owners were self-funding their endeavors. With regard to a local business changing hands, newcomer Maria Setzer commented:

> I think the business is just breaking even this year. It's been subsidized by [the previous owner].... They're a couple that, she—they had a lot of money. She had a huge trust fund. They could just dump money into it if it was not making enough. It took them seven years, finally, to get to a place where it's like, "OK, we're breaking even. We're paying our employees, and that's it. There's not a profit after that."

A separate interview with the previous owner confirmed this story. He explained:

> The thing that probably most people don't have is, [my wife] had regular income, so we didn't have to make money from the [business].
>
> *Q: Where did her income come from?*
>
> From her family.

12. Teaching (n= 6); construction/carpentry (n = 4); nonprofits (n = 3); medical professions (n = 3); subsistence activities (n = 4); and retired (n = 8).

13. Pedulla and Newman 2011.

14. Philip Moss and Chris Tilly (1996: 253) have defined soft skills "as skills, abilities, and traits that pertain to personality, attitude, and behavior rather than to formal or technical knowledge."

15. For more on color-blind racism, see Andersen 2001; Bonilla-Silva 2009; Ferber 2012; Gallagher 2003; Hartmann et al. 2017. With regard to class blindness, Joan Williams (2017: 2) has described a similar phenomenon that she calls "class cluelessness" and explains that in the United States liberal middle-class whites have become more conscious of racial inequality over time, while systematically ignoring class differences and even callously insulting the white working class.

16. For more on American individualism, see Bellah et al. 1996; Pugh 2016.

17. Andrew Sayer (2005: 4) has argued that people of differing class statuses "are likely to feel obliged to justify their differences.... Many may attempt to distinguish themselves from others through moral boundary drawing, claiming virtues for themselves and imputing vices to their others." The ideological stance of class blindness plays a very similar role to that of color blindness for whites, which, according to Eduardo Bonilla-Silva (2009: 2) "exculpate[s] them from any responsibility for the status of people of color." Bonilla-Silva (2009: 4) goes on to

assert that "shielded by color blindness, whites can express resentment toward minorities, criticize their morality, values, and work ethic; and even claim to be victims of 'reverse racism.'"

18. Hochschild 1989.

19. The childcare "crisis" was the subject of much local concern during my time in Paradise Valley and was the subject of inquiry by local organizations, as well as being covered in depth by the local newspaper. The superintendent of the local schools explained:

> We also have a lack of high quality affordable childcare. And I heard from a lot of parents—surprisingly not just single moms but single dads and working families that—where they are having to make hard choices about who works, and do they work, because of the lack of high quality affordable childcare.

Adding to these concerns, one of the larger daycare providers closed during the summer of 2015, leaving many parents without another reliable or affordable option. However, as is discussed in chapter 7, efforts by multiple community nonprofit organizations did result in an additional daycare option being created several years after I concluded my fieldwork.

20. In cases of single-parent and same-sex parent households, parents of both genders used this strategy.

21. For more on middle-class parents opting out of the workforce, see Covert 2013; Deason 2010; Percheski 2008; Stone 2008.

22. Field Notes, October 13, 2014.

23. This included several who had returned to Paradise Valley after leaving for years to pursue education and training elsewhere, as well as the common pattern of retired parents relocating to Paradise Valley to be closer to their adult children and grandchildren who had moved there.

24. Including a number who lived on private, usually unpaved roads that did not receive services and needed both winter snow removal and year-round maintenance.

25. Field Notes, November 3, 2014.

26. Field Notes, October 17, 2014.

27. For more on second-shift chores and "traditional" division of labor, see Hochschild 1989.

28. Campbell and Bell 2000; Campbell, Bell, and Finney 2006; Connell 1995.

29. Hochschild 1989.

30. Campbell et al. 2006.

31. West and Zimmerman 1987.

32. Campbell, Bell, and Finney 2006: 2; West and Zimmerman 1987.

33. Hochschild 1989.

34. Field Notes, October 13, 2014.

35. Hochschild 1989; Sherman 2009a.

36. See previous research by Mederer 1999; Sherman 2009a, 2009b.

37. A friend recounted being turned down for a leadership position at a local nonprofit organization and being told that they were really looking for someone from Seattle who had social connections there that could be mobilized for fundraising (Field Notes, July 25, 2015).

38. A number of prominent local nonprofits had boards that were more than half women, and almost entirely recent in-migrants. For example, the board of one of the largest and most active organizations in the valley, according to their 2018 website, had fourteen members, only one of whom had lived in the valley as a child.

39. Field Notes, October 13, 2014.

40. The notable exceptions to this pattern included several holiday-specific community-oriented events such as the free Easter egg hunt at a public park, as well as several events that provided food for needy families and gifts for children during the Thanksgiving and Christmas holidays.

41. As is discussed in more depth in chapter 7, the Angel Food organization stood out as an important contrast to this pattern in multiple ways. It was also common for a small number of well-resourced, well-educated, and liberal-minded local adults from families with long histories in the valley to play important leadership roles in nonprofit organizations.

42. Becker 2009; Bourdieu 1977; Lamont 1992; Lareau 2003.

43. Bourdieu 1986; Lareau 2003; Putnam 2001.

CHAPTER 4. TROUBLE IN PARADISE

1. Bellah et al. 1996; Hauhart 2015.

2. Halfacree 1995; Howarth 1995; Wuthnow 2015.

3. Robert Wuthnow (2018: 15) has argued that for rural populations "so much of everyday life occurs within the bounded, socially and culturally identified community that the community itself takes on the characteristics of home."

4. See Sherman 2009b for more on the various shades of meaning of safety, home, and "family friendliness" in rural communities, including signaling a preference for whiteness and racial homogeneity.

5. Sonya Salamon (Salamon 2003a:11) has observed similarly in a rural town experiencing suburbanization: "Oldtimers can envision living no place else, but many newcomers, loosely attached, often expect to move on."

6. Bellah et al. 1996; Sherman 2009b; Wuthnow 2015.

7. For more on issues of working poverty and underemployment, see Edin and Lein 1997; Ehrenreich 2001; Newman 1999; Pedulla and Newman 2011; Seefeldt 2016; Shipler 2005; Shulman 2003.

8. The links between poverty and social exclusion have long been noted, particularly in the European Union (Nolan and Whelan 2010). Shucksmith (2012,

2016; Shucksmith and Schafft 2012) has noted the importance of looking at both of these issues with regard to understanding rural inequality.

9. See Kelly 2013 for more on these issues.

10. Campbell and Bell 2000; Campbell et al. 2006.

11. Field Notes, February 12, 2015; March 12, 2015; April 2, 2015.

12. Unemployment insurance provides temporary benefits to workers who are laid off through no fault of their own.

13. With regard to the "digital divide" and inequality, Bridgette Wessels (2013: 17–18) has explained:

> It is not only the networked structuring of [digital] technology and the ability to access and use it that are contributing factors in inequality but it also provides access to information and the public sphere, which is a key resource in an information society. . . . Inclusion into digitally enabled networks is significant in terms of the opportunities people have to engage in economic life and to participate in political, social, and cultural life.

14. Halfacree 1995; Howarth 1995; Wuthnow 2015.

15. In only one case in this fieldwork did I observe that an old-timer's volunteer work led to a leadership position with a local organization. However, it should be noted that a number of very well-resourced valley natives, including the owners of prominent local businesses and some very large landowners, were repeatedly sought for leadership roles including board memberships and input on the direction of the community. Those with long ties to the valley *and* significant wealth to donate toward initiatives did often have considerable power within the community.

16. Becker 2009.

17. Field Notes, February 12, 2015.

18. Sherman 2006, 2009b.

19. Sherman 2006, 2009b.

20. Among 38 old-timers, 18 were homeowners; 63 percent of old-timers lived in houses (n = 24, 7 of which were rented and all but 2 of which were older homes); 29 percent lived in single-wide or travel trailers (n = 11, 6 of which were rented); and 8 percent (n = 3) lived in rented apartments, 2 of which were subsidized housing units.

21. Bellah et al. 1996; Hauhart 2015; Michaelson 2009.

22. Housing stress is defined as unaffordability, crowding, or lack of basic amenities (Mikesell 2004), and housing insecurity as lacking sufficient, stable, and/or permanent residences (Coleman-Jensen and Steffen 2017).

23. Field Notes, April 14, 2015. The valley had four housing complexes specifically designated as affordable, consisting of eighty-nine subsidized apartments. Despite these units, significant rental overburdening occurred throughout the valley, and many of its lowest-income residents could not find stable housing. According to Census estimates, in Eagle Flat and Reliance, 23 percent and

40 percent, respectively, of renting tenants are overburdened, meaning that they pay more than 30 percent of their gross income in rent. One local assessment conducted in 2016 found that nearly 40 percent of residents put more than 35 percent of their income toward housing, and 20 percent spend more than half. It also found that 41 percent of houses in the valley are occupied only seasonally (other sources maintain that this number is even higher). In response to this report, in 2016 a new land trust was formed to work on housing issues, with plans to build more than two dozen affordable single-family homes for people earning 60 percent to 100 percent of the area's median income. There are also plans for mixed developments that may include rental housing.

24. Field Notes, March 13, 2015; May 14, 2015.

25. Desmond 2012.

26. Field Notes, December 22, 2016.

27. Field Notes, May 23, 2014.

28. Field Notes, September 9, 2014.

29. Field Notes, October 30, 2014.

30. For more on restrictions and surveillance within trailer park housing, see Desmond 2016 and Salamon and MacTavish 2006, 2017.

31. Field Notes, June 25, 2015.

32. Field Notes, December 22, 2016.

33. Researchers have found similar dynamics to operate in urban settings as well (Desmond 2016; Purser 2016; Seefeldt 2016).

34. Field Notes, December 22, 2016.

35. A full 37 percent of working-age old-timers interviewed reported not working, while just 7 percent of newcomers did.

36. Desmond 2016; Edin and Lein 1997; Hays 2003; Newman 1999; Roy and Burton 2007; Stack 1974.

37. Brown and Lichter 2004; Hofferth and Iceland 1998; Nelson 2000, 2005; Sherman 2009b; Tickamyer and Henderson 2011.

38. Brewster and Padavic 2002; Desmond 2012; Edin and Kefalas 2005; Heflin and Pattillo 2006; Levine 2013; Smith 2010.

39. Nelson and Smith 1999; Sherman 2009b; Tickamyer and Wood 1998.

40. Just 12.5 percent of newcomers mentioned receiving help from friends or family recently, compared to 54 percent of old-timers. However, it was common for newcomers to reference the potential for family help, particularly with regard to major expenses like children's college educations. Old-timers, however, often reported very small amounts of available help and expectations that they repay debts quickly.

41. Several local and county organizations helped to distribute aid and assistance that could be used for help with rent, utilities, gas, and auto repairs. Clients could apply for aid up to $150 per year, per family or household. Particularly in

the winter months, this was an extremely common request received at both Angel Food and Home Front.

42. Medical aid (n = 29); food bank (n = 15); utilities (n = 11); SNAP (n = 9); TANF (n = 1).

43. Fong, Wright, and Wimer 2016; Hays 2003; Kissane 2012; Rogers-Dillon 1995; Seccombe 2010; Sherman 2006, 2013.

44. Given that income was among the variables factored into the newcomer/ old-timer distinction, it is not surprising that newcomers' rates of aid receipt were much lower: 57 percent received subsidized medical care (n = 24); 5 percent reported food bank usage (n = 2); 10 percent reported being a SNAP receipt (n = 4); and no newcomers reported receiving utilities aid. None reported having ever received TANF.

45. In his classic work, Erving Goffman (1959) describes social interactions through the metaphor of dramatic performance, in which social actors attempt to manipulate impressions and interpretations through their presentations of self.

46. Field Notes, October 30, 2014; November 6, 2014; December 11, 2014; November 20, 2014; January 8, 2015; January 22, 2015; March 2, 2015.

47. Field Notes, October 30, 2014.

48. Field Notes, November 20, 2014.

49. Field Notes, February 5, 2015.

50. Field Notes, December 11, 2014; March 12, 2015.

51. Beisel 1992; Bourgois 1995; Duneier 1999; Gowan 2010; Kissane 2012; Lamont 1992, 2000; Sherman 2006, 2009b, 2013.

52. For more on wealth as a cushion against shocks, see Conley 1999; Oliver and Shapiro 2006; Spilerman 2000.

53. In addition to rising taxes on existing properties, homeowners also reported finding themselves in conflict with new neighbors who demanded that a dirt road be paved, at private cost to those who owned property along it. There were reports of lawsuits being filed against those who refused or could not contribute to these shared expenses (Field Notes, April 26, 2015).

CHAPTER 5. "CERTAIN CIRCLES"

1. Quandt et al. 1999; Sherman 2009b.

2. Field Notes, September 28, 2014.

3. With regard to the roles of social and cultural capital, see Bourdieu 1977, 1984, 1986; Lamont and Molnar 2002; Putnam 2001.

4. Sherman 2006, 2009b.

5. Beisel 1992; Lamont and Fournier 1992; Lamont and Molnar 2002.

6. Duncan 1999; Flora and Flora 2013, 2014.

7. Sherman 2009b.

8. Larsen and Hutton 2012; Ooi, Laing, and Mair 2015; Salamon 2003a.

9. Sherman 2006, 2009b.

10. Debertin and Goetz 2013; Duncan 1999; Flora and Flora 2014; Hofferth and Iceland 1998; Sherman 2009b.

11. Nelson 2005; Sherman 2009b; Slack 2007; Tickamyer and Henderson 2011.

12. Field Notes, June 30, 2015.

13. See Desmond 2012 for more on "disposable" social ties.

14. See Salamon and MacTavish 2017 for more on mobile home parks and the failure to create community.

15. Mark Granovetter (1973) has discussed the importance of weak versus strong ties for bridging social circles and providing access to new social networks.

16. It was common for the Angel Food staff to call and check up on regular clients who were known to be socially isolated if they failed to visit on distribution days. In several cases they were concerned for clients' physical as well as mental health.

17. Field Notes, December 11, 2014.

18. Field Notes, May 14, 2015.

19. Halfacree 1995; Howarth 1995; Wuthnow 2015.

20. Smith and Krannich 2000.

21. Bourdieu 1984; Lamont 1992.

22. Fischer 1975; Sherman 2009b.

23. Armstrong and Stedman 2013; Ulrich-Schad and Qin 2018.

24. Crowley and Lichter 2009; Devine 2006; Hochschild 2016; Stein 2001.

25. For more on the "high culture" versus "low culture" distinction, see Bourdieu 1984.

26. Lamont et al. 2016; Williams 2012, 2017.

27. Numerous sociologists argue the opposite: that cultural tastes are very much shaped by social class (Bourdieu 1977, 1984; Lamont 1992; Lareau 2003; Small, Harding, and Lamont 2010; Williams 2012).

28. Field Notes, September 13, 2014.

29. Field Notes, November 10, 2014.

30. James Coleman (1988) has argued that "closure" of social networks is necessary for the emergence of effective norms that allow for collective sanctioning of undesired behavior.

31. Although I did not work for pay locally, my volunteer jobs occasionally allowed me a firsthand window into these dynamics. My field notes from May 22, 2015, describe working the bar for a local fundraising event for wealthy donors, in which "a number of people ... demanded drinks from us without saying 'please' or 'thank-you.' [One guest] got our attention by just holding out his glass and saying, 'white wine' authoritatively, without any acknowledgement of us at all." At the end of the night, despite having worked for several hours (in my case as an unpaid volunteer), we discovered that "we had just $5.25 in the tip jar."

32. The Easter egg hunt to which Wendy referred did draw a cross-section of families from around the valley. However, some of its most elite families carefully planned and executed their own exclusive "special" Easter picnic and egg hunt on privately owned land (Field Notes, April 1, 2015; April 5, 2015).

33. Becker 2009; Coleman 1988.

34. School officials at the time were aware of these concerns and actively engaged in projects to increase access to educational opportunities, as is discussed more in chapter 7.

35. Calarco 2014; Lareau 2003; McHenry-Sorber and Schafft 2015; Sherman and Sage 2011.

36. Budge 2006; Carr and Kefalas 2009; Corbett 2007; Petrin et al. 2014; Sherman and Sage 2011.

37. Newcomers (n = 10) and old-timers (n = 4).

38. Newcomers (n = 16) and old-timers (n = 14).

39. Previous researchers have found that differing aspirations for children are a key part of social class–based differences in parenting styles and resources that provide middle-class children with advantages over working-class and poor children within educational systems and institutions (Kohn 1959; Lareau 2003; Lareau and Calarco 2012).

40. Calarco 2014; Fan and Chen 2001; Lareau 2003.

41. Field Notes March 19, 2015; April 15, 2015.

42. For more on these issues, see Calarco 2014; Cooper 2014; Kohn 1959; Lareau 2003; Lareau and Calarco 2012.

43. Just over a quarter (26 percent) of newcomers expressed frustrations with local schools or educational opportunities versus 39 percent of old-timers (n = 11 newcomers and 15 old-timers).

44. Particularly controversial over my time in Paradise Valley was the school board's decision to pursue the International Baccalaureate (IB) program for kindergarten through tenth grades. The debate around the program was virulent at times, with newcomer parents generally supporting the initiative, and old-timers—as well as many retirees without children in the schools—harshly opposing it. Complaints revolved around its cost for the community; its rigorousness being too much for kids who already struggled in school, and for less educated parents to be able to help with homework; and its international focus and ties to the United Nations, which irked many political conservatives. A number of old-timers chose to remove their children from Paradise Valley's public schools over this issue (Field Notes, February 20, 2015; April 15, 2015). Despite these protests, the school board went on to apply for authorization for the IB program, which it received in 2017. It was implemented at both the elementary and high schools soon thereafter.

45. Gerarld and Haycock 2006; Jencks et al. 1979; Lareau 2003; Parcel and Dufur 2001; Sewell and Hauser 1975.

46. Calarco 2014; Kohn 1959; Lareau 2003; Sherman and Harris 2012.

47. Cobb, McIntire, and Pratt 1989; Corbett 2007; Mette et al. 2016; Petrin, Schafft, and Meece 2014; Sherman and Sage 2011.

48. These issues were acknowledged as serious by the newly hired superintendent of schools, who was attempting to remedy some concerns. He commented in an interview:

> When I first arrived I heard numerous stories about families who are challenged by the fees associated with public education, [including] pay-to-play, enrichment fees, course fees, supply fees—you know for a family of four that begins to add up really quickly. In fact, we started to look at what does it cost to send a child to—or to support a family that attends a public school in Paradise Valley, and the numbers are significant. And we know we have families that can't afford that.

49. Sherman 2006, 2009b; Sherman and Sage 2011.

50. Barnard 2016; Bourgois 1995; Gowan 2010; Purser 2009.

51. Sherman 2006, 2009b.

52. Bellah et al. 1996; Lamont et al. 2016.

53. Carpenter-Song, Ferron, and Kobylenski 2016; Pied 2019; Sage and Sherman 2014; Sherman 2009b; Whitley 2013.

54. Bellah et al. 1996; Lobao 2006.

55. Field Notes May 26, 2015.

56. Sherman 2006, 2009b.

57. Japonica Brown-Saracino has made a distinction between in-migrants who attempt to gentrify rural social spaces and those who focus on preserving them. She explains: "Gentrifiers seek to tame the 'frontier,' while social preservationists work to preserve the wilderness, including its inhabitants, despite their own ability to invest in and benefit from 'improvements' or revitalization" (Brown-Saracino 2004: 136). While not quite self-conscious preservationists, earlier waves of in-migrants to Paradise Valley did more closely resemble this group, including tendencies toward "a set of interactional practices, such as befriending old-timers, patronizing old-timers' businesses, and the decision to stay in the neighborhood or town, rather than to sell property for profit" (Brown-Saracino 2004: 153).

58. A report released by the US Census Bureau in 2019 found that income inequality in the United States had reached its highest level in more than fifty years (US Census Bureau 2019), which analysts blamed on "the long-running trend of the wealthy seeing far larger income growth than middle- or lower-income earners" (Telford 2019). Andrea Armstrong and Richard Stedman (2013: 323) have asserted: "Social interaction between residents of differing backgrounds helps to minimize the sense of otherness, overcome perceived differences, and facilitate trust among diverse groups," and that more frequent interaction helps reduce "othering" and incidence of culture clash.

CHAPTER 6. PARADISE LOST

1. Field Notes, October 24, 2014.
2. Lichter and Brown 2011; Lichter and Ziliak 2017.
3. Golding 2014b; Kondo, Rivera, and Rullman 2012; Nelson et al. 2010; Salamon 2003a; Kondo, Rivera, and Rullman 2012: 181.
4. For more on this, see also Cramer 2016; Hochschild 2016; Wuthnow 2018.
5. See also Williams 2010, 2017.
6. N = 35 of 40 newcomers for whom information was collected on voting interests.
7. Brehm, Eisenhauer, and Krannich 2004; Brown and Glasgow 2008; Jennings and Krannich 2013; Jobes 2000; Lichtenstein 2004; Stedman 2006; Ulrich-Schad, Henly, and Safford 2013.
8. Putnam 2001; Wuthnow 2018.
9. Field Notes, November 22, 2014.
10. Bourdieu 1984; Lamont 2000; Lamont and Fournier 1992.
11. Small, Harding, and Lamont 2010.
12. Sherman 2006, 2009b.
13. In explaining his theory of stigma management, Erving Goffman (1963:107) has asserted: "The stigmatized individual exhibits a tendency to stratify his 'own' according to the degree to which their stigma is apparent and obtrusive. He can then take up in regard to those who are more evidently stigmatized than himself the attitudes the normal take to him." See also Bourgois 1995; Burton, Garrett-Peters, and Eason 2011; Cohen, Krumer-Nevo, and Avieli 2017; Duneier 1999; Gowan 2010; Hashemi 2015; Hays 2003; Kissane 2012; Lamont 2000; Purser 2009; Sherman 2009, 2013; Small, Harding, and Lamont 2010; Woodward 2008; Wray 2006.
14. Concern with rural opioid use has been growing in recent years, as rural areas are heavily impacted by "deaths of despair," including those related to opioid use and addiction (Case and Deaton 2017; Monnat 2018; Monnat and Rigg 2016; Rigg, Monnat, and Chavez 2018).
15. For more on these dynamics, see Wray 2006.
16. Sherman 2009.
17. This is also a common theme for low-income populations more generally, given the individualistic landscape of modern neoliberal America (Levine 2013; Seefeldt 2016; Silva 2013).
18. N = 26 of 36 old-timers for whom voting information was collected. A lack of social capital is believed to be a key factor contributing to lowered civic engagement and voting among the poor (Piven and Cloward 2000; Rosenstone 1982).
19. Hochschild 2016; Wuthnow 2018. While these researchers argue that much of rural conservatism is directly linked to racism and racial resentment, this was not the dominant narrative in Paradise Valley. To the contrary, with this popula-

tion political conservatism was much more consciously linked to economic issues than to racial ones.

20. Paige Kelly and Linda Lobao (2019) have found that social status and socio-cultural values help explain conservative voting patterns in rural areas. Despite often describing conservative leanings, however, the majority of old-timers (59 percent) expressed no explicit party preference.

21. Other themes that have been described as common to rural populations as a whole, including racism and anger at perceptions of disrespect (Cramer 2016; Hochschild 2016; Wuthnow 2018), were not strong themes in either the interviews or the ethnographic data. This does not suggest that racism or resentment were completely absent in Paradise Valley, but rather that in this particular community and region these are not experienced as the main sources of threat for rural populations. Given their low level of exposure to nonwhite populations and the geographic remoteness of the valley, other aspects of the antigovernment discourse were more clearly relevant to their most proximate concerns.

22. Frank 2004; Hochschild 2016.

23. Wuthnow (2018: 102) has similarly found that farmers are "more informed than the average townsperson" with regard to federal policies, because their "livelihoods were directly influenced by government agricultural policies."

24. These terms refer to General Schedule pay scales for federal government jobs, with salary levels starting at step 1 and rising with each additional step.

25. Loka Ashwood (2018: 10) has asserted similarly that "the democratic state has long enforced a utilitarian logic where those considered the least important . . . were sacrificed for those considered to be the most important." She goes on to explain that this logic has led to "'for-profit democracy,' in which the utilitarian rule of the most people and the greatest profit defines the government's purpose" (Ashwood 2018: 24).

26. Ashwood (2018: 203) also connects this type of focus on self-protection to the invalidity of the state: "When centralized authorities are seen largely as invalid, either as part of the system or as part of the government, citizens need some way to cope with that insecurity. Guns hold power, power that expands beyond a person's reach. Gun ownership and self-defense become more important as state legitimacy wanes, and perhaps even further, as the state is seen as a threat."

27. According to the industry website irrigation.education,

> As the name suggests, center pivots irrigate in a circular pattern around a central pivot point. Pivots are capable of applying water, fertilizer, chemicals, and herbicides. This versatility can improve the efficiency of irrigation practices by using a single piece of machinery to perform several functions.
>
> Most center pivot machines are electrically powered, using either a generator or a public power source. Pivots use both 120 and 480 volts of alternating current (VAC) to operate. 120 VAC is used as the control circuit, powering the safety circuit, the forward and reverse movement of the pivot, and, more precisely, the movement of the Last Regular Drive Unit (LRDU). The 480 VAC is the power circuit and supplies the needed energy for the drive units to move. (irrigation.education 2016)

28. Estimated costs of installing a pivot system, including pump, well, and pipelines, are about $150,000 (North Dakota State University 2013).

29. Joan Williams (2017: 101) has noted the tendency for working-class Americans to fail to understand or see the ways in which the government subsidizes the middle class and working class through a variety of programs. She argues for the need for education and "publicizing to working-class Americans how they themselves benefit from government programs."

30. Many also complained about decreased access to private land, as immigrants erected fences and denied grazing access (Field Notes, August 26, 2014).

31. Sherman 2009.

32. Scholars and pundits have argued that among Donald Trump's most successful political strategies has been his ability to appeal to white men's sense of victimhood (Johnson 2017; Rucker 2018).

33. For more on these issues, see Cramer 2016; Hochschild 2016; Wuthnow 2018.

34. Duncan 1999; Fitchen 1991; Schafft 2006; Sherman 2009.

35. Gans 1996; Kittay 1999; Rogers-Dillon 1995; Seccombe 2010.

36. McCall et al. 2017; Piketty and Saez 2014; US Census Bureau 2019.

CHAPTER 7. CROSSING THE DIVIDE AND RECLAIMING THE DREAM

1. Armstrong and Stedman 2013; Brehm, Eisenhauer, and Krannich 2004; Crowe 2006; Deller 2010; Hunter et al. 2005; Jennings and Krannich 2013; Krannich and Petrzelka 2003; McGranahan 1999; Reeder and Brown 2005; Stedman 2006; Ulrich-Schad 2018; Ulrich-Schad and Qin 2018.

2. Armstrong and Stedman 2013; Jobes 2000; Krannich and Petrzelka 2003; Ooi, Laing, and Mair 2015; Salamon 2003b; Smith and Krannich 2000; Ulrich-Schad and Qin 2018; Winkler 2013.

3. Calarco 2014; Cooper 2014; Hacker, Rehm, and Schlesinger 2010; Hays 1996.

4. Gest 2016; Williams 2017; Bryer and Prysmakova-Rivera 2018; Gans 1996; Hays 2003; Kissane 2012; Seccombe 2010; Sherman 2009b.

5. Lamont 2000; Williams 2017; Wray 2006.

6. Burton et al. 2013; Gilbert 2014; Lichter and Ziliak 2017; McCall et al. 2017; Morris and Western 1999; Piketty and Saez 2014; Wodtke 2016.

7. Neckerman and Torche 2007; Telford 2019; US Census Bureau 2019.

8. Chetty et al. 2016.

9. David Autor (2019: 4) has discussed a four-decade process of "occupational polarization," which has contributed to falling non-college graduate wages in the following ways:

It has shunted non-college workers from middle-skill career occupations that reward specialized and differentiated skills into traditionally low-education occupations that demand primarily generic skills; it has disproportionately depressed middle-wage employment among non-college workers in urban labor markets, thus directly reducing average non-college wages and—to a startling degree—attenuating the urban non-college wage premium that prevailed in earlier decades; and it has created an excess supply of less-educated workers that serves to depress non-college wages across occupations and geographic areas.

10. Cramer 2016; Hamilton et al. 2008.

11. Golding 2014a; Lichter and Ziliak 2017.

12. Neckerman and Torche 2007: 340.

13. Association with those most like ourselves is often referred to by sociologists as "homophily."

14. Neckerman and Torche 2007: 344.

15. Pettigrew and Tropp 2008.

16. Case and Deaton 2017; Monnat and Rigg 2016; Rigg, Monnat, and Chavez 2018.

17. Putnam and Feldstein 2003: 9.

18. Calarco 2014; Logan and Burdick-Will 2017; Sherman and Sage 2011.

19. Flora and Flora 2013; Putnam 2001; Putnam and Feldstein 2003.

20. Field Notes, September 18, 2014.

21. Field Notes, October 2, 2014.

22. Field Notes, December 11, 2014.

23. Field Notes, December 12, 2014; December 13, 2014.

24. Carr and Kefalas 2009; Golding 2014b.

25. Pew Research Center 2015; Williams 2017.

26. Autor 2019; Chetty et al. 2016; Wodtke 2016.

27. Ashwood 2018; Chetty et al. 2016; Cooper 2014; Sherman 2017.

28. Cramer 2016; Frank 2004; Hochschild 2016; Wuthnow 2018.

EPILOGUE

1. Monnat 2020; Peters 2020; Schafft and Maselli 2021.

2. Ames 2020; Siegler 2020.

3. Berliner 2020; Tan 2020.

4. Burawoy 1998: 5.

5. Burawoy 1998: 7.

6. Minnesota Population Center 2016; US Census Bureau 2016.

7. Office of Financial Management 2016; US Census Bureau 2016.

8. US Census Bureau 2012.

References

Ames, Michael. 2020. "Why an Idaho Ski Destination Has One of the Highest COVID-19 Infection Rates in the Nation." *The New Yorker*, April 3.

Andersen, Margaret L. 2001. "Restructuring for Whom? Race, Class, Gender, and the Ideology of Invisibility." *Sociological Forum* 16(2):181–201.

Armstrong, Andrea, and Richard C. Stedman. 2013. "Culture Clash and Second Home Ownership in the U.S. Northern Forest." *Rural Sociology* 78(3):318–45.

Ashwood, Loka. 2018. *For-Profit Democracy: Why the Government Is Losing the Trust of Rural America*. New Haven, CT: Yale University Press.

Autor, David H. 2019. "Work of the Past, Work of the Future." *AEA Papers and Proceedings 2019* 109:1–32.

Barnard, Alex V. 2016. "Making the City 'Second Nature': Freegan 'Dumpster Divers' and the Materiality of Morality." *American Journal of Sociology* 121(4):1017–50.

Becker, Gary S. 2009. *Human Capital: A Theoretical and Empirical Analysis, with Special Reference to Education*. Chicago: University of Chicago Press.

Beisel, Nicola. 1992. "Constructing a Shifting Moral Boundary." In *Cultivating Differences: Symbolic Boundaries and the Making of Inequality*, edited by M. Lamont and M. Fournier, 104–28. Chicago: University of Chicago Press.

Bellah, Robert N., Madsen Richard, M. Sullivan William, Swidler Ann, and M. Tipton Steven. 1996. *Habits of the Heart: Individualism and Commitment in American Life*. Berkeley: University of California Press.

Berliner, Uri. 2020. "COVID-19 Pandemic Pushes Many in New York City to Suburbs." National Public Radio, July 4, Weekend Edition Saturday.

Biddle, Catharine, and Ian Mette. 2017. "Education and Information." In *Rural Poverty in the United States*, edited by A. R. Tickamyer, J. Sherman, and J. Warlick, 322–38. New York: Columbia University Press.

Bonilla-Silva, Eduardo. 2009. *Racism without Racists: Color-Blind Racism and the Persistence of Racial Inequality in America*. 3rd edition. Lanham, MD: Rowman & Littlefield Publishers.

Bourdieu, Pierre. 1977. "Cultural Reproduction and Social Reproduction." In *Power and Ideology in Education*, edited by J. Karabel and A. H. Halsey, 487–510. New York: Oxford University Press.

———. 1984. *Distinction: A Social Critique of the Judgement of Taste*. Cambridge, MA: Harvard University Press.

———. 1986. "The Forms of Capital." In *Handbook of Theory and Research for the Sociology of Education*, edited by J. G. Richardson, 241–58. New York: Greenwood Press.

Bourgois, Philippe. 1995. *In Search of Respect: Selling Crack in El Barrio*. Cambridge, UK: Cambridge University Press.

Brehm, Joan M., Brian W. Eisenhauer, and Richard S. Krannich. 2004. "Dimensions of Community Attachment and Their Relationship to Well-Being in the Amenity-Rich Rural West." *Rural Sociology* 69(3):405–29.

Brewster, Karin L., and Irene Padavic. 2002. "No More Kin Care? Change in Black Mothers' Reliance on Relatives for Child Care, 1977–94." *Gender & Society* 16(4):546–63.

Brown, David L., and Nina Glasgow. 2008. *Rural Retirement Migration*. Dordrecht: Springer.

Brown, David L., and Kai A. Schafft, eds. 2019. *Rural People and Communities in the 21st Century: Resilience and Transformation*. 2nd edition. Cambridge, UK: Polity.

Brown, J. Brian, and Daniel T. Lichter. 2004. "Poverty, Welfare, and the Livelihood Strategies of Nonmetropolitan Single Mothers." *Rural Sociology* 69(2):282–301.

Brown-Saracino, Japonica. 2004. "Social Preservationists and the Quest for Authentic Community." *City & Community* 3(2):135–56.

Bryer, Thomas A., and Sofia Prysmakova-Rivera. 2018. *Poor Participation: Fighting the Wars on Poverty and Impoverished Citizenship*. Lanham, MD: Lexington Books.

Budge, Kathleen. 2006. "Rural Leaders, Rural Places: Problem, Privilege, and Possibility." *Journal of Research in Rural Education* 21(13):1–10.

Burawoy, Michael. 1998. "The Extended Case Method." *Sociological Theory* 16(1):4–33.

Burton, Linda, Raymond Garrett-Peters, and John Major Eason. 2011. "Morality,

Identity, and Mental Health in Rural Ghettos." In *Communities, Neighbor-hoods, and Health: Expanding the Boundaries of Place, Social Disparities in Health and Health Care*, edited by L. Burton, S. P. Kemp, M. Leung, S. A. Matthews, and D. T. Takeuchi, 91–110. New York: Springer.

Burton, Linda M., Daniel T. Lichter, Regina S. Baker, and John M. Eason. 2013. "Inequality, Family Processes, and Health in the 'New' Rural America." *American Behavioral Scientist* 57(8):1128–51.

Calarco, Jessica McCrory. 2014. "Coached for the Classroom: Parents' Cultural Transmission and Children's Reproduction of Educational Inequalities." *American Sociological Review* 79(5):1015–37.

Campbell, Hugh, and Michael Mayerfeld Bell. 2000. "The Question of Rural Masculinities." *Rural Sociology* 65(4):532–46.

Campbell, Hugh, Michael Mayerfeld Bell, and Margaret Finney. 2006. "Masculinity and Rural Life: An Introduction." In *Country Boys: Masculinity and Rural Life*, edited by H. R. Campbell, M. M. Bell, and Finney, 1–22. University Park: Pennsylvania State University Press.

Carpenter-Song, Elizabeth, Joelle Ferron, and Sara Kobylenski. 2016. "Social Exclusion and Survival for Families Facing Homelessness in Rural New England." *Journal of Social Distress and the Homeless* 25(1):41–52.

Carr, Patrick J., and Maria J. Kefalas. 2009. *Hollowing out the Middle: The Rural Brain Drain and What It Means for America*. Boston: Beacon Press.

Case, Anne, and Angus Deaton. 2017. "Mortality and Morbidity in the 21st Century." *Brookings Papers on Economic Activity* (Spring):397–476.

Chetty, Raj, David B. Grusky, Maximilian Hell, Nathaniel Hendren, Robert Manduca, and Jimmy Narang. 2016. *The Fading American Dream: Trends in Absolute Income Mobility since 1940*. NBER Working Paper 22910. Cambridge, MA: National Bureau of Economic Research.

Christofides, C. A., Pats Neelakantan, and Todd Behr. 2006. *Examining the Rural-Urban Income Gap*. Harrisburg: Center for Rural Pennsylvania.

Clark, Madilynne. 2017. "Why Rural Washington Is Fed-up with Olympia and Seattle." *Washington Policy Center*. Accessed November 12, 2018. www.washingtonpolicy.org/publications/detail/why-rural-washington-is-fed-up-with-olympia-and-seattle.

Cloke, Paul, and Jo Little. 1990. *The Rural State? Limits to Planning in Rural Society*. Oxford, UK: Oxford University Press.

Cobb, R. A., W. G. McIntire, and P. A. Pratt. 1989. "Vocational and Educational Aspirations of High School Students: A Problem for Rural America." *Journal of Research in Rural Education* 6(2):11–16.

Cohen, Yael, Michal Krumer-Nevo, and Nir Avieli. 2017. "Bread of Shame: Mechanisms of Othering in Soup Kitchens." *Social Problems* 64(3):398–413.

Coleman, James Samuel. 1988. "Social Capital in the Creation of Human Capital." *American Journal of Sociology* 94(supp.):S95–120.

Coleman-Jensen, Alisha, and Barry Steffen. 2017. "Food Insecurity and Housing Insecurity." In *Rural Poverty in the United States*, edited by A. Tickamyer, J. Sherman, and J. Warlick, 256–97. New York: Columbia University Press.

Collins, Patricia Hill. 2008. *Black Feminist Thought: Knowledge, Consciousness, and the Politics of Empowerment*. 1st edition. New York: Routledge.

Conley, Dalton. 1999. *Being Black, Living in the Red: Race, Wealth, and Social Policy in America*. 1st edition. Berkeley: University of California Press.

Connell, R. W. 1995. *Masculinities*. Berkeley: University of California Press.

Cooper, Marianne. 2014. *Cut Adrift: Families in Insecure Times*. Berkeley: University of California Press.

Corbett, Michael. 2007. *Learning to Leave: The Irony of Schooling in a Coastal Community*. Halifax, Nova Scotia: Fernwood Publishing Co., Ltd.

Covert, Bryce. 2013. "How the 'Opt-Out Revolution' Changed Men." *The Nation*, August 8.

Cramer, Katherine J. 2016. *The Politics of Resentment: Rural Consciousness in Wisconsin and the Rise of Scott Walker*. Chicago: University of Chicago Press.

Crowe, Jessica A. 2006. "Community Economic Development Strategies in Rural Washington: Toward a Synthesis of Natural and Social Capital." *Rural Sociology* 71(4):573–96.

Crowley, Martha, and Daniel T. Lichter. 2009. "Social Disorganization in New Latino Destinations?" *Rural Sociology* 74(4):573–604.

Curran, D. 2016. *Risk, Power, and Inequality in the 21st Century*. New York: Palgrave Macmillan.

Deason, Grace. 2010. "Opting Out: Strategic Choice, Social Protest, or Feminism's Dead End?" *Sex Roles* 63(11–12):897–99.

Debertin, David L., and Stephan J. Goetz. 2013. *Social Capital Formation in Rural, Urban and Suburban Communities*. University of Kentucky Staff Paper 474. University of Kentucky.

Deller, Steven. 2010. "Rural Poverty, Tourism and Spatial Heterogeneity." *Annals of Tourism Research* 37(1):180–205.

Desmond, Matthew. 2012. "Disposable Ties and the Urban Poor." *American Journal of Sociology* 117(5):1295–1335.

———. 2016. *Evicted: Poverty and Profit in the American City*. 1st edition. New York: Crown.

Devine, Jennifer. 2006. "Hardworking Newcomers and Generations of Poverty: Poverty Discourse in Central Washington State." *Antipode* 38(5):953–76.

Dolsak, Nives, and Aseem Prakash. 2018. "Seattle's Smoky Summers Are Becoming the New Normal." *The Hill*, August 22.

Duncan, Cynthia M. 1999. *Worlds Apart: Why Poverty Persists in Rural America*. New Haven, CT: Yale University Press.

Duneier, Mitchell. 1999. *Sidewalk*. New York: Farrar, Strauss and Giroux.

Edin, Kathryn, and Maria Kefalas. 2005. *Promises I Can Keep: Why Poor Women Put Motherhood before Marriage*. Berkeley: University of California Press.

Edin, Kathryn, and Laura Lein. 1997. *Making Ends Meet: How Single Mothers Survive Welfare and Low-Wage Work*. New York: Russell Sage Foundation.

Ehrenreich, Barbara. 2001. *Nickel and Dimed: On (Not) Getting By in America*. New York: Metropolitan Books.

Fan, Xitao, and Michael Chen. 2001. "Parental Involvement and Students' Academic Achievement: A Meta-Analysis." *Educational Psychology Review* 13:1–23.

Ferber, Abby L. 2012. "The Culture of Privilege: Color-Blindness, Postfeminism, and Christonormativity." *Journal of Social Issues* 68(1):63–77.

Fischer, Claude S. 1975. "Toward a Subcultural Theory of Urbanism." *American Journal of Sociology* 80(6):1319–41.

Fitchen, Janet M. 1991. *Endangered Spaces, Enduring Places: Change, Identity, and Survival in Rural America*. Boulder, CO: Westview Press.

Flora, Cornelia Butler, and Jan L. Flora. 2013. *Rural Communities: Legacy and Change*. 4th edition. Boulder, CO: Westview Press.

———. 2014. "Community Organization and Mobilization in Rural America." In *Rural America in a Globalizing World: Problems and Prospects for the 2010s*, edited by E. Ransom, C. Bailey, and L. Jensen, 609–25. Morgantown: West Virginia University Press.

Fong, Kelley, Rachel A. Wright, and Christopher Wimer. 2016. "The Cost of Free Assistance: Why Low-Income Individuals Do Not Access Food Pantries." *Journal of Sociology & Social Welfare* 43(1):71–93.

Fortmann, Louise, and Jonathan Kusel. 1990. "New Voices, Old Beliefs: Forest Environmentalism among New and Long-standing Rural Residents." *Rural Sociology* 55(2):214–32.

Frank, Thomas. 2004. *What's the Matter with Kansas? How Conservatives Won the Heart of America*. New York: Metropolitan Books.

Freudenburg, William R. 1992. "Addictive Economies: Extractive Industries and Vulnerable Localities in a Changing World Economy." *Rural Sociology* 57(3):305–32.

Freudenburg, William R., Lisa J. Wilson, and Daniel J. O'Leary. 1998. "Forty Years of Spotted Owls? A Longitudinal Analysis of Logging Industry Job Losses." *Sociological Perspectives* 41(1):1–26.

Gallagher, Charles A. 2003. "Color-Blind Privilege: The Social and Political Functions of Erasing the Color Line in Post Race America." *Race, Gender & Class* 10(4):22–37.

Gans, Herbert. 1996. *The War against the Poor: The Underclass and Antipoverty Policy*. New York: Basic Books.

Gerald, Danette, and Kati Haycock. 2006. *Engines of Inequality Diminishing Equity in the Nation's Premier Public Universities*. The Education Trust.

Accessed February 17, 2018. https://edtrust.org/wp-content/uploads/2013/10/EnginesofInequality.pdf.

Gest, Justin. 2016. *The New Minority: White Working Class Politics in an Age of Immigration and Inequality*. Oxford, UK: Oxford University Press.

Ghose, Rina. 2004. "Big Sky or Big Sprawl? Rural Gentrification and the Changing Cultural Landscape of Missoula, Montana." *Urban Geography* 25(6):528–49.

Gilbert, Dennis L. 2014. *The American Class Structure in an Age of Growing Inequality*. 9th edition. Los Angeles: Sage Publications.

Goffman, Erving. 1959. *The Presentation of Self in Everyday Life*. 1st edition. New York: Anchor.

———. 1963. *Stigma: Notes on the Management of Spoiled Identity*. Englewood Cliffs, NJ: Prentice Hall.

Golding, Shaun A. 2014a. "Migration and Inequality in the Rural United States: Connecting Urban to Rural and Local to Global." *Sociology Compass* 8(3):324–35.

———. 2014b. "Moving Narratives: Using Online Forums to Study Amenity Out-migration in the American Midwest." *Journal of Rural Studies* 33:32–40.

Gowan, Teresa. 2010. *Hobos, Hustlers, and Backsliders: Homeless in San Francisco*. Minneapolis: University of Minnesota Press.

Granovetter, Mark S. 1973. "The Strength of Weak Ties." *American Journal of Sociology* 78(6):1360–80.

Grusky, David B., Bruce Western, and Christopher Wimer. 2011a. "The Consequences of the Great Recession." In *The Great Recession*, edited by Grusky, Western, and Wimer, 3–20. New York: Russell Sage Foundation.

———, eds. 2011b. *The Great Recession*. New York: Russell Sage Foundation.

Hacker, Jacob S., Philipp Rehm, and Mark Schlesinger. 2010. *Standing on Shaky Ground: Americans' Experiences with Economic Insecurity. Publications*. New York: Rockefeller Foundation.

Halfacree, Keith H. 1995. "Talking about Rurality: Social Representations of the Rural as Expressed by Residents of Six English Parishes." *Journal of Rural Studies* 11(1):1–20.

Hamilton, Lawrence C., Leslie R. Hamilton, Cynthia M. Duncan, and Chris R. Colocousis. 2008. "Place Matters: Challenges and Opportunities in Four Rural Americas." *Carsey Institute Reports on Rural America* 1(4):2–32.

Hartmann, Douglas, Paul R. Croll, Ryan Larson, Joseph Gerteis, and Alex Manning. 2017. "Colorblindness as Identity: Key Determinants, Relations to Ideology, and Implications for Attitudes about Race and Policy." *Sociological Perspectives* 60(5):866–88.

Hashemi, Manata. 2015. "Waithood and Face: Morality and Mobility among Lower-Class Youth in Iran." *Qualitative Sociology* 1–23.

Hauhart, Robert C. 2015. "American Sociology's Investigations of the American Dream: Retrospect and Prospect." *American Sociologist* 46(1):65–98.

Hays, Sharon. 1996. *The Cultural Contradictions of Motherhood*. New Haven, CT: Yale University Press.

———. 2003. *Flat Broke with Children: Women in the Age of Welfare Reform*. Oxford, UK: Oxford University Press.

Heflin, Colleen M., and Mary Pattillo. 2006. "Poverty in the Family: Race, Siblings, and Socioeconomic Heterogeneity." *Social Science Research* 35(4):804–22.

Hines, J. Dwight. 2010. "In Pursuit of Experience: The Postindustrial Gentrification of the Rural American West." *Ethnography* 11(2):285–308.

Hochschild, Arlie. 1989. *The Second Shift*. New York: Penguin Books.

Hochschild, Arlie Russell. 2016. *Strangers in Their Own Land: Anger and Mourning on the American Right*. New York: New Press.

Hofferth, Sandra, and John Iceland. 1998. "Social Capital in Rural and Urban Communities." *Rural Sociology* 63(4):574–98.

Hout, Michael, Asaf Levanon, and Erin Cumberworth. 2011. "Job Loss and Unemployment." In *The Great Recession*, edited by D. B. Grusky, B. Western, and C. Wimer, 59–81. New York: Russell Sage Foundation.

Howarth, William. 1995. "Land and Word: American Pastoral." In *The Changing American Countryside: Rural People and Places*, edited by E. N. Castle, 13–35. Lawrence: University Press of Kansas.

Hunter, Lori M., Jason D. Boardman, and Jarron M. Saint Onge. 2005. "The Association between Natural Amenities, Rural Population Growth, and Long-Term Residents' Economic Well-Being." *Rural Sociology* 70(4):452–69.

irrigation.education. 2016. "How a Center Pivot Irrigation Machine Works." Accessed September 24, 2018. http://blog.irrigation.education/blog/how-a-center-pivot-works.

Jencks, Christopher, Susan Bartlett, Mary Corcoran, James Crouse, David Eaglesfield, Gregory Jackson, Kent McClelland, Peter Mueser, Michael Olneck, Joseph Schwartz, Sherry Ward, and Jill Williams. 1979. *Who Gets Ahead? The Determinants of Economic Success in America*. New York: Basic Books.

Jennings, Brian M., and Richard S. Krannich. 2013. "A Multidimensional Exploration of the Foundations of Community Attachment among Seasonal and Year-Round Residents." *Rural Sociology* 78(4):498–527.

Jensen, Leif, and Danielle Ely. 2017. "Measures of Poverty and Implications for Portraits of Rural Hardship." In *Rural Poverty in the United States*, edited by A. R. Tickamyer, J. Sherman, and J. Warlick, 67–83. New York: Columbia University Press.

Jensen, Leif, and Eric B. Jensen. 2011. "Employment Hardship Among Rural Men." In *Economic Restructuring and Family Well-Being in Rural America*, edited by K. E. Smith and A. R. Tickamyer, 40–59. University Park: Penn State University Press.

Jensen, Leif, Diane K. McLaughlin, and Tim Slack. 2003. "Rural Poverty: The Persisting Challenge." In *Challenges for Rural America in the Twenty-First Century*, edited by D. Brown and L. E. Swanson, 118–31. University Park: Penn State University Press.

Jensen, Leif, Ann R. Tickamyer, and Tim Slack. 2019. "Rural-Urban Variation in Informal Work Activities in the United States." *Journal of Rural Studies* 68:276–284.

Jobes, Patrick C. 2000. *Moving Nearer to Heaven: The Illusions and Disillusions of Migrants to Scenic Rural Places*. Westport, CT: Praeger.

Johnson, Paul Elliott. 2017. "The Art of Masculine Victimhood: Donald Trump's Demagoguery." *Women's Studies in Communication* 40(3):229–50.

Jones, Robert Emmet, J. Mark Fly, James Talley, and H. Ken Cordell. 2003. "Green Migration into Rural America: The New Frontier of Environmentalism?" *Society & Natural Resources* 16(3):221–38.

Judt, Tony. 2011. *Ill Fares the Land*. 1st edition. London: Penguin Books.

Kelly, E. Brooke. 2013. "Working at Getting to Work: Negotiating Transportation and Low-Wage Work in Rural Michigan." *Sociation Today* 11(2). www.ncsociology.org/sociationtoday/v112/work.html.

Kelly, Paige, and Linda Lobao. 2019. "The Social Bases of Rural-Urban Political Divides: Social Status, Work, and Sociocultural Beliefs." *Rural Sociology* 84(4):633–870.

Kissane, Rebecca Joyce. 2012. "Poor Women's Moral Economies of Nonprofit Social Service Use: Conspicuous Constraint and Empowerment in the Hollow State." *Sociological Perspectives* 55(1):189–211.

Kittay, Eva Feder. 1999. "Welfare, Dependency, and a Public Ethic of Care." In *Whose Welfare?*, edited by G. Mink, 189–213. Ithaca, NY: Cornell University Press.

Kohn, Melvin L. 1959. "Social Class and Parental Values." *American Journal of Sociology* 64(4):337–51.

Kondo, Michelle C., Rebeca Rivera, and Stan Rullman. 2012. "Protecting the Idyll but Not the Environment: Second Homes, Amenity Migration and Rural Exclusion in Washington State." *Landscape and Urban Planning* 106(2):174–82.

Koricich, Andrew, Xi Chen, and Rodney P. Hughes. 2018. "Understanding the Effects of Rurality and Socioeconomic Status on College Attendance and Institutional Choice in the United States." *Review of Higher Education* 41(2):281–305.

Krannich, Richard S., and Peggy Petrzelka. 2003. "Tourism and Natural Amenity Development: Real Opportunities?" In *Challenges for Rural America in the*

Twenty-First Century, edited by D. L. Brown and L. E. Swanson, 190–99. University Park: Penn State University Press.

Kusmin, Lorin. 2014. *Rural America at a Glance, 2014 Edition. Economic Brief.* EB-26. Washington, DC: US Department of Agriculture.

Lamont, Michèle. 1992. *Money, Morals, and Manners: The Culture of the French and American Upper-Middle Class.* Chicago: University of Chicago Press.

———. 2000. *The Dignity of Working Men: Morality and the Boundaries of Race, Class, and Immigration.* New York: Russell Sage Foundation.

Lamont, Michèle, and Marcel Fournier. 1992. *Cultivating Differences: Symbolic Boundaries and the Making of Inequality.* Chicago: University of Chicago Press.

Lamont, Michèle, and Virag Molnar. 2002. "The Study of Boundaries in the Social Sciences." *Annual Review of Sociology* 28:167–95.

Lamont, Michèle, Graziella Moraes Silva, Jessica Welburn, Joshua Guetzkow, Nissim Mizrachi, Hanna Herzog, and Elisa Reis. 2016. *Getting Respect: Responding to Stigma and Discrimination in the United States, Brazil, and Israel.* Princeton, NJ: Princeton University Press.

Lareau, Annette. 2003. *Unequal Childhoods: Class, Race, and Family Life.* 1st edition. Berkeley: University of California Press.

Lareau, Annette, and Jessica McCrory Calarco. 2012. "Class, Cultural Capital, and Institutions: The Case of Families and Schools." In *Facing Social Class: How Societal Rank Influences Interaction*, edited by S. T. Fiske and H. R. Markus, 61–86. New York: Russell Sage Foundation.

Larsen, Soren, and Craig Hutton. 2012. "Community Discourse and the Emerging Amenity Landscapes of the Rural American West." *GeoJournal* 77(5):651–65.

Levine, Judith. 2013. *Ain't No Trust: How Bosses, Boyfriends, and Bureaucrats Fail Low-Income Mothers and Why It Matters.* Berkeley: University of California Press.

Lichtenstein, Grace. 2004. "Part-Time Paradise." *High Country News.* Accessed January 30, 2017. www.hcn.org/issues/285/15070.

Lichter, Daniel T., and David L. Brown. 2011. "Rural America in an Urban Society: Changing Spatial and Social Boundaries." *Annual Review of Sociology* 37(1):565–92.

Lichter, Daniel T., and Deboarah Roempke Graefe. 2011. "Rural Economic Restructuring: Implications for Children, Youth, and Families." In *Economic Restructuring and Family Well-Being in Rural America*, edited by K. E. Smith and A. R. Tickamyer, 25–39. University Park: Penn State University Press.

Lichter, Daniel T., and Kai A. Schafft. 2016. "People and Places Left Behind: Rural Poverty in the New Century." In *The Oxford Handbook of the Social*

Science of Poverty, edited by D. Brady and L. M. Burton, 317–40. Oxford, UK: Oxford University Press.

Lichter, Daniel T., and James P. Ziliak. 2017. "The Rural-Urban Interface: New Patterns of Spatial Interdependence and Inequality in America." *ANNALS of the American Academy of Political and Social Science* 672(1):6–25.

Lobao, Linda. 2006. "Gendered Places and Place-Based Gender Identities: Reflections and Refractions." In *Country Boys: Masculinity and Rural Life*, edited by H. Campbell, M. M. Bell, and M. Finney, 267–75. University Park: Penn State University Press.

Logan, John R., and Julia Burdick-Will. 2017. "School Segregation and Disparities in Urban, Suburban, and Rural Areas." *ANNALS of the American Academy of Political and Social Science* 674(1):199–216.

Lorah, Paul, and Rob Southwick. 2003. "Environmental Protection, Population Change, and Economic Development in the Rural Western United States." *Population and Environment* 24(3):255–72.

Mattingly, Marybeth J., Kristin E. Smith, and Jessica A. Bean. 2011. *Unemployment in the Great Recession: Single Parents and Men Hit Hard*. Issue Brief. 35. Carsey Institute, New Hampshire.

McCall, Leslie, Derek Burk, Marie Laperrière, and Jennifer A. Richeson. 2017. "Exposure to Rising Inequality Shapes Americans' Opportunity Beliefs and Policy Support." *Proceedings of the National Academy of Sciences* 114(36):9593–98.

McCoy, Terrence. 2017. "Disabled, or Just Desperate? Rural Americans Turn to Disability as Jobs Dry Up." *Washington Post*, March 30.

McDermott, Monica, and Frank L. Samson. 2005. "White Racial and Ethnic Identity in the United States." *Annual Review of Sociology* 31(1):245–61.

McGranahan, David. 1999. *Natural Amenities Drive Rural Population Change. Agricultural Economic Report*. AER-781. US Department of Agriculture Economic Research Service.

McHenry-Sorber, Erin, and Kai A. Schafft. 2015. "'Make My Day, Shoot a Teacher': Tactics of Inclusion and Exclusion, and the Contestation of Community in a Rural School–Community Conflict." *International Journal of Inclusive Education* 19(7):733–47.

Mederer, Helen J. 1999. "Surviving the Demise of a Way of Life: Stress and Resilience in Northeastern Commercial Fishing Families." In *The Dynamics of Resilient Families*, edited by H. I. McCubbin, E. A. Thompson, A. I. Thompson, and J. A. Futrell, 203–35. Thousand Oaks, CA: Sage Publications.

Mette, Ian M., Catharine Biddle, Sarah V. Mackenzie, and Kathy Harris-Smedberg. 2016. "Poverty, Privilege, and Political Dynamics within Rural School Reform Unraveling Educational Leadership in the Invisible America." *Journal of Cases in Educational Leadership* 19(3):62–84.

Michaelson, Adam. 2009. *The Foreclosure of America: The Inside Story of the*

Rise and Fall of Countrywide Home Loans, the Mortgage Crisis, and the Default of the American Dream. 1st edition. New York: Berkley Hardcover.

Mikesell, James. 2004. "One in Four Rural Households Are Housing Stressed." *Amber Waves*, November 1.

Minnesota Population Center. 2016. "National Historical Geographic Information System: Version 11.0 [Database]." Accessed January 27, 2017. www.nhgis.org/.

Monnat, Shannon M. 2018. "Factors Associated with County-Level Differences in U.S. Drug-Related Mortality Rates." *American Journal of Preventive Medicine* 54(5): 611–19.

———. 2020. "Why Coronavirus Could Hit Rural Areas Harder." *Lerner Center for Public Health Promotion, Syracuse University.* Accessed July 23, 2020. https://lernercenter.syr.edu/2020/03/24/why-coronavirus-could-hit-rural-areas-harder/.

Monnat, Shannon M., and David L. Brown. 2017. "More Than a Rural Revolt: Landscapes of Despair and the 2016 Presidential Election." *Journal of Rural Studies* 55:227–36.

Monnat, Shannon M., and Khary K. Rigg. 2016. "Examining Rural/Urban Differences in Prescription Opioid Misuse among US Adolescents." *Journal of Rural Health* 32(2):204–18.

Morris, Martina, and Bruce Western. 1999. "Inequality in Earnings at the Close of the Twentieth Century." *Annual Review of Sociology* 25:623–57.

Moss, Philip, and Chris Tilly. 1996. "'Soft' Skills and Race: An Investigation of Black Men's Employment Problems." *Work and Occupations* 23(3):252–76.

Neckerman, Kathryn M., and Florencia Torche. 2007. "Inequality: Causes and Consequences." *Annual Review of Sociology* 33(1):335–57.

Nelson, Lise, and Peter B. Nelson. 2011. "The Global Rural: Gentrification and Linked Migration in the Rural USA." *Progress in Human Geography* 35(4):441–59.

Nelson, Margaret K. 2000. "Single Mothers and Social Support: The Commitment to, and Retreat from, Reciprocity." *Qualitative Sociology* 23(3):291–317.

———. 2005. *The Social Economy of Single Motherhood: Raising Children in Rural America.* New York: Routledge.

Nelson, Margaret K., and Joan Smith. 1999. *Working Hard and Making Do: Surviving in Small Town America.* Berkeley: University of California Press.

Nelson, Peter B., Alexander Oberg, and Lise Nelson. 2010. "Rural Gentrification and Linked Migration in the United States." *Journal of Rural Studies* 26(4):343–52.

Newman, Katherine S. 1999. *No Shame in My Game: The Working Poor in the Inner City.* New York: Vintage Books.

Nolan, Brian, and Christopher T. Whelan. 2010. "Using Non-Monetary Deprivation Indicators to Analyze Poverty and Social Exclusion: Lessons from Europe?" *Journal of Policy Analysis and Management* 29(2):305–25.

North Dakota State University. 2013. "Irrigation—Frequently Asked Questions." Accessed September 24, 2018. www.ag.ndsu.edu/irrigation/faqs.

Office of Financial Management. 2016. "Decennial Census." Accessed October 11, 2016. www.ofm.wa.gov/pop/census.asp.

Oliver, Melvin, and Thomas Shapiro. 2006. *Black Wealth / White Wealth: A New Perspective on Racial Inequality*. 2nd edition. New York: Routledge.

Ooi, Natalie, Jennifer Laing, and Judith Mair. 2015. "Sociocultural Change Facing Ranchers in the Rocky Mountain West as a Result of Mountain Resort Tourism and Amenity Migration." *Journal of Rural Studies* 41:59–71.

Parcel, Toby L., and Mikaela J. Dufur. 2001. "Capital at Home and at School: Effects on Student Achievement." *Social Forces* 79(3):881–911.

Parker, Timothy S., Lorin D. Kusmin, and Alexander W. Marre. 2010. *Economic Recovery: Lessons Learned from Previous Recessions*. US Department of Agriculture Economic Research Service.

Pedulla, David S., and Katherine S. Newman. 2011. "The Family and Community Impacts of Underemployment." In *Underemployment: Psychological, Economic, and Social Challenges*, edited by D. C. Maynard and D. C. Feldman, 233–52. New York: Springer.

Percheski, Christine. 2008. "Opting Out? Cohort Differences in Professional Women's Employment Rates from 1960 to 2005." *American Sociological Review* 73(3):497–517.

Peters, David J. 2020. "Rural America Is More Vulnerable to COVID-19 Than Cities Are, and It's Starting to Show." *The Conversation*. Accessed July 23, 2020. http://theconversation.com/rural-america-is-more-vulnerable-to-covid-19-than-cities-are-and-its-starting-to-show-140532.

Petrin, Robert A., Kai A. Schafft, and Judith L. Meece. 2014. "Educational Sorting and Residential Aspirations among Rural High School Students: What Are the Contributions of Schools and Educators to Rural Brain Drain?" *American Educational Research Journal* 51(2):1–33.

Pettigrew, Thomas F., and Linda R. Tropp. 2008. "How Does Intergroup Contact Reduce Prejudice? Meta-Analytic Tests of Three Mediators." *European Journal of Social Psychology* 38(6):922–34.

Pew Research Center. 2015. *Most Say Government Policies since Recession Have Done Little to Help Middle Class, Poor*.

Phillips, Martin. 2004. "Other Geographies of Gentrification." *Progress in Human Geography* 28(1):5–30.

Pied, Claudine M. 2019. "The Problem People and the Hard Workers: Whiteness and Small Town Response to Economic Decline." *Identities* 26(1):33–50.

Piketty, Thomas, and Emmanuel Saez. 2014. "Inequality in the Long Run." *Science* 344(6186):838–43.

Pilgeram, Ryanne. 2019. "'How Much Does Property Cost Up There?': Exploring the Relationship between Women, Sustainable Farming, and Rural Gentrification in the US." *Society & Natural Resources* 32(8):911–27.

Piven, Frances Fox, and Richard A. Cloward. 2000. *Why Americans Still Don't Vote: And Why Politicians Want It That Way.* Boston: Beacon Press.

Porter, Eduardo. 2018. "The Hard Truths of Trying to 'Save' the Rural Economy." *New York Times*, December 14.

Prasad, Monica, Steve G. Hoffman, and Kieran Bezila. 2016. "Walking the Line: The White Working Class and the Economic Consequences of Morality." *Politics & Society* 44(2):281–304.

Pugh, Allison J., ed. 2016. *Beyond the Cubicle: Job Insecurity, Intimacy, and the Flexible Self.* New York: Oxford University Press.

Purser, Gretchen. 2009. "The Dignity of Job-Seeking Men." *Journal of Contemporary Ethnography* 38(1):117–39.

———. 2016. "The Circle of Dispossession: Evicting the Urban Poor in Baltimore." *Critical Sociology* 42(3):393–415.

Putnam, Robert D. 2001. *Bowling Alone: The Collapse and Revival of American Community.* New York: Simon & Schuster.

Putnam, Robert D., and Lewis Feldstein. 2003. *Better Together: Restoring the American Community.* New York: Simon and Schuster.

Quandt, Sara A., Juliana McDonald, Ronny A. Bell, and Thomas A. Arcury. 1999. "Aging Research in Multi-Ethinic Rural Communities: Gaining Entrée through Community Involvement." *Journal of Cross-Cultural Gerontology* 14(2):113–30.

Reeder, Richard J., and Dennis M. Brown. 2005. *Recreation, Tourism, and Rural Well-Being.* Economic Research Report 7. US Department of Agriculture Economic Research Service.

Rigg, Khary K., Shannon M. Monnat, and Melody N. Chavez. 2018. "Opioid-Related Mortality in Rural America: Geographic Heterogeneity and Intervention Strategies." *International Journal of Drug Policy* 57:119–29.

Rogers-Dillon, Robin. 1995. "The Dynamics of Welfare Stigma." *Qualitative Sociology* 18(4):439–56.

Rosenstone, Steven J. 1982. "Economic Adversity and Voter Turnout." *American Journal of Political Science* 26(1):25–46.

Roy, Kevin, and Linda Burton. 2007. "Mothering through Recruitment: Kinscription of Nonresidential Fathers and Father Figures in Low-Income Families." *Family Relations* 56(January 2007):24–39.

Rucker, Phillip. 2018. "The President as the Persecuted: Donald Trump's Strategy of Self-Victimization." *Washington Post*, June 4.

Sage, Rayna, and Jennifer Sherman. 2014. "'There Are No Jobs Here': Opportunity Structures, Moral Judgment, and Educational Trajectories in the Rural Northwest." In *Dynamics of Social Class, Race, and Place in Rural Education,* edited by C. B. Howley, A. Howley, and J. Johnson, 67–94. Charlotte, NC: Information Age Press.

Salamon, Sonya. 2003a. "From Hometown to Nontown: Rural Community Effects of Suburbanization." *Rural Sociology* 68(1):1–24.

———. 2003b. *Newcomers to Old Towns: Suburbanization of the Heartland.* Chicago: University of Chicago Press.

Salamon, Sonya, and Katherine MacTavish. 2006. "Quasi-Homelessness among Rural Trailer Park Families." In *International Perspectives on Rural Homelessness*, 45–87. London: Routledge Press.

———. 2017. *Singlewide: Chasing the American Dream in a Rural Trailer Park.* 1st edition. Ithaca, NY: Cornell University Press.

Sayer, Andrew. 2005. *The Moral Significance of Class.* Cambridge, UK: Cambridge University Press.

Schafft, Kai A. 2006. "Poverty, Residential Mobility, and Student Transiency within a Rural New York School District." *Rural Sociology* 71(2):212–31.

Schafft, Kai A., and A. Maselli. 2021. "Shifting Population Dynamics in the United States, and the Implications for Rural Schools." In *Handbook on Rural Education in the United States*, edited by A. P. Azano, K. Eppley, and C. Biddle. London, UK: Bloomsbury.

Schafft, Kai A., Erin McHenry-Sorber, Daniella Hall, and Ian Burfoot-Rochford. 2018. "Busted amidst the Boom: The Creation of New Insecurities and Inequalities within Pennsylvania's Shale Gas Boomtowns." *Rural Sociology* 83(3):503–31.

Schwalbe, Michael, Sandra Godwin, Daphne Holden, Douglas Schrock, Shealy Thompson, and Michele Wolkomir. 2000. "Generic Processes in the Reproduction of Inequality: An Interactionist Analysis." *Social Forces* 79(2):419–52.

Seccombe, Karen. 2010. *"So You Think I Drive a Cadillac?" Welfare Recipients' Perspectives on the System and Its Reform.* 3rd edition. Upper Saddle River, NJ: Prentice Hall.

Seefeldt, Kristin S. 2016. *Abandoned Families: Social Isolation in the Twenty-First Century.* 1st edition. New York: Russell Sage Foundation.

Sewell, William H., and Robert M. Hauser. 1975. *Education, Occupation, and Earnings: Achievement in the Early Career.* New York: Academic Press.

Sherman, Jennifer. 2006. "Coping with Rural Poverty: Economic Survival and Moral Capital in Rural America." *Social Forces* 85(2):891–913.

———. 2009a. "Bend to Avoid Breaking: Job Loss, Gender Norms, and Family Stability in Rural America." *Social Problems* 56(4):599–620.

———. 2009b. *Those Who Work, Those Who Don't: Poverty, Morality, and Family in Rural America.* Minneapolis: University of Minnesota Press.

———. 2013. "Surviving the Great Recession: Growing Need and the Stigmatized Safety Net." *Social Problems* 60(4):409–32.

———. 2014. "Rural Poverty: The Great Recession, Rising Unemployment, and the Underutilized Safety Net." In *Rural America in a Globalizing World: Problems and Prospects for the 2010s*, edited by C. Bailey, L. Jensen, and E. Ransom, 523–39. Morgantown: West Virginia Press.

———. 2018. "'Not Allowed to Inherit My Kingdom': Amenity Development and Social Inequality in the Rural West." *Rural Sociology* 83(1):174–207.

Sherman, Jennifer, and Elizabeth Harris. 2012. "Social Class and Parenting: Classic Debates and New Understandings." *Sociology Compass* 6(1):60–71.

Sherman, Jennifer, and Rayna Sage. 2011. "'Sending Off All Your Good Treasures': Rural Schools, Brain-Drain, and Community Survival in the Wake of Economic Collapse." *Journal of Research in Rural Education* 26(11):1–14.

Sherman, Rachel. 2017. *Uneasy Street: The Anxieties of Affluence*. Princeton, NJ: Princeton University Press.

Shipler, David K. 2005. *The Working Poor: Invisible in America*. Reprint edition. New York: Vintage.

Shirley, Carla D. 2010. "'You Might Be a Redneck If...' Boundary Work among Rural, Southern Whites." *Social Forces* 89(1):35–61.

Shucksmith, Mark. 2012. "Class, Power and Inequality in Rural Areas: Beyond Social Exclusion?" *Sociologia Ruralis* 52(4):377–97.

———. 2016. "Social Exclusion in Rural Places." In *Routledge International Handbook of Rural Studies*, edited by M. Shucksmith and D. L. Brown, 433–49. New York: Routledge.

———. 2018. "Re-Imagining the Rural: From Rural Idyll to Good Countryside." *Journal of Rural Studies* 59:163–72.

Shucksmith, Mark, and Kai A. Schafft. 2012. "Understanding Social Exclusion in European and U.S. Rural Contexts." In *Rural Transformations and Rural Policies in the US and UK*, edited by M. Shucksmith, D. L. Brown, S. Shortall, J. Vergunst, and M. Warner, 100–116. New York: Routledge.

Shulman, Beth. 2003. *The Betrayal of Work: How Low-Wage Jobs Fail 30 Million Americans and Their Families*. 1st edition. New York: New Press.

Siegler, Kirk. 2020. "Sun Valley, Idaho: 'No One Should Come Here.'" NPR. org. Accessed on July 20, 2020. www.npr.org/2020/03/27/822122059/sun-valley-idaho-no-one-should-come-here.

Silva, Jennifer M. 2013. *Coming up Short: Working-Class Adulthood in an Age of Uncertainty*. New York: Oxford University Press.

———. 2019. *We're Still Here: Pain and Politics in the Heart of America*. New York: Oxford University Press.

Slack, Tim. 2007. "The Contours and Correlates of Informal Work in Rural Pennsylvania." *Rural Sociology* 72(1):69–89.

Small, Mario Luis, David J. Harding, and Michèle Lamont. 2010. "Reconsidering Culture and Poverty." *ANNALS of the American Academy of Political and Social Science* 629(1):6–27.

Smith, Kristin. 2017. "Changing Gender Roles and Rural Poverty." In *Rural*

Poverty in the United States, edited by A. R. Tickamyer, J. Sherman, and J. Warlick, 117–32. New York: Columbia University Press.

Smith, Kristin E. 2011. "Changing Roles: Women and Work in Rural America." In *Economic Restructuring and Family Well-Being in Rural America*, edited by K. E. Smith and A. R. Tickamyer, 60–81. University Park: Penn State University Press.

Smith, Kristin E., and Ann R. Tickamyer, eds. 2011. *Economic Restructuring and Family Well-Being in Rural America*. University Park: Penn State University Press.

Smith, Michael D., and Richard S. Krannich. 2000. "'Culture Clash' Revisited: Newcomer and Longer-term Residents' Attitudes toward Land Use, Development, and Environmental Issues in Rural Communities in the Rocky Mountain West." *Rural Sociology* 65(3):396–421.

Smith, Sandra Susan. 2010. *Lone Pursuit: Distrust and Defensive Individualism among the Black Poor*. New York: Russell Sage Foundation.

Spilerman, Seymour. 2000. "Wealth and Stratification Processes." *Annual Review of Sociology* 26(1):497–524.

Stack, Carol B. 1974. *All Our Kin: Strategies for Survival in a Black Community*. New York: Basic Books.

Stedman, Richard C. 2006. "Understanding Place Attachment among Second Home Owners." *American Behavioral Scientist* 50(2):187–205.

Stein, Arlene. 2001. *The Stranger Next Door: The Story of a Small Community's Battle over Sex, Faith, and Civil Rights*. Boston: Beacon Press.

Stone, Pamela. 2008. *Opting Out?: Why Women Really Quit Careers and Head Home*. Berkeley: University of California Press.

Tan, Anjelica. 2020. "Americans Leave Large Cities for Suburban Areas and Rural Towns." *The Hill*. Accessed July 6, 2020. https://thehill.com/opinion/finance/505944-americans-leave-large-cities-for-suburban-areas-and-rural-towns.

Telford, Taylor. 2019. "Income Inequality in America Is the Highest It's Been since Census Bureau Started Tracking It, Data Shows." *Washington Post*, September 26.

Thiede, Brian, and Tim Slack. 2017. "The Old versus the New Economies and Their Impacts." In *Rural Poverty in the United States*, edited by A. R. Tickamyer, J. Sherman, and J. Warlick, 231–56. New York: Columbia University Press.

Thompson, Cameron, Teresa Johnson, and Samuel Hanes. 2016. "Vulnerability of Fishing Communities Undergoing Gentrification." *Journal of Rural Studies* 45:165–74.

Thompson, Steve. 2006. "Gateway to Glacier: Will Amenity Migrants in North-Western Montana Lead the Way for Amenity Conservation?" In *The Amenity*

Migrants: Seeking and Sustaining Mountains and Their Cultures, edited by
L. A. G. Moss, 108–19. Oxford, UK: CABI.

Tickamyer, Ann R., and Debra A. Henderson. 2011. "Livelihood Practices in the
Shadow of Welfare Reform." In *Economic Restructuring and Family Well-
Being in Rural America*, edited by K. E. Smith and A. R. Tickamyer, 294–319.
University Park: Penn State University Press.

Tickamyer, Ann R., Jennifer Sherman, and Jennifer Warlick, eds. 2017. *Rural
Poverty in the United States*. New York: Columbia University Press.

Tickamyer, Ann R., and Teresa A. Wood. 1998. "Identifying Participation in
the Informal Economy Using Survey Research Methods." *Rural Sociology*
63(2):323–39.

Ulrich-Schad, Jessica D. 2018. "'We Didn't Move Here to Move to Aspen': Community Making and Community Development in an Emerging Rural Amenity
Destination." *Journal of Rural and Community Development* 13(4):43–66.

Ulrich-Schad, Jessica D., Megan Henly, and Thomas G. Safford. 2013. "The Role
of Community Assessments, Place, and the Great Recession in the Migration
Intentions of Rural Americans." *Rural Sociology* 78(3):371–98.

Ulrich-Schad, Jessica D., and Hua Qin. 2018. "Culture Clash? Predictors of
Views on Amenity-Led Development and Community Involvement in Rural
Recreation Counties." *Rural Sociology* 83(1):81–108.

U.S. Census Bureau. 2012. "American FactFinder Results." Accessed December
25, 2013. http://factfinder2.census.gov.

———. 2015. "American Community Survey 5-Year Estimates." Accessed June 6,
2014. http://factfinder2.census.gov/.

———. 2016. "American FactFinder Results." Accessed October 11, 2016. http://
factfinder.census.gov/faces/nav/jsf/pages/index.xhtml#.

———. 2019. *ACS Provides New State and Local Income, Poverty and Health
Insurance*. CB19-152. US Census Bureau.

Wessels, Bridgette. 2013. "The Reproduction and Reconfiguration of Inequal-
ity: Differentiation and Class, Status, and Power in the Dynamics of Digital
Divides." In *The Digital Divide: The Internet and Social Inequality in
International Perspective*, edited by M. Ragnedda and G. W. Muschert, 17–28.
New York: Routledge.

West, Candace, and Don H. Zimmerman. 1987. "Doing Gender." *Gender &
Society* 1(2):125–51.

Whitley, Sarah. 2013. "Changing Times in Rural America: Food Assistance and
Food Insecurity in Food Deserts." *Journal of Family Social Work* 16(1):36–52.

Williams, Joan. 2010. *Reshaping the Work-Family Debate: Why Men and Class
Matter*. Cambridge, MA: Harvard University Press.

Williams, Joan C. 2012. "The Class Culture Gap." In *Facing Social Class: How
Societal Rank Influences Interaction*, edited by S. T. Fiske and H. R. Markus,
39–58. New York: Russell Sage Foundation.

———. 2017. *White Working Class: Overcoming Class Cluelessness in America.* Boston: Harvard Business Review Press.

Winkler, Richelle. 2013. "Living on Lakes: Segregated Communities and Inequality in a Natural Amenity Destination." *Sociological Quarterly* 54(1):105–29.

Winkler, Richelle, Donald R. Field, A. E. Luloff, Richard S. Krannich, and Tracy Williams. 2007. "Social Landscapes of the Inter-Mountain West: A Comparison of 'Old West' and 'New West' Communities." *Rural Sociology* 72(3):478–501.

Wodtke, Geoffrey T. 2016. "Social Class and Income Inequality in the United States: Ownership, Authority, and Personal Income Distribution from 1980 to 2010." *American Journal of Sociology* 121(5):1375–1415.

Woodward, Kerry. 2008. "The Multiple Meanings of Work for Welfare-Reliant Women." *Qualitative Sociology* 31(2):149–68.

———. 2013. *Pimping the Welfare System: Empowering Participants with Economic, Social, and Cultural Capital.* Lanham, MD: Lexington Books.

Wray, Matt. 2006. *Not Quite White: White Trash and the Boundaries of Whiteness.* Durham, NC: Duke University Press Books.

Wuthnow, Robert. 2015. *In the Blood: Understanding America's Farm Families.* Princeton, NJ: Princeton University Press.

———. 2018. *The Left Behind: Decline and Rage in Rural America.* Princeton, NJ: Princeton University Press.

Yardley, William. 2011. "Washington Becomes Only State to Close Its Tourism Office." *New York Times*, July 11.

Yarwood, Richard. 2005. "Beyond the Rural Idyll: Images, Countryside Change and Geography." *Geography* 90:19–31.

Zweig, Michael. 2007. *The Working Class Majority—America's Best Kept Secret.* Ithaca, NY: Cornell University Press.

Index

capital); importance, 11; reducing gaps in, 198–99; "turning their back on kids," 141

Edwards, Marilyn, 43, 89

elections. *See* voting

employment: cultural capital and, 61, 82, 152; in-migrants and, 9, 26, 28, 62; by industry, 214–15, 215t; at nonprofits, 27, 62, 76, 79; in tourism industry, 28, 60, 86, 215. *See also under* women

Engle, Maura, 43

ethnicity. *See* racial/ethnic diversity

families, supporting all. *See* Home Front

family–work trade-offs, 66–71, 108–12

Farley, Amy, 42–43, 89, 101, 102, 110

Farley, Emmet, 42, 89, 100, 101, 110

Feldstein, Lewis, 198

feminism, 73

feminized occupations, 5, 226n12

Fern, Lea, 162, 164–65, 194

Ferrer, Maya, 53–54, 161

fishing, 40, 41

food bank. *See* Angel Food

food distribution with dignity, 200–204. *See also* Angel Food

forest industry, 6, 25. *See also* logging

Foster, Doris, 43, 181–82

Foster, Fred, 173, 181–83

gender roles (and norms), 41–42, 66, 68, 71–76, 111, 114; daily chores, challenges, and, 71–76. *See also* women

gentrification, 35, 101, 238n57

Gilbert, Brooke, 55–56, 77, 126

Girard, Kristine, 168

Goffman, Erving, 235n45, 239n13

Gough, Nadine, 134–35, 143–44

government. *See* antigovernment discourse; political system; voting

Graham, Katrina, 56, 58

Graham, Matt, 51

Great Recession, 5, 22, 56, 58, 111; recovery period, 24; and unemployment, 215

Griffen, Sabena, 32, 78–79, 126, 160

grocery stores, 14, 22, 132, 157

gun control, 181

Hammond, Jody, 92, 116, 129

Harris, Ted, 110–11, 137

Harris, Wendy, 40, 87, 110, 111, 127–28, 137, 142–43, 202

help seeking, 118, 147, 148; "We don't ask for help," 148. *See also* social support

helping without interacting: class blindness and, 159–68; "We try to give back to the community," 162

Hill, Emily, 144, 149

Hill, Jason, 144

"hippie-rednecks," 32

Hobson, Asa, 31, 89, 141, 142, 166–67, 178

"home," 86–87

Home Front (family support center), 14, 164, 199, 235n41; ongoing efforts, 200; volunteering at, 14, 162, 163, 200

homeownership: dreams of, 101, 102, 107; letting go of, 101

housing, 211, 233n23

housing insecurity, 99–108; "I wasn't allowed to inherit my kingdom," 100

human capital: education and, 11–12, 138–46, 154; lack of, 97, 98, 143, 150; nature of and components of, 11, 82; newcomers and, 61, 67, 82, 139, 141, 144–46, 150, 154; old-timers and, 123, 139, 143, 145, 146, 150, 154; and the social divide, 138–46. *See also* symbolic capital

hunting, 39–41

income. *See* wages

industrialization, 4

inequality, 12, 187, 189; come home, 194–97; effects, 195–97; increasing, 194, 195; reproduction of, 10–12, 46, 138, 146, 154, 155, 190, 191, 195, 196, 198, 199, 205. *See also* economic inequality; social boundaries; social class

in-migrants, 2, 31, 155; characteristics, 26–31, 155, 161–62; early waves of, 28, 29; employment and, 9, 26, 28, 62; gentrifiers vs. social preservationists, 238n57; new/recent waves of, 29, 212. *See also* newcomers and old-timers

in-migration, 7, 8, 190; and housing, 100–101; impact, 8–9, 35, 45, 46, 155, 191; motivations for, 51–53

irrigation, center pivot, 182, 240–41nn27–28

Jenkins, Howard, 29, 31, 50, 161

Jessica (Ryan Boyle's partner. *See* Wheeler, Jessica

Kelly, Jim, 149, 161

labor market, 24–28, 64, 242n9

labor market successes, career sacrifices and, 57–66

land, 38–40; public, 25, 38–40, 183
Larson, Edna, 28, 39, 88
last settler syndrome, 158
liberalism, 56, 57, 160, 161, 206; among newcomers, 30, 53, 160, 163; Paradise Valley
as an oasis of, 55; "rednecks" and, 31; on
west side, 176. *See also* conservatism;
political views
Lloyd, Allison, 109, 115, 128, 136–39, 175, 177,
182
Lloyd, Chad, 39, 87, 97, 115, 137–39, 175, 177,
182
logging, 24, 25, 30, 31, 44, 45, 94, 180
Long, Julie, 93, 94
Lowry, Hannah, 52–53, 55, 68, 70, 71, 77, 108,
134, 145, 150

marginalization, 129, 159; access to resources
and, 8; class divide/social divide and, 158,
205; morality and, 116; old-timers and,
85–86, 116, 119, 122, 137, 156, 169, 171, 176,
184
Martin, Kevin, 63, 73, 74, 133
mills, 25
mining, 24
Mitchell, Lillian, 170–71
moral capital, 146, 147; basis of and components of, 11, 122–23, 147, 150; devaluation
of, 123, 150, 152, 154–55, 191; education
and, 146; and housing, 106–8; importance, 11, 123; and the labor market, 11–12,
98; lack of, 98, 106–8, 123, 124, 150;
nature of, 11, 122–23; newcomers and,
122–23, 150, 152, 154–55, 169–70; old-
timers and, 122–23, 150–52, 154–55, 169–
70, 191. *See also* symbolic capital
morality, 116, 146
Morris, Joyce, 45
Moss, Philip, 230n14
Murphy, Shawn, 27, 52, 54, 58–59, 62, 64, 70,
140, 143, 161, 197

Native Americans, 2, 24, 34, 216. *See also* Paradise Valley: native residents
Neckerman, Kathryn M., 195
Nelson, Irene, 39–41, 169
neoliberalism, 4, 5, 163
newcomers and old-timers, 8, 33, 219, 220–
23t; characteristics, 33–34; definitions,
meanings, and uses of the terms, 30–32;
dividing paradise, 29–35; exploring Paradise Valley's divide, 45–47. *See also*
in-migrants

news media, 161, 179, 180; anger discourse
and, 185, 193
nonprofits, 27, 62, 76, 134, 164, 164–66, 203–4,
232n37; boards, 77–79, 134, 232n38;
childcare and, 199, 231n19; class blindness
and, 167; donations to, 76, 162–63;
employment at, 27, 62, 76, 79; forces sustaining, 165–66; leadership roles in, 77–78,
232n41; newcomers and, 62, 77–79, 186–
87, 193; number of, 27, 77; volunteering at,
14, 67, 76–79, 162 (*see also* volunteer work)

occupational polarization, 241n9
old-newcomers, 32
old-timers: attachment to Paradise Valley,
86–91. *See also* newcomers and
old-timers
orchards, 24–25, 31, 63, 182, 217

Paradise Valley (Washington State): and the
American Dream, 85, 86, 91; building a
future in a divided community and
nation, 204–7; constructing and maintaining paradise, 80–83; demographics,
214–17; description and overview, 7,
21–23; divide (*see* newcomers and old-
timers); enduring paradise and downsizing dreams, 117–20; exemplary efforts
from, 197–204; giving back to (*see* volunteer work); history, 4, 24; "it's home,"
86–87; location, 7; loss and resilience in,
4–7; motivations for moving to, 49–57, 80;
native residents, 37, 42, 98, 233n15 (*see
also* Native Americans; old-timers);
struggles to survive in, 91–112; surviving
in, 57–66; symbolic resources and social
boundaries, 8–13; triumphs and challenges, 7–13
Paradise Valley High School, 141
Parker, Beverly, 127, 175
Patterson, Audrey, 36, 42, 86–87, 147–48, 173
Perry, Walter, 160, 165
philanthropy, 67, 165–68. *See also* charity
Phillips, Barbara, 45, 183
pivot irrigation system, 182, 240–41nn27–28
political system, distrust in the, 176–78; "my
vote doesn't count for much," 176 (*see also*
voting)
political views, 32–33, 57, 161, 175, 176, 181; of
newcomers, 30, 32, 33, 155, 160, 163, 220–
23t; of old-timers, 32, 33, 178, 220–23t.
See also conservatism; liberalism
politics, 161, 179, 193–94

Poole, Kate, 59–60
poverty, 112–13, 185, 215, 216t; "It is way
  hand-to-mouth," 92. *See also* economics of
  Paradise Valley; wages
poverty alleviation, Angel Food's efforts
  toward, 113, 200–204, 212, 235n41
protectionism, 157, 158, 180. *See also* anger
  discourse; self-protection
Putnam, Robert D., 198

race, 10, 34, 63, 212
racial breakdown for towns in Paradise Valley,
  216, 216t
racial/ethnic diversity (vs. homogeneity), 10,
  34, 55, 88, 132, 216, 232n4. *See also*
  segregation
racism, 34–35, 185, 239n19, 240n21; color-
  blind, 34, 63, 228n20, 230n15, 230n17
ranchers and ranching, 25, 38, 43–44, 181,
  183
"rat race," 87; getting out of the, 49–50
"rednecks," 31–32
Reed, Aspen, 73, 74, 133
resilience. *See under* Paradise Valley
Rhodes, Pam, 92, 108, 114, 116, 148, 170, 173,
  176
Roberts, Owen, 30, 40, 41, 88, 92, 96, 171–72
Rossi, Greg, 31, 42–44, 147, 176, 180
rural dream, 2, 50, 51, 57
"rural man," image of the, 73

sawmills, 25
Sayer, Andrew, 230n17
school system, 141, 144, 198. *See also*
  education
seasonal work, 91–93, 95–97, 100–102
segregation, 132, 154, 195, 196
self-protection, 175, 177, 181, 206, 240n26. *See
  also* protectionism
Setzer, Maria, 31, 51, 71, 78, 126–27, 162,
  230n11
Silver, Sharon, 134
social boundaries, 132, 167; class blindness
  and, 193; "different ideologies and ways
  of life," 135; efforts to minimize, 202–3;
  interaction across, 187; managing marginalization through, 168–74; moral capital and, 11; old-timers and, 9, 168–72,
  174, 175; resources, divisions, symbolic
  capital and, 123–52; symbolic resources
  and, 8–13; volunteer work and, 114, 187,
  202–4
social capital, 147, 200; acquiring/building,

127, 130–31, 153, 198, 204; cultural capital
  in the creation of, 11, 131–38, 154; disparities in, 92, 123–31, 195; importance, 11, 82,
  123–24; lack of, 92, 103–4, 107, 124, 125,
  127, 137–38, 150, 153, 239n18; nature of,
  11; newcomers and, 61, 67, 72, 82, 122,
  124, 127, 131, 137, 150, 153, 154, 191; old-
  timers and, 92, 103–4, 111, 125, 150, 174,
  191; reproduction, 123, 130–31; social isolation and, 123–31; substituting for economic capital, 123, 124. *See also* symbolic
  capital
social class, 10, 26, 28, 32–33, 48, 55, 138, 143,
  196, 204–5; ignoring/overlooking, 10, 50,
  135, 205 (*see also* class blindness). *See also*
  inequality; social boundaries
social distancing, 201, 202
social divide, 32, 63, 130, 151, 153, 158, 169,
  187, 196–97; Angel Food and, 203; bridg-
  ing/crossing the, 163, 167, 187, 198, 200,
  203, 207; charity, philanthropy and, 167,
  187, 200; class blindness and, 167, 168,
  196; culture and, 131, 132, 137 (*see also*
  cultural divide); human capital and the,
  138–46; types of social division, 9. *See also
  under* newcomers and old-timers; Paradise Valley
social isolation, 129–30, 175, 192, 210; "not
  there to help you," 178; "pretty much on
  our own," 128; social capital and, 123–31.
  See also social support
social mobility. *See* upward mobility
social preservationists, 238n57
social reproduction. *See* inequality: reproduction of
social services, 112–13, 215, 216t; "you don't
  ask for outside help," 115
social stigma. *See* stigma
social support: childcare challenges and,
  67–71; "everybody helps with everything,"
  70; giving and receiving, 66–80; survival,
  aid, and self-denial, 112–17. *See also* social
  isolation; social services
soft skills, 61; defined, 230n14
sports, after-school, 142–43
Stedman, Richard, 238n58
Stevens, Phillip, 30, 58
Stewart, Molly, 74–75
Stewart, Todd, 53, 62, 74, 75
stigma, 239n13; associated with aid receipt,
  112–14, 146–52
stigma management, 17, 239n13
symbolic boundaries, 10, 63, 116, 123, 153, 174

Founded in 1893,
UNIVERSITY OF CALIFORNIA PRESS
publishes bold, progressive books and journals
on topics in the arts, humanities, social sciences,
and natural sciences—with a focus on social
justice issues—that inspire thought and action
among readers worldwide.

The UC PRESS FOUNDATION
raises funds to uphold the press's vital role
as an independent, nonprofit publisher, and
receives philanthropic support from a wide
range of individuals and institutions—and from
committed readers like you. To learn more, visit
ucpress.edu/supportus.